Fatima, the First Hundred Years

The Complete Story from Visionaries to Saints

✠ ✠ ✠

CENTENARY CELEBRATION EDITION

FATIMA
The First Hundred Years

*The Complete Story
from Visionaries to Saints*

CENTENARY CELEBRATION EDITION

✠✠✠

BARRY R. PEARLMAN

 Angelico Press

First published in the USA
by Angelico Press 2017
© Barry R. Pearlman 2017

For information, address:
Angelico Press
4709 Briar Knoll Dr.
Kettering, OH 45429
angelicopress.com
info@angelicopress.com

ISBN 978 1 62138 276 8 pb
ISBN 978 1 62138 277 5 cloth
ISBN 978 1 62138 278 2 ebook

Cover design: Michael Schrauzer

CONTENTS

To Our Lady of the Rosary

You are altogether beautiful, my love,
there is no blemish in you...
You have ravished my heart,
my sister, my bride,
You have ravished my heart
with a glance of your eyes,
with one jewel of your necklace.

(Song of Songs 4:7, 10)

Preface to the Centenary Celebration Edition

In 1917, DURING THE MONTHS of May to October, on the thirteenth of each month, the Virgin Mary appeared to three shepherd children in the Cova da Iria, near Fatima, in central Portugal. The sublime message she brought and the awesome miracle she wrought there were so extraordinary that many books have been written about them. The purpose of this book is to retell the story of Fatima and, at the same time, explain in familiar language the profound and momentous message which has been given to the entire world. To commemorate the centenary anniversary of Fatima, this entirely revised and updated edition has been produced.

I would like to express my thanks to John Riess of Angelico Press, for bringing out this centenary edition at this juncture. His advice and encouragement have been invaluable. Thanks also to the editor, Allie Gunther, for her expert and painstaking enhancement of the text.

I also acknowledge with special gratitude the donation by Mrs. Bowskill of photographs taken in 1951 by her late husband, Dennis.

Finally, for my wife, Anne, and for my mother, both of whose wisdom and encouragement have supported me in so many ways, my heartfelt affection. Without their solicitude and constancy this work could not have been completed.

Unless otherwise indicated all Scriptural quotations are from *The Holy Bible: Revised Standard Version* (second edition), published by Thomas Nelson Inc., 1971.

Mary:
Mother of the Faithful

A T OUR COMMENCEMENT into the story of Fatima let us prepare ourselves to embark on a spiritual voyage. Even though we may not be making an actual pilgrimage, whereby we transport ourselves from one physical place to another, nevertheless we shall be moving from one spiritual state to another—from one interior world to another. Not for mere curiosity should we come to Fatima, but for a deeper friendship with Our Lord. We come to Fatima so that we may somehow be renewed, transformed, completed. For our spiritual passage is made for similar reasons as those who make the physical pilgrimage: to strengthen our faith; to pray better, for ourselves or for others; to obtain understanding, guidance, or consolation; to find forgiveness, offer thanks, celebrate our joy; to come close to God.

Our heavenly Father has created us so that we may also come into that fellowship of love which He shares with His Son in the Holy Spirit: for we were made for God. The entire history of salvation is nothing more than a manifestation of the profound desire on the part of God to seek and to restore His lost sheep to their proper estate. And this would be impossible if there were not something already in each of us which could respond to His call. Our Lady was sent to Fatima for just this purpose: to speak to our hearts. Therefore, it would be profitable for us firstly to explore the heart of Mary if we are fully to understand the message Our Lady of Fatima will be bringing to us.

There is a mystery in Mary that is bound up with the mystery of salvation in which we in turn are implicated. This mystery involves the communion of hearts. The life of the Mother of our Lord and Savior is so intimately linked with that of her Son that it is impossible to reflect upon the mystery of salvation without considering her obedient participation in its unfolding. "For when the fullness of time came, God sent forth his Son, born of a woman . . . so that we might receive adoption as sons" (Gal. 4:4–5). He who "was destined before the foundation of the world" (1 Pet. 1:20) to take on human flesh, but without sin, was also destined by the sovereign will and consummate foreknowledge of the Father to be the seed of the woman who in the end time would crush the head of the serpent (Gen. 3:15; Ro. 16:20; Rev. 12:1–9). There exists an intimate and unbreakable bond between the mission of the obedient Son of God and His devoted mother that is also bound up with the eternal will of the Father and the destiny of the Church.

This bond was foreshadowed in the Old Testament prophecy that a virgin would conceive and bear a son who would be called Emmanuel, "God with us" (Is. 7:14; Mt. 1:23). Already taking form in Isaiah is the image of the holy city of Zion as a virgin who is to bring forth the Redeemer of the people Israel and, through Him, become the mother of many:

> Before she was in labor she gave birth; before her pain came upon
> her she was delivered of a son…
> For as soon as Zion was in labor
> she brought forth her sons…
> For thus says the Lord:
> "Behold, I will extend prosperity to her like a river,
> and the wealth of nations like an overflowing stream;
> and you shall suck, you shall be carried upon her hip,
> and dandled upon her knees." (66:7–8, 12)

The identification of Mary as the Daughter of Zion evokes the insight that Mary, a daughter of Israel by birth and by faith, embodies within herself both the Old Testament expectation and the New Testament fulfillment.

What binds Mary's life to that of her Son is the consent she gave when the angel announced to her that "The Holy Spirit will come upon you, and the power of the Most High will overshadow you; therefore the child to be born will be called holy, the Son of God" (Lk. 1:35). Her response, "Behold, I am the handmaid of the Lord; let it be to me according to your word"—a fiat freely offered to the

2

angel—sets in motion a series of events which will ultimately lead to the "falling and rising of many." For this reason the Holy Spirit, speaking through her cousin Elizabeth, pronounces her "blessed . . . among women." The Spirit also inspires Mary herself to proclaim that she is to be called blessed by "all generations" because of the "great things" the Almighty One has done for her. Thus she rejoices in God her savior who has "recognized the low estate of His handmaiden." Mary in turn recognizes in what has been done to her the hand of the One who "exalts those of low degree." It is God himself who exalts her by predestining her to be the Mother of Emmanuel. For although Jesus had come to us for a definite purpose—a purpose which he had consummated supremely on the cross—we still have to bear our own crosses (a task which needless to say is not easy in our fallen human condition). Therefore, Christ has provided a Mother for His children—a Mother who has tread the same path as us, albeit in an exemplary manner, yet one who never leaves our side. Our Lord has given us Our Lady who is both the exemplary disciple of faith and the spiritual mother of all believers.

The Exemplary Disciple of Faith

Mary is the handmaid of the Lord. As such she has come to personify the exemplary disciple—the one favored by God. This is even more remarkable when her humanity is fully acknowledged. Mary, like us, is a creature of God. Although she is uniquely favored to be the Mother of "God with us," nevertheless, she is a finite and historical being. She had to cultivate her discipleship in the same manner as we who must also live by faith and obedience. Moreover, her earthly estate was an impoverished one. She epitomizes the poor of the Lord, designated the *anawim* in the Old Testament. These poor are seen as the faithful residue, that remnant among the children of Israel who, though oppressed and shunned by the world, continued to remain steadfast throughout the history of their covenant.[1] "For I

---

1. Anthony Tambasco, *What Are They Saying About Mary?*, 33.

3

will leave in the midst of you a people humble and lowly. They shall seek refuge in the name of the Lord" (Zeph. 3:12). This tiny remnant of the anawim, who kept alive the hopes of Israel, are associated in Zephaniah 3:14–20 with the Daughter of Zion. They are pictured as oppressed, outcast, shamed, and impoverished, like us, yet expectantly awaiting their deliverance. There can be little doubt that Mary in her poverty and faithfulness represents this group (LG55).

> Luke casts his entire infancy narrative in the mould of the poor of [the Lord]. The characters of these stories, such as Zechariah and Elizabeth, Simeon and Anna, all represent the last of the Old Testament anawim awaiting the Messiah with hope. The stories are designed, however, to culminate in Mary as the perfection of the anawim. She contrasts with Zechariah's doubt by her faithfulness as the handmaid of the Lord, open to whatever the Lord wants (1:38). She keeps all things in her heart, pondering them (2:19, 51), the image of the faithful anawim who receive and reflect on God's revelation. She brings the offering of the poor—turtle doves—as her sacrifice to the Lord in the temple, and she hears from Simeon that the sword of God's word in her Son will penetrate her heart especially (2:22–40).[2]

When the angel, Gabriel, announces to Mary that she has been chosen by God to be the Mother of the Christ, the whole composition of her soul is laid out before us. The reason for her election is not given. Yet we are told in a seminal verb that she is already perfectly favored, fully graced because of the nature of her election. Gabriel says to Mary in the Greek of Luke's Gospel: "*Kaire, kecharitomene*" (in Latin *Ave, gratia plena*) meaning "Hail, one having been completely (or fully) graced (or favored)" by God.

In Greek the perfect tense denotes an action that has been completed or perfected in the past, but whose effects continue into the present. The adoption of the perfect tense demonstrates a completed action of grace effected upon Mary *which continues to be manifested in her.* This is the meaning understood by the Latin Fathers when they translated the same Greek passage as *gratia plena*, "grace-filled." Furthermore, this greeting is in the form of a

---

2. Ibid.

proper name: "Hail, full of grace." Therefore, the full meaning of Gabriel's greeting to Mary is that she, herself, is now the one who has been and continues to be completely favored by God so much so that she is in fact "blessed among (all) women."

"But she was greatly troubled at the saying, and considered in her mind what sort of greeting this might be" (Lk. 1:29). Confronted by a supernatural apparition greeting her in such an extraordinary manner, it is no wonder that Mary should be troubled, even fearful. Such is her humility that she can find no reason within herself for such favor. She has only one concern: "How shall this be, since I know not a man." For Mary has vowed her virginity to God,[3] thus abandoning the expectation of every Jewish maiden's heart: that of being the Mother of the Messiah.

The answer given by the angel is decisive: "Do not be afraid, Mary, for you have found (aorist) favor with God." Here the aorist form indicates that Mary's *finding* of grace is a once and for all action that has already been accomplished. Furthermore, she is reassured by the angel that the past bestowal of grace upon her is foreordained by God, solely because of her election to be the Mother of the Messiah. But when was Mary so graced?

It has been an accepted tradition among the Jews that God's elective purpose is effected from even before the moment of birth: "Before I formed you in the womb I knew you, and before you were born I consecrated you. . . ." (Jer. 1:5; cf. Ps. 139:15–16; Is. 49:1; Ro. 9; Gal. 1:15). It could not be otherwise, given the foreknowledge and sovereignty traditionally attributed to the God of Israel. That Luke knew this tradition is evidenced by the angel's previous announcement to Zechariah concerning John the Baptist: "and he will be filled with the Holy Spirit, *even from his mother's womb*" (1:15). Moreover, Luke associates Mary, "full of grace," with the joyous response of the elected babe in Elizabeth's womb: "when the voice of your greeting came to my ears, the babe in my womb leaped for joy" (v. 44).

Under the inspiration of the Holy Spirit, Mary is understood, not

---

3. That it was customary for Jewish maidens to vow their chastity to God, see *The Temple Scroll* (11QT) in G. Vermes, *The Dead Sea Scrolls in English*, 149.

only by Elizabeth, but by herself, to be the one upon whom devolved the entire destiny of the *anawim,* the poor among the Daughters of Zion, who expectantly await the fulfillment of the promises made to her. Luke places Mary at the consummation of God's elective purposes. Into her surges the confluence of Israel's entire history of election and covenant, promise and fulfillment, suffering and redemption. When the reader attends to the number of prophetic allusions which Luke packs into the first two chapters of his gospel and acknowledges his interweaving of their themes, the entire tapestry of God's sovereign purposes and divine fore-knowledge unfolds in an eternal plan of momentous magnitude and wondrous glory. From the apparitions of the angel to Mary to the appearance of the angelic host before the shepherds in the field, from the promises made to Zachariah to the prophecies of Simeon and Anna, we are compelled to recognize Mary's election as being part of an eternal and grand design.

> Since God the Father has chosen us in Christ before the creation of the world, it is simply logical that the first willed, the first loved, the first elected one of the Father is Jesus Christ. Now since Jesus Christ, the Incarnate Word and Lord of the universe and particularly of humanity, is Himself a man and, therefore, our Brother, He had to have a Mother. And, as Pope Pius IX appropriately said, by the same eternal decree in which God willed the Incarnation of His Only-begotten Son, He also willed specifically His Son's Immaculate Mother. . . .[4]

The utter simplicity and majesty of God is such that he is not subject to the flow of temporal events and, therefore, does not will according to the succession of time but from eternity. In one deliberate act He wills the whole of salvation history with all its efficacy and grandeur. Like Elizabeth, we can only cower before the full weight of it: "Why is this granted me that the mother of my Lord should come to me?" (1:43).

Thus, from the moment of her conception Mary is full of grace. That is the Old Testament tradition in which Luke is writing. From

4. Ven. Fr. Gabriel Allegra, OFM, *Mary's Immaculate Heart: A Way to God* (Chicago: Franciscan Herald Press, 1982), 19–20.

the very instant of Mary's conception, indeed, even before her conception in the mind of God, Mary was predestined to be fully graced. She was preserved from subjection to original sin through a special privilege bestowed upon her by God out of the special love he had for his only begotten Son, and from the necessity and exigency of her place in the divine plan of redemption. The Subtle Doctor, Bl. John Duns Scotus, had affirmed this in his *Commentary on the Third Book of the Sentences:* "Since the Passion of Christ was immediately and principally ordered to delete original guilt as well as actual guilt, in such a way that all the Trinity, since it had the foresight of the merits of the Passion of Christ, applied them to the Virgin and preserved her from all actual sin, and also from all original sin."

The force of this truth is even more striking when we acknowledge the freedom with which she offered her consent: "Behold, I am the handmaid of the Lord; let it be to me according to your word." For how is it that Mary, predestined before the foundation of the world to be the Mother of our Lord, could also possess that free will to render her fiat, her "let it be"?

The solution to the question of how Mary could be predestined and free at the same time is to be found in her singular holiness. For all her actions flowed from those very graces which formed her immaculate heart. Mary *is* the one who was composed through grace so as to freely will, out of the nature divinely bestowed upon her, that very thing which God had predestined in her. Mary's sanctity was such that her consent to God's word was foreseeable, even though it was free, simply because she was graced to be the sort of person who would so freely choose.

Mary remained true to herself, reassured by the angel that if she did so she would be acting in accordance with the graces bestowed upon her by God's eternal favor and foreknowledge. For Mary to do otherwise would have put her in a state of alienation both from her own self and from her God: that very state that we call original sin. But Mary, by the grace of God, was preserved free from such alienation. This fact, that she was predisposed freely and obediently to consent to God's word, means that she was in perfect union with her God with whom she has found favor and who has done great things for her in making her the Mother of "God with us." She *knows* that thenceforth all generations will call her blessed! For only one so blessed could have been so chosen.

Indeed so, for it would have been unseemly for God to have acted upon her if there had been the slightest reluctance or unwillingness on her part. Because of this, we should not be surprised to see Mary manifesting, throughout her pilgrimage on earth, the supreme virtues and gifts of a life so uniquely graced. In fact, such a life would only serve to fill out the nature of that grace. "He will rejoice over you with gladness, he will renew you in his love. . . . I will make you renowned and praised among all the peoples of the earth. . . ." (Zeph. 3:17, 20). When we examine Mary's life as portrayed in the Holy Scriptures, we find her exemplifying those characteristics which have traditionally been prized as Christian virtues: the theological virtues of faith, hope, and charity; the cardinal virtues of prudence, justice, temperance, and fortitude; and the religious virtues of poverty, chastity, and obedience. We also witness in her exemplary life evidence of the spiritual fruits mentioned by Paul in Gal. 5:22 ff: love, joy, peace, patience, kindness, generosity, fidelity, meekness, and self-control. We may contemplate these several virtues as they are expressed throughout the various stages of Mary's life with her Son, remembering that it is God who calls all things into being.

In the annunciation of the angel and in the visitation to Elizabeth, we have already witnessed Mary's obedience, faith, joy, hope, meekness, and self-control. Her generosity toward Elizabeth in rejoicing with her in what they have come to share adds to her readiness to make her visitation "with haste." For after the angel drew Mary's attention to what had been also done for Elizabeth (Lk. 1:36), Mary, moved by charity, hastened to the house of her kinswoman, only to find herself once more being blessed. But the response "why is this granted me, that the mother of my Lord should come to me?" gives a deeper dimension to Mary's gift of grace: because of her act of belief "there would be fulfillment of those things told her of the Lord" (Lk. 1:43–45).

This is the moment when Mary pronounces her *Magnificat*, in which she rejoices in her Savior, who has blessed her to be the Mother of the One who from generation to generation will fulfill those promises made to Abraham and his children. This is the moment when Mary, breathing the atmosphere of eternity, expresses her obeisance before the majesty of the unfolding panorama in which she is encompassed. Her prayer reveals her joy, gratitude, and gladness for the future recipients of God's merciful promises: the poor, the oppressed, those enslaved by power, riches, pleasure, the empty, the lonely. Already the "handmaiden of the Lord" has begun to express her maternal solicitude for her spiritual children.

That Mary represents the *anawim*, the poor in the Lord, is also emphasized in Luke's birth narrative: "And she gave birth to her first-born son and wrapped him in swaddling cloths, and laid him in a *phatne* (manger, feeding-trough) because there was no place for them in the inn" (2:7). Those who witness this spectacle in Luke's gospel are not the stately wise men in Matthew's tradition, but simple shepherds keeping a nightly vigil over their sheep. They too receive an angelic annunciation that in the city of David, a Savior, their Messiah and Lord, is born that day. But the sign that is given to them is the mere fact that he is "wrapped in swaddling cloths and lying in a manger" (v.12). The sign that this is "Christ the Lord" (cf. Is. 9:6–7) is no more than the very circumstances of His impoverished birth within the city of David! "And they went with haste, and found Mary and Joseph, and the babe lying in a manger" (v.16). Luke tells us that after witnessing the "thing" which the "Lord has made known" to them, the shepherds tell others, evoking wonder in all who hear them. Meanwhile, Mary silently and patiently reflects upon these things "within her heart" (Lk. 2:19, 51).[5]

Forty days later, in obedience to the Jewish law, the Holy Family journey to the Temple of Jerusalem, where Mary undergoes the ritual of purification (Lev. 12:2–5). Then they bring the infant, whom they have named Jesus, to be consecrated to God (Ex. 13:2, 12). Their offering of a pair of turtle doves (Lk. 2:24) is that of the poor people (Lev. 2:8). Among these poor people is also Simeon who is "righteous and devout, looking for the consolation of Israel, and the Holy Spirit was upon him" (v.25).

5. Frederick M. Jelly, *Madonna: Mary in the Catholic Tradition* (Huntington: Our Sunday Visitor, 1986), 166–68.

Upon hearing the name Jesus, which means "Savior," Simeon offers his inspired improvisation upon its meaning: "mine eyes have seen thy salvation which thou hast prepared in the presence of all peoples, a light for revelation to the Gentiles, and for glory to thy people Israel" (vv. 30–32). Both Mary and Joseph marvel at this outburst. In accordance with the tradition, Simeon turns to bless them, directing to Mary—now thrice blessed—the prophecy that her child will occasion decision and dissension, leading to the "fall and rising of many." This "sign that is spoken against" will reveal the hidden thoughts and intentions of many hearts. His words will provoke division, cutting through the land like a sword (Ez. 21:1–17; Mt. 10:34; Heb. 4:12; Rev. 1:6): a sword that will also penetrate the soul of Mary. Her Son, the Messiah, must suffer.

Instructed by an angel of God to flee Herod's wrath, Joseph takes Mary and the infant Jesus to make the arduous and dangerous venture down to Egypt, a journey of four or five days. After a stay of about a year, upon the death of Herod they return, this time to Nazareth, because Archelaus, scion and stamp of Herod, is ruling over Bethlehem. For thirty years they dwell in Nazareth. These are the silent years, the time of nurturing, of responsibility, of intimacy, and of education in the traditions, prayers, and history of the children of Israel—a time to carry out the commonplace duties of a Jewish mother. The ideal mother is eulogized in the Book of Proverbs, ch. 31:

> The heart of her husband trusts in her,
> and he will have no lack of gain.
> She does him good, and not harm,
> all the days of her life.
> She seeks wool and flax,
> and works with willing hands…
> she brings her food from afar.
> She rises while it is yet night
> and provides food for her household…
> Her lamp does not go out at night.
> She puts her hands to the distaff,
> and her hands hold the spindle.
> She opens her hand to the poor,
> and reaches out her hands to the needy.

Mary: Mother of the Faithful

Strength and dignity are her clothing...
She opens her mouth with wisdom,
and the teaching of kindness is on her tongue.
Her children rise up and call her blessed;
her husband also, and he praises her.

The ordinariness of Mary's life at this time sounds the depths of her humility beneath the light of all the remarkable things God had accomplished in her. Truly "the sanctity of Our Lady was great indeed, but so great that it cannot be adequately be expressed in anything other than the ordinary ways of human existence."[6] In Nazareth she manifests her sanctity through humble and loving charity towards the two men of her household who loved her. However banal or arduous her life may have been, she was always giving thanks to her heavenly Father: "Blessed are you Lord God, King of the Universe, who gives us work for our hands."

Jesus is hardly twelve years old when Mary experiences another wound. It is the feast of Passover, and Mary and Joseph devoutly observe the custom of making an annual pilgrimage to Jerusalem. But when the time comes for the family to return home, Jesus, unknown to them, remains behind to discuss the Law and the Prophets with the teachers in the Temple. They, counting on Jesus's obedience to them (2:51), suppose him to be somewhere among the company of travelers. Anxiously Mary and Joseph search among their kinfolk and acquaintances for their only son. Discovering after a day's journey that he is not among any of the bands making up the caravan party, they return to Jerusalem, where they continue to seek him. On the third day they are astonished to find him, sitting among the temple scholars—something which he could not have been allowed to do unless he had already been made *bar mitzvah*, or Son of the Commandment, according to Jewish law.

Jesus's gentle and masterly response to their astonishment corrects, with a single utterance, both Joseph's and Mary's misunderstanding of where His priorities lie: "Did you (plural) not know that I must be in my Father's house?" Joseph and Mary would have each received these words in a different way. Jesus, who has achieved his

6. Thomas Merton, quoted in E.K. Lynch, *The Scapular of Carmel*, 37.

II

majority, is firstly saying to Joseph: "Dear Father, you have taught me well the Torah and my righteous duty before God. And do you not therefore know that I must now take on this responsibility as a son of Israel?" And at the same time he is implying to Mary: "Mother, have we not often remembered together how, through your saintly consent, I was conceived by the Holy Spirit; and that God is my Father?"

From the beginning, when the angel first announced to Mary that she was favored to bear a special Son, through the eulogy of Elizabeth and the revelations of the Shepherd, to the prophecies of Simeon and Anna, Mary did not understand the full significance of what was unfolding around her. Her natural reaction was to reflect quietly upon all these occurrences. Even at this juncture she did not understand what Jesus had said to them, but "kept all these things in her heart" (50–51). Mary, like the rest of us, has to walk by faith. Unlike her son, she was not given that divine knowledge which so amazed the rabbis. The graces given to her were those of obedience and faith, patience and self-control, meekness and solicitude, loving kindness and generosity—graces which she would continue to display.

The next scene from Mary's pilgrimage of faith expands on this issue of priorities. "Then his mother and his (brethren)[7] came to him, but they could not reach him for the crowd. And he was told, 'Your mother and your brothers are standing outside, desiring to

---

7. The term "brothers of Jesus" should not be taken as indicating further children of Mary. The term "brothers" (brethren) has been used in the Old and New Testaments to mean kinsmen or disciples (Gen. 14:16; 29:12; Lev. 10:4; Mt. 28:10; Jn. 20:17; Acts 1:15; 2:29; 6:3). Furthermore, recent scholarship has shown that there is no firm evidence in the New Testament to warrant the conclusion that they do represent further offspring of Mary. In fact, a close reading of the finding of Jesus in the Temple implies that Jesus is their only son, as does John's account of Jesus's entrusting Mary to the "beloved disciple," which would be unusual if there were other children to look after her (Jn. 19:26–27). Moreover, early Church fathers going back to the second century, such as Irenaeus, Clement of Alexandria, and Gregory of Nyssa, maintained the perpetual virginity of Mary. The tradition continued through Basil, Ambrose, Jerome, Augustine, Peter Chrysologus and Leo the Great. After the Council of Ephesus in 431, it was accepted *de fide* by all Christians until the Reformation. See R.E. Brown (et al.), *Mary in the New Testament*; Michael O'Carroll, *Theotokos*, articles "Brothers" and "Virginity"; and Ronald Lawler, *The Teaching of Christ*, 108.

see you.' But He said to them, 'My mother and my brothers are those who hear the word of God and do it.'" (Lk. 8:19–21.) As in the previous incident, we are again shown Mary, this time with relatives other than Joseph, seeking for Jesus.

Luke locates this passage after Jesus's discourse on the nature of true discipleship in the parable of the sower, while in Matthew and Mark it is placed immediately before that parable (Mt. 12:46–50 = Mk. 3:31–35). While Matthew and Mark strive to demonstrate that the "real" *family* of Jesus is to be found among his believing disciples, Luke simply depicts Jesus utilizing the occasion as the basis for teaching the nature of a *true* disciple. It is the crowd only that prevents the family from gaining access to Jesus. They are standing on the outside, desiring to come in (v.20). Jesus essentially acknowledges that insofar as anyone hears the word and does it, that person, whether inside the circle of disciples or desiring to come inside, is already a brother of Jesus.

The implication of this for Mary is that she who has been repeatedly praised and exalted is already a faithful disciple. We have already been prepared for this by the parable of the sower, wherein Jesus concludes that the good soil denotes "those who, hearing the word, hold it fast in an honest and good heart, and bring forth fruit with patience" (v.15). This is precisely the description that Luke has hitherto made of Mary. He is unlikely to contradict himself after having so painstakingly portrayed such an obedient and responsive heart. Once more Luke draws attention to Mary, the handmaid of the Lord, as the exemplary disciple of enduring faith.

A similar situation to the above arises when a woman impressed by Jesus's casting out a dumb demon cries out, "Blessed is the womb that bore you, and the breasts that you sucked!" Jesus replies, "Even more (*menoun*) blessed are those who hear the word of God and keep it!" (11:27–28) Here Jesus is "directing our attention to the fact that the primary reason for calling his mother blessed is not to be seen in her physical relationship to him, but in her faithful discipleship."[8] Those who belong to his family must evidence those same graces which Mary possesses in such abundance. For Mary is

8. Jelly, 54.

blessed not just because of her physical motherhood, which is of divine origin, but because of the exemplary faith graciously bestowed upon her. "Blessed is she who believed that there would be fulfillment of what was spoken from the Lord . . . and his mother kept all these things in her heart." Certainly, Luke includes Mary among those who "hear the word of God and keep it."

Especially so, for at the end of her life we find Mary praying among the faithful of Jerusalem in the city of Zion, awaiting the coming of the Holy Spirit (Acts 1:14). Having witnessed the life, death, and resurrection of Jesus, she is now as faithful as ever in maintaining her prayerful vigil. As a final tribute to the constancy of her discipleship, Mary is portrayed as kneeling in prayerful solidarity with the nascent Church. The consistent portrait of the Madonna, painted by Luke, is that of one who from the first moment believed and followed her Lord with a perfect and enduring faith. Her vision and understanding have matured, so that at the end of her splendid, but painful life, we find her at one in prayer with the faithful community—a community that is only at the beginning of its pilgrimage.

Our Spiritual Mother

When we turn to John's gospel, we find the source of another tradition about the Blessed Virgin Mary: that she is the Mother of God's people. We already saw that implicit in the Daughter of Zion motif was Isaiah's image of the virgin of Zion giving birth to a son and to sons: "before her pain came upon her she was delivered of a son . . . For as soon as Zion was in labor she brought forth her sons" (66:7, 8). This tradition—that, through Jesus, Mary is the spiritual Mother of the Church—has its source in John's gospel, although it is implied in the synoptics. After all, the other evangelists went to great pains to establish that followers of Jesus are His spiritual brothers and sisters. Luke implies that Mary is not only Jesus's physical mother, but His spiritual Mother also, by virtue of her fiat and her continued faithfulness towards him: "Even more blessed are those who hear the word of God and keep it." This faithful devotion to Jesus is likewise the basis for John's portrait of the Madonna; it is

14

significant to note that he places Mary at the beginning of Jesus's ministry, when he works his first miracle at Cana, and at the end, at the foot of the cross.

The Cana pericope in John 2:1–11 is rich in symbolism. However, our intention here is to explore only the theme of spiritual Motherhood. The essential feature of that theme is the image of Mary interceding for the wedding guests. Jesus and his disciples are invited to a wedding together with Mary. In the course of the celebration the wine runs out. Mary draws Jesus's attention to this fact and, undaunted by his apparent reluctance, directs the servants: "Do whatever he tells you." He orders the servants to fill with water six stone jars each holding about twenty to thirty gallons. Miraculously, the water becomes very fine wine, even better than that originally served by the steward of the ceremony.

It is Mary who asks Jesus for this gift on behalf of the wedding guests. She manifests her concern to alleviate the humility of the newlyweds when the loss of wine threatens to spoil their nuptial celebrations. At the same time, she spontaneously displays her ingenuous and serene confidence in her Son's powers. The suspense is understated. Jesus's response seems disjunctive: "O woman, what have you to do with me? My hour has not yet come" (2:3–4). Significantly, Jesus addresses His Mother as "woman." But we should not be surprised at the starkness of this contrast between "woman" and mother, given John's penchant for symbolism, since it links naturally with the "woman" at the cross (19:26). John seems in both places to be deemphasizing the physical motherhood of Mary in favor of her spiritual Motherhood—the same tendency that we noted in the other evangelists. Mary is, in the abstract, the woman who appeals on behalf of the people. The substitution of the term "woman" for the more natural term "mother" serves to distance Mary from her physical relationship with Jesus and to place her in the more representative role of a woman expressing solicitude for human beings. Moreover, this question about Mary's role is asked by Jesus himself: "O woman, what have you to do with me?" John is directing us, as Jesus directs Mary, to consider just what her motherhood really means.

Jesus's next statement, "My hour has not yet come," refers unequivocally to his passion and crucifixion (12:23, 27; 13:1; 17:1). And it is at that hour that we next see Mary standing with the "beloved disciple" at the foot of the cross (19:26). Not only has Jesus's hour not yet come, but neither, as it were, has Mary's "hour." Her adoption of the role of mother to the "beloved disciple" has yet to occur, therefore: "O woman, what have you to do with me? My hour has not yet come." In this *tête a' tête* between Jesus and Mary, Jesus confronts his mother with a new role. She is invited to relinquish her ordinary physical motherhood for the wider mothering of all human beings. And Mary obeys. She adopts that role when she instructs the servants to "do whatever he tells you." Her intercession with Jesus on behalf of the wedding guests procures for them in abundance that good fruit of the vine that only the keeper of the best wine can give. As a direct result of Mary's intercession, then, the disciples are able to "behold his glory" (1:14). "And his disciples believed in him" because of it.

When, at the foot of the cross, Jesus again calls her "woman," we are immediately reminded of Mary's maternal willingness to intercede on behalf of Jesus's disciples. No doubt Mary, having already taken on this mantle at Cana, is also reminded of Jesus's commission to her. Recollecting as well Simeon's prophecy that the Messiah must suffer, Mary finds herself associated with something at once solemn, glorious, and crushingly painful.

At the foot of the cross, Mary certainly does not experience the pain she feels as a personal punishment for sin, for there is nothing in her which is disagreeable to God. Rather, the Virgin Mary suffers primarily as a Mother. It is her compassion for her stricken son that wounds her, intensified by having once more to repeat that "yes" to God before the horror of what is unfolding before her. She hears her son's despondent cry from the cross: "My God, my God, why have you forsaken me?" And the same cry reverberates in Mary, wringing from her heart the lament: "Behold the handmaid of the Lord. Be it done to me according to Thy word." Christ conquers death, Mary overcomes suffering.[9]

9. A. Martinez Sierra, *Maria, Caminho do Homem*, 144.

16

Mary triumphs over suffering because it is endured in accordance with the will of God. Therefore, her resignation in the face of affliction expands in sublimity and dignity. She remains standing at the foot of the cross, sharing in her Son's immolation offered for the sake of the lost. She partakes of the passion of Christ and, through that sacrifice, gives birth to another extension of her motherhood. Because she knows that God will abandon neither His Son nor her, the light of hope can never be extinguished in her. She stands at the cross in union with her Son and in solidarity with those poor who had also trusted in the God of Israel. The servant, Mary, drinks from the fountain of that same love which the Son held for the human beings for whom he died. And in that love, displayed in the outspread arms of the Son of God, Mary could know, through her anguish, the magnitude of the love the Father also had for estranged and oppressed humanity. Mary's collaborative work is sustained in that compassion, for it is through and by that very compassion that her ordeal gains in majesty. Not only through her Motherhood, but by her steadfastness at the foot of the cross for love's sake, Mary is united with Jesus's macerating thirst for the lost. At Calvary, for the first time, human pain becomes redemptive.[10]

The Church has always understood the exigency of such suffering. Saint Paul confirms this in his letter to the Colossians: "Now I rejoice in my sufferings for your sake, and in my flesh I complete what is lacking for the sake of his body, that is, the Church" (v. 1:24). Not only Mary, but every Christian, can be certain that suffering, though unavoidable in this fallen world, is not useless. It has a redemptive value in union with and by virtue of Christ's holy cross. "For God is not so unjust as to overlook your work and the love which you showed for his sake in serving the saints" (Heb. 6:10). Therefore, "if one suffers as a Christian, let him not be ashamed, but under that name let him glorify God" (1 Pt. 4:16).

But who is the beloved disciple of Jesus, this mysterious figure "who had lain close to his breast at the supper" and asked "who is it that is going to betray you" (21:20; 13:23)? We are never given the actual name of this disciple. However, Peter asks of Jesus, "Lord,

10. Ibid., 146.

17

what about this man?" and Jesus answers, "If it is my will that he remain until I come, what is that to you?" (21:21). Even the brethren of Jesus speculated who he might be, wondering if he was not going to die. However, John does not tell us that he will not die—but that if Christ *should wish* that he remain until Christ comes again, what is that to them (v. 23).

Who then is this beloved disciple who lays his head on the Savior's breast? The answer, given in the gospel itself, is that "it is the disciple who is bearing witness to these things, *and* who has written these things" (v. 24). This character, who has no particular identity within the narrative, seems to float ghostlike above it. We are already familiar with this artifice in John's gospel. He is drawing the reader into the narrative in such a way as to challenge him to see a wider and more abstract role for the character. Just as we were challenged to see a wider role for the "woman," so we are here challenged to discover a wider identity for the faithful witness. And we are to do that by seeing him standing in solidarity with Mary at the foot of the cross being summoned to take the Mother of God to himself. Such a beloved disciple would always respond with obedience. "And from that hour the disciple took her to his *own* home" (19:27).

In this brief reflection on Mary, we have examined those traditions which most directly contribute to understanding the message of Fatima. We have discovered that Mary is the exemplary disciple who embodies for us those virtues we need as we, like her, fulfill our own pilgrimage of faith: the virtues of faith, hope, love, gentleness, simplicity, humility, obedience, solicitude, etc. But we have also penetrated the nature of Mary's heart. Her heart, immaculate by the grace of God, reveals to us two essential predispositions for those seeking sanctity: contemplation upon the word of God and the consent to do His will. Mary, who preserved God's word in her heart, has, from the moment of her conception, been kept Immaculate. She has been preserved free from the stain of original sin. But for us this is not so. Tragically, in us the stain of Adam's fall is an ever-present affliction. Nevertheless, in those who are to be saved, there is a seed which "abides in him, and he cannot sin because he is born of God" (1 Jn. 3:9; 5:18). In those "born of God" who, in His eternal foreknowledge, are to be saved, there is a "seed"—from God—which is kept from wholeheartedly embracing sin, so that they are enabled efficaciously, *though not irresistibly*, to consent to God's sanctifying grace (1 Cor. 1:7–8; Phil. 1:6; 1 Thess. 3:13; 5:23). It is a tradition in Marian theology that devotion to Mary is a sign of our predestination. At Fatima we will hear Our Lady say, "My Immaculate Heart will be the way that will lead you to God." Therefore, because Mary is also our spiritual Mother, we have confidence that in her we possess someone who avidly desires to help us, her children, as we make our spiritual journey—especially when we consider the response that she asks of us.

However, the events at Fatima are of such an extraordinary nature, and have such pressing repercussions in our time, that it is essential to touch on one other tradition about Mary, namely that of her appearances to various individuals. Throughout the history of the Church, Mary has been solicitous in appearing at moments of historical urgency. Since many of these appearances go back to the Church Fathers,[11] we shall only describe three of those more recent events which have a link with Fatima, all of which take place within the nineteenth century.

Mary in the Life of the Faithful

The first of these notable apparitions took place in Paris in 1830. On the 27th of November, Catherine Labouré, a Sister of Charity of St. Vincent de Paul, was awakened from sleep by the voice of a young child inviting her to go to the chapel She entered and found it aglow with burning candles. Then she saw the Virgin Mary standing on a

11. Michael O'Carroll, *Theotokos*, "Apparitions." (See for example Francis Johnston, *The Wonder of Guadalupe*.) There have also been many other alleged apparitions which the Church has not approved. Since 1928 and 1991 there have been over 210 reported apparitions, the vast majority of which the Church has repudiated.

globe with a halo of twelve stars surrounding her head and rays of light extending from her hands. The entire image was surrounded with the words, "Mary, conceived without sin, pray for us who have recourse to thee." Mary's image disappeared and was replaced with a large "M." Through the center of the M was a bar supporting a cross. Beneath the bar were two hearts. One, surrounded by thorns, symbolized the Sacred Heart of Jesus; the other, pierced with a sword, represented the Immaculate Heart of Mary. Again, twelve stars surrounded this image.

An inner locution instructed Catherine to have a medal struck with these images on its front and back. The promise was given that all who wore the medal with confident devotion would receive great graces through Mary's prayerful intercession for them. She was further cautioned to tell no one except her confessor about these visions. The medal was struck and made available to many people. After diligent investigations into the miraculous cures, which followed the faith people placed in Our Lady's promises, the Archbishop de Quelen of Paris gave the medal his official approval. For our purposes, the importance of this medal is simple: it led to a popular swell of petitions asking the Church to issue a proclamation concerning the Immaculate Conception of Mary.

On September 19, 1846, Mary appeared to two children on a mountain near La Salette in France. The boy, Maximin Giraud, age 11, and the girl, Melanie Calvat, age 15, were watching cattle when an unusual light in the form of a globe appeared before them. Inside the globe, they could make out the image of a woman seated as though on a rock with her head bowed in her hands. She was weeping. Lamenting the terrible irreligion that prevailed in the decadent and turbulent France of Louis Napoleon Bonaparte III, she made a number of prophecies warning of disasters to come and predicting a time of evil when the Church would experience a great tribulation. "The Vicar of my Son will suffer a great deal, because for a while the Church will yield to large persecution, a time of darkness, and the Church will witness a frightful crisis."[12] There followed

---

12. Melanie Calvat, *Apparition . . . on the Mountain of LaSalette*, 14.

prophecies concerning the rise of an evil doctrine and the wars that would ensue, an increase in atheism, materialism, and vice of all kinds. Afterwards, the lady predicted a brief period of peace and "unity among the workers of Jesus Christ." She implored the return of the people of France to true religious devotion.

As a direct result of the growth in popular piety and petitioning, on 8 December 1854, St. Pius IX defined the doctrine of the Immaculate Conception: "The most Blessed Virgin Mary, in the first instant of her Conception, by a singular grace and privilege granted by Almighty God, in view of the merits of Jesus Christ, the Savior of the human race, was preserved free from all stain of original sin."[13] Thus the tradition implicit in Scripture and held from the beginning by many in the Church both Catholic and Orthodox, as well as some Reformers, finally became dogma as a direct result of the popular movement created by the visions of Catherine Labouré and the children of La Salette.

As if in confirmation of this decree (Mt. 16:19), yet another apparition occurred, this time to one Bernadette Soubirous of Lourdes. In 1858 fourteen-year-old Bernadette, the daughter of a poor family, went to look for firewood with her sister, Antoinette, and a mutual friend, Jeanne Abadie. The month was February, and it was bitterly cold. The children made their way to the Grotto of Massabielle, a garbage dump. Antoinette and Jeanne decided to cross the nearby river Gave in search of wood. However, Bernadette, being quite frail and subject to asthmatic attacks, was unable to enter the freezing river. She remained behind at Massabielle to gather the wood littering the cave.

Suddenly, there was a rush of wind which rustled a liana bush. Above the bush, a brilliant light appeared which enveloped a very beautiful young lady, no taller than Bernadette and of a similar age. She seemed to step out of the light. She was dressed in a long white mantle with a blue girdle around her waist. Upon her arm, a Rosary was suspended. The beautiful apparition took the Rosary and crossed herself with it, thus inviting Bernadette to pray along with

13. This teaching was declared as *de fide* in the Apostolic Constitution *Ineffabilis Deus.*

her. Bernadette knelt before the image and, imitating her movements, also made the sign of the cross with her Rosary and began to pray: "Hail Mary, full of grace..." The Lady remained silent during the decade of Aves, joining with Bernadette only at the "Our Father" and the "Glory be." A quarter of an hour passed—just enough time for five decades of the Rosary. The beautiful young Lady smiled approvingly. Then she vanished.

Between February 11 and July 16, 1858, the Lady appeared eighteen times. On the occurrence of the seventh apparition (February 25), Bernadette was directed by the Lady, as a penance for sinners, to eat a wild herb growing in the grotto and to drink from the spring. Bernadette began to scratch a hole in the mud, and a trickle of water bubbled up and filled the hole. Overflowing, it spread out to form the present spring which continues to flow at Lourdes.

The sixteenth apparition revealed the dignity of the person. It was March 25, the Feast of the Annunciation, when Bernadette asked the Lady her name. She answered, "I am the Immaculate Conception." The Virgin spoke in the Bigorre dialect words which were of momentous significance to the Church, but utterly incomprehensible to Bernadette. Being uneducated she could scarcely pronounce the word "conception." Certainly she did not know of the Papal Decree made only four years before: it was not part of her catechism, nor had it filtered down to the common people. Bernadette did not even know what the word meant.

We might pause to reflect upon this unusual utterance. It even struck Fr. Peyramale, the local Curé, as odd, for surely the Blessed Virgin would say, "I am the one who was conceived immaculate!" Conception is an event, not a person. However, we note a similarity in its construction to Jesus's statement in John 11:25: "I am the resurrection and the life..." Jesus utilizes the same grammatical construction as Our Lady of Lourdes, but goes on to explain what he means by it: "he who believes in me, though he die, yet shall he live." In other words, Jesus is the resurrection not only because he will experience this event, but because he has the power to accomplish it for others. We also note that this passage occurs in the context of the raising of Lazarus from the dead. Our Lady, in using this construction, is similarly implying that she has been given the role of intercession on our behalf for those graces that will enable us to become immaculate.

During the last visitation, Our Lady told Bernadette, "I cannot promise you happiness in this world, only in the next." Bernadette never saw Mary again until her death in the convent of Nevers on April 16, 1879. She had lived a life of intense suffering from a tubercular tumor on the knee. Her last words were "Holy Mary, Mother of God, pray for me a poor sinner… sinner…" Her body was exhumed thirty years after her death and found to be incorrupt. Her hair, teeth, eyes, and hands, indeed her whole body, though emaciated, was "entire and without the least trace of corruption."[14] It is on display in the Mother House at Nevers for anyone to see.

Having briefly described the traditions concerning those apparitions that Mary has made in our time, we now have the background necessary to understand the message and events of Fatima. Later, we shall see how all this relates to Fatima and to our own spiritual pilgrimage. We now turn to describe the historical and political background behind the Fatima events. For it will be evident that the extraordinary phenomena of Fatima have direct repercussions on our own times and for our future.

14. Joan Carroll Cruz, *The Incorruptibles*, 289. This is a remarkable catalogue with photographs of many saints who have shared this extraordinary preservation such as: St. Clare, St. Agnes, St. Francis Xavier, St. John of the Cross, St. Theresa of Avila, St. Francis de Sales, St. Catherine Labouré, along with some ninety-five others.

The Dawn of Tribulation

URING THE SUMMER OF 1914, the most disastrous war to inflame the western world exploded in Europe.[1] It was ignited by the murder of the heir to the Austrian throne, the Archduke Francis Ferdinand, and his wife, who were shot to death in their car while on a state visit to Sarajevo, Bosnia on June 28, 1914. The assassin was a Bosnian student named Gavrilo Princip. He was a member of the "Black Hand," a Pan-Slavic movement to free the countries of Bosnia and Herzegovina annexed by Austria in 1908. His intention was to foment a republican uprising against the Archduke. Russia and Serbia had previously insisted that Austria withdraw from the Balkans. However, Austria reacted by demanding that Serbia allow Austrian officials to enter its territory to hunt down the Pan-Slavic organizers. Though conciliatory, Serbia refused to allow Austria to enter, and Austria-Hungary declared war on Serbia on July 28. Serbia appealed to Russia for support. Impoverished and militarily weak, yet fearful of Austrian expansion, Russia reluctantly agreed. Czar Nicholas II ordered Russian mobilization on her southern frontier, fully realizing that this action would lead to world war.

Two great alliances divided Europe: the Entente (France, Britain, and Russia) and the Central Powers (Germany, Austria-Hungary, and Turkey). They had emerged from the nationalist aspirations and economic imperialism that had arisen after the Napoleonic wars. Europe was in its birth throes. The jockeying of nations for military power, economic ascendancy, and more extensive frontiers had eventually produced these two great alliances. Thus, when Russia came to the defense of Serbia against Austria-Hungary, France began to mobilize also. Germany declared war on France and Russia and, seeing an opportunity to increase its naval supremacy over Britain in order to pursue its own interests in Africa, deliberately

---

1. J.J. Cosgrove and J.K. Kreiss, *Two Centuries*, 301.

invaded the neutral country of Belgium in direct violation of the Treaty of London of 1839. This would draw Britain into the war and simultaneously outflank the French defenses on the Alsatian frontier. With France out of the war and the weak Russian army routed, Germany would be left as the strongest power on the continent. The Kaiser could then bring the might of the German navy against Britain. On August 4, after the invasion of Belgium, Britain declared war on Germany. Europe was at war.

For two years, the alliances were deadlocked in trench warfare. Thousands upon thousands of men slaughtered each other for gains of only a kilometer of blood-soaked turf. These muddy, disease-infested trenches determined the battle lines from the English Channel to Switzerland. This was the notorious Western front where each side lost over 1,200,000 men at places such as Somme and Verdun. The armies were also bogged down at two other fronts: the Italo-Austrian front from Switzerland to the Adriatic and the Russian front from Rumania to the Baltic Sea, where casualties were just as terrible.

Submarines, aircraft, and poison gas were the new tools of terror. Unrestricted submarine warfare was directed against merchant shipping. For the first time, air raids were inflicted upon civilians. Mustard gas blanketed the trenches. The cost in human lives was terrible: over 8,530,000 men died. The conflict wreaked havoc and destruction throughout Europe and the Near East. Cities, towns, villages, and farmlands were laid waste. Starvation, homelessness, and disease were endemic. Transport and industry were disrupted, generating financial turmoil. Vast war debts accrued and many currencies collapsed. But the real human misery remained hidden within the unremembered lives of innumerable, ordinary individuals who day by day had to carry on in the face of this hellish nightmare.

This war would radically transform Europe. Three ruling dynasties were to disappear: the Hapsburg, Hohenzollern, and Romanov. Four empires would fall: the Austro-Hungarian, the German, the Ottoman, and the Russian. The Austro-Hungarian Empire disintegrated into various states which (Austria excepted) were destined to become communist satellites. The German Empire, considerably reduced, became the Weimar Republic. The Ottoman Empire crumbled into a number of warring Arabic principalities. And the Russian empire, also severely diminished, was on the verge of becoming a communist republic.

Present day Russia was born from this war. What had been a feudal country dominated by a weak Czar under the influence of a depraved, self-styled "holy man" was destined to become the ill-fated promulgator of those "evil doctrines" prophesied by Our Lady of La Salette. But in 1916, at the commencement of our story of Fatima, Russia was merely an impoverished, backward, yet fervently religious nation, suffering from grave economic mismanagement and autocratic incompetence.

Since 1900, strikes, mass meetings, riots and assassinations were commonplace in Russia. The Industrial Revolution had come to this feudal country like an imperious intruder. It inflicted economic exploitation and oppression upon the mass of Russian people now displaced from their rural roots. Discontent and militant unionism were everywhere. In the winter of 1905, a priest led a band of workers to the Winter Palace in St. Petersburg to present Czar Nicholas II a petition requesting the creation of a popular assembly. They approached the Palace singing "God save the Czar." His Cossacks replied by discharging their rifles into the crowd, massacring a thousand defenseless citizens. It was 22 January, 1905, "Bloody Sunday."

The general unrest and national strikes which followed led Nicholas II to capitulate to the citizens' petition. A *Duma* (parliament) was convened. But the Czar refused to comply with its demands. Rather, he conspired to gradually weaken its powers until it was reduced to a mere forum for discontent. The disasters brought about by military defeat—first at the hands of Japan during the Russo-Japanese conflict, then at the hands of Germany in the early months of the World War—only increased the citizens' disillusionment. The wars, which had exacted a heavy toll on human life, considerably impoverished the country. Famine was widespread. Frustration grew as the populace could see no immediate alleviation for their conditions. Desperately, people turned to

Marxist socialism, which had promised them deliverance from their bourgeois overlords. Two parties emerged: the Bolsheviks (or majority), who sought socialism through armed revolution, and the Mensheviks (or minority), who wanted to introduce socialism through parliamentary means.

Why was Nicholas II so blind to the resentment that was festering among the people? The principal reason was that he and the Czarina Alexandra had become enthralled by a dissolute mystic named Rasputin who had ingratiated himself into their favors through his uncanny ability to improve the haemophilia of their son Alexey, future heir to the throne.

Rasputin was not his real name. His original name was Grigorii Yefimovich Novykh, and he was born in Pokrovskoe near Tyumin in Siberia *c.*1864. He came from peasant stock and, although he had attended school, he remained illiterate. He adopted the name Rasputin (meaning *dissolute*) after having joined the sect of the *khlysti* (flagellants), whose rites combined sexual expression with religious devotion, earning the name through early dissipation and frequent drinking bouts. Rasputin himself promoted the belief that prolonged debauchery was the best way to purge oneself of sin in order to produce that state of passionless purity which was a prerequisite for the true seeker of God. He described himself as a *staretz* or "self-proclaimed holy man," although he was never a monk. In fact, he had been married since 1883 to Praskovia Dubrovina and had three children. But marriage did not satisfy him. In 1892 he left his family in order to join the numerous displaced mystics who spent their lives wandering Russia, visiting holy shrines and forming groups of disciples.

The Church in Russia is ancient, going back to King St. Vladimir of Kiev, who in 987 first accepted Christ on behalf of the people. Far from any contact with Rome, Russia simply followed the Eastern Church, who sent her many patriarchs and missionaries. When Constantinople fell to the Muslim Turks in 1453, Moscow came to see itself as the "third Rome." Separation of Church and state had never occurred in Russia, so that the authority of the Czar was preeminent over the Bishops. From the beginning, Russia had produced many mystics. It was an extremely religious country, more in harmony with Eastern mysticism than with Western rationalism. Popular superstition continued to produce numerous shamans and healers.

Rasputin was one of these. He roamed over the vastness of Russia, promoting his devotional path and gaining many adherents. He wandered even as far as Jerusalem and Greece, visiting the monastery at Mount Athos. In 1903 he turned up in St. Petersburg, where he was accepted as a *staretz* by Fr. John of Kronstadt, who then introduced him to Theophan, the inspector of the religious academy of St. Petersburg, and Hermogen, the Bishop of Saratov. Feeling that his background uniquely fitted him to be a strong and articulate link with the Russian peasants and that his charisma predisposed him to nurture their ardent faith, they warmly accepted him as a mystic, acknowledging his healing abilities.

In fact, it was because of his healing reputation that he became enamored by two Montenegrin princesses, Militsa and Anastasia. They were leaders of one of those sundry spiritualist groups that were in vogue among Russian society. Séances were the new craze, and clairvoyants were enthusiastically esteemed. It was during one of these occult gatherings that Rasputin met Militsa and Anastasia, when he had occasion to reveal the secret of his religion to each of them. Thinking that he would also be of value in curing the young heir of his haemophilia, Princess Militsa introduced him to their spiritual guide, who in turn, on 1 November, 1905 introduced him to the Czar and his family.

Rasputin met the family dressed in polished boots, a silk blouse, and an expensive overcoat. Nicholas and Alexandra were utterly impressed. "In Rasputin's presence," they said of him, "one immediately sensed the wisdom, gravity, deep comprehension of life, and majesty of thought which he possessed to a remarkable degree."[2] Rasputin spent the following three years ingratiating himself with clerical and aristocratic authorities.

Foremost among these admiring socialites was Mme. Olga V. Lokhtina, who was "cured" by Rasputin of neurasthenia. He moved into her house, where he was introduced to many society person-

2. Ibid.

ages among the salon set who assembled there. He learned to perfume his beard, which was necessary, given his habit of preferring it to table napkins. He continued to dress in peasant garb, but only of the finest materials. Yet he rarely bathed, and his hair and beard were filthy and unkempt. His reputation as a holy man continued to increase simply because none of those who had submitted to him wanted to admit that they had been abused. Rather than abandon pride and confess that they had been duped by him, they sang his praises all the more.

> He would be surrounded by his admirers, with whom he also slept ... quite openly and without shame.... I often heard his views, a mixture of religion and debauchery. He would sit there and give instructions to his female admirers. "Do you think I degrade you? I don't degrade you, I purify you." That was his basic idea. He also used the word "grace" meaning that by sleeping with him a woman came into the grace of God.[3]

Popular opinions about Rasputin's occult abilities range between the two extremes of outright charlatanry and satanic possession. It is extremely difficult to separate truth from legend. There is little doubt that he had an inordinate charisma, eliciting that faith in him which induced various healings. This becomes even more likely when one appreciates that the general decadence and hedonism of life within Russian courtly society provoked personality disturbances that manifested themselves in various psychosomatic symptoms—real and imagined. However, Rasputin's magnetism must not be underestimated, since he also had the ability to induce trances in people, especially in the nervous types who were drawn to the séances and spiritualist gatherings so popular at that period. We have already noted his ability to hold people in thrall to his will; we also note his prophetic abilities. When Rasputin was young—before he began his wanderings—he prophesied that he would die a violent death, and that the royal family would also die violently soon after.

At that time, 1908, the four-year-old Alexey was suffering from

---

3. N.A. Sakolov, a contemporary journalist, quoted in ibid., 170.

serious bleeding in his leg. The pain induced by the pressure of the blood that accumulated through the internal haemorrhaging was intense. Nicholas and Alexandra were beside themselves with worry for their much beloved and only son. Neither their doctors nor their spiritual advisers could do anything to ease the young boy's agony. In desperation, they remembered Rasputin. Alexandra sought the advice of the Montenegrin family, who convinced her she should allow Rasputin to heal the child.

Rasputin arrived, striking an imposing figure in his peasant boots and overcoat. He was tall and heavyset, with a massive head displaying a broad nose, full lips, and a long, black beard, matted and thick with grime. His nervous eyes quickly glanced around the room, penetrating the characters of the Czar the Czarina and their daughters gathered around little Alexey's bed. Kneeling before the boy, he began to pray over him softly. Gradually the pain eased and the accumulated blood dispersed. By the time he had finished ministering to the boy, young Alexey was sitting up in bed cheerfully chatting with his sisters. Upon leaving the palace, Rasputin warned the Czar and Czarina that the fate of Russia, the boy, and the dynasty were inextricably entwined with him.

From this moment, Rasputin's prestige was firmly established. "Seeing in Rasputin, the 'man of God,' the answer to her prayers in a sure protection for her son from agony and death, Alexandra drew him into the bosom of her family and lavished upon him all the ardent outpouring gratitude and love of her whole-hearted personality, so rarely displayed in public."[4] Rasputin could do no wrong in her eyes. Nicholas, who was weak and submissive and just as devoted to his son, also refused to countenance the lurid reports concerning Rasputin's blatant behavior.

Social success did nothing to check his appetites. His drinking bouts increased in intensity, so that he was often embroiled in fights. He betrayed intimacies about the royal family and fabricated stories of his relationships with the Czarina. He boasted that they had fallen completely under his control, believing him to be the Christ. His promiscuity increased, and he indulged himself with

4. Warren H. Carroll, 1917: *Red Banners, White Mantle,* 18.

both society ladies and prostitutes: "He would regularly gather them up in the streets or places of entertainment, and wearing the heavy gold pectoral cross which the Czarina had given him, take them home or to public bathhouses."[5] To society figures, he maintained the posture of a *staretz,* promising sanctification for anyone allowing themselves contact with his person. But with the common people, he was merely another one of those dissipated satyrs (so aptly described by Tolstoy and Dostoevsky) that one frequently encountered in Russian life.

In the presence of the imperial family, Rasputin behaved with the utmost civility and devotion. He was loved by the children, especially Alexey. Rasputin was often seen carrying the little Czarovich, the heir of all the Russias, about the palace on his enormous shoulders. Whenever accounts of his scandalous behavior reached the ears of Nicholas, the Czar refused to accept that Rasputin was anything other than a humble and pious *staretz.* Anxious not to displease his wife or to endanger his son, Nicholas rejected these allegations, to the extent that many of Rasputin's accusers eventually found themselves transferred to the remotest parts of the empire or demoted from any position of influence.

Meanwhile, Rasputin used his power over the family to secure the appointment of those loyal to him to influential positions in return for special favors. These appointments ranged from church officials to cabinet ministers. One of these was V. K. Sabler, who was made the over-procurator of the Holy Synod. With Sabler in his pocket, Rasputin could make or break any church official he pleased. The first to experience Rasputin's weight of authority were Bishop Hermogen and a priest named Illiodor. When Rasputin's scandalous behavior became too brazen to be ignored—he had recently raped a nun—he was summoned before the Bishop in the presence of a number of Church officials. "The imposing group cowed Rasputin, for once; he admitted the rape of the nun and other grave sexual sins. But he showed no contrition, only fear. Bishop Hermogen was suddenly overcome by the almost irresistible urge—felt and described by many good men when they came in contact with Ras-

5. Alex De Jonge, *The Life and Times of Grigorii Rasputin,* 170.

putin—to attack him physically, to make a sudden maximum effort to destroy a monstrous presence."[6] The Bishop punched Rasputin in the face and repeatedly struck his head with an iron cross. The entire assemblage made him swear on an icon to cease liaisons with women and to keep away from the Czar's family. Rasputin asked forgiveness, but the Bishop replied "Never and nowhere."[7] Within a few weeks, Bishop Hermogen was relinquished of his ecclesial office and exiled to a monastery. Illiodor was arrested, stripped of his priestly duties, and forced out of the country.

When war engulfed the country, Rasputin took advantage of the general distraction. The Russian defeats of 1915 had effected the withdrawal of Russia from all of Poland, and Nicholas II took it upon himself to relieve Grand Duke Nicholas of his command. With the Czar out of the way, Rasputin's dominance over the Czarina was complete. He took the opportunity to consolidate his powers over the government. He appointed a corrupt official, Sturmer, as prime minister in February, 1916, using him to weed out any who opposed Rasputin. However, Sturmer's incompetence brought the government dangerously close to another uprising. Rasputin got rid of Sturmer, replacing him with the half-mad Protopopov. A senior minister, Trepov, was asked by Nicholas to form a caretaker government in his absence. Trepov, being an opponent of Rasputin, refused to accept unless Protopopov was removed. The Czar agreed determining to oust Protopopov. But Rasputin inveigled Alexandra to dissuade Nicholas. She pressed him with several letters—even visited him at army headquarters. Her personal presence won the moment, but upon returning to the palace she continued to write:

> I shall stand against them [Trepov and Rodzyank, president of the Duma] with God's holy man. . . . He has kept you where you are. . . . Only believe more in Our Friend. . . . We must give a strong country to Baby [Alexey], and dare not be weak for his sake . . . draw the reins in tightly which you let loose. . . . Take no big steps without warning me. . . . Russia loves to feel the whip. . . . How I wish I could pour my will into your veins. . . . Listen to me,

6. Carroll, 19.
7. Ibid.

which means Our Friend. I suffer over you as a tender, soft-hearted child. Pardon, believe, and understand.[8]

On December 16, 1916 Alexandra received the following reply from a broken and submissive husband.

Tender thanks for the severe written scolding. I read it with a smile, because you speak to me as though I was a child. . . . Your poor little weak-willed hubby.[9]

The last Czar of all the Russias, responsible for one hundred and fifty million people, capitulated in the midst of a potentially over-whelming war to the designs of a depraved shaman. Trepov was ordered to remain as Transport Minister under the Chief Minister, Protopopov. Rasputin had become in effect the most powerful man in Russia.[10] With an incompetent and futile caretaker government, and military defeat staring Russia in the face; with starvation and panic in the streets and a government manipulated by a dissipated Machiavellian, it is no wonder that Russia was on the verge of revolution. In order to save Russia it was mandatory, therefore, that Rasputin be destroyed.

It was the night of 29/30 December, 1916.[11] Snow blanketed the city of St. Petersburg. In the pitch-black darkness a car was making its way through the frozen streets. In it were four men: Grand Duke Dmitri Pavlovich, first cousin to the Czar; Vladimir Purishkevich, an ardent monarchist and member of the Duma; S. S. Lazavert, a doctor; and Captain Sukhotin of the Russian army. They were on their way to the villa of Prince Felix Yusupov, husband of the Czar's niece, Irina. Their intention was to save Russia in the only way they could: by assassinating Rasputin.

Rasputin, who thought he had been invited to meet Irina, kept them waiting for half an hour while he dressed himself in a white silk blouse and black velvet trousers. It was two o'clock in the morning when they returned to Prince Yusupov's house. Rasputin was

8. De Jonge, 259.

9. Quoted in Carroll, 22.

10. Quoted in ibid.

11. The description of the killing of Rasputin comes mainly from Carroll ibid., 29–34, but it is essentially the same as that described by De Jonge.

immediately taken to the wine cellar while a phonograph played upstairs, suggesting that the ladies were diverting themselves with music. Of course, no ladies were in the house: Irina was visiting in the Crimea at the time.

Yusupov was alone with Rasputin in the cellar. Nervously, he offered him a poisoned cake. Rasputin took the cake and two others as well. Yusupov then suggested he try a glass of wine. Rasputin drank it in one gulp, followed by two poisoned glassfuls, which he downed thirstily. Nothing happened. Although he had taken enough cyanide to kill several men, Rasputin merely wanted Yusupov to play him a song on his guitar.

Yusupov went upstairs and found that Dr. Lazavert had fainted under the stress, while the other three men were brandishing their revolvers, ready to rush down and fire upon Rasputin. Instead, Yusupov persuaded them to let him have one more try and, taking Dmitri's revolver, descended the stairs to confront their victim. Rasputin was admiring a cabinet of valuable trinkets while quietly drinking another glass of Madeira. Yusupov told him to offer up his prayers before the crucifix which hung on the wall. Then, producing the revolver, he fired a single shot at Rasputin's heart. Rasputin bellowed and collapsed heavily onto a thick mat on the floor. The other men, hearing the crash, rushed down and helped Yusupov roll Rasputin off the rug. There was a bullet hole in the chest, but no blood.

Captain Sukhotin then disguised himself in Rasputin's coat and, together with the Doctor and the Grand Duke, drove away in the car toward Rasputin's home. Only the Prince and Purishkevich now remained in the house with the murdered man. They reveled awhile about the future prospects for Russia now that Rasputin's tyranny was ended. Elated, Yusupov went back down to the cellar to look upon the creature who had corrupted Russia for so many years. Impulsively, he reached out and shook the body. Rasputin opened his eyes, fixing them upon Yusupov. Rising up, he clutched Yusupov by the shoulder, hissing "Felix... Felix..."

Freeing himself from his grip Yusupov scrambled upstairs shrieking: "Purishkevich! Shoot! Shoot! He's alive! He's getting away!"[12]

12. Ibid., 32.

Behind him was Rasputin, crawling up the stairs. Before they could compose themselves, he had staggered out into the courtyard. Purishkevich ran after him and fired four shots, two of which hit Rasputin in the shoulder and neck. Roaring, he fell headlong into the snow. Two soldiers in the street heard the shots, but when they learned who had been fired upon, they agreed to remain silent. They helped drag the massive body back into the house. Then the soldiers left.

Still Rasputin was not dead! Yusupov heard him wheezing and, when he noticed one of his eyes opening, he fell upon Rasputin in terror, pummeling him with a two-pound, lead walking stick. By this time the other conspirators had returned. They bundled the still-warm body in a curtain and bound it with rope. Heaving the carcass into the car, they drove to the Petrovsky Bridge and dumped it into the freezing torrent of the Neva River...

> [T]he shape of Rasputin bobbed and writhed. The cyanide from the three poisoned cakes, and then from two poisoned glasses of wine, had long since passed from its stomach to the inner tissues of its body, where it kills swiftly and unerringly, most surely of all when in a lethal dose prepared by a doctor. Yusupov's bullet lay near its heart, Purishkevich's fourth bullet in its neck, both wounds later pronounced surely mortal by medical examiners. Its head, battered by the blows of Yusupov's lead-weighted stick, was broken open in several places by the impact of the head-first fall from the bridge; blood from the gaping wounds eddied the water. Grigorii, son of Efim, the Dissolute, the dark angel of Russia, had already died at least five times that night. Now came the sixth death, drowning and freezing.[13]

When Rasputin's corpse was discovered two hundred feet from the bridge, it was encased in ice. The lungs were later found to be filled with water, which indicated that he had been breathing. The right arm, free of its bonds, was reaching out.

Rasputin was buried in a small chapel in the Imperial Park in Petrograd on January 3, 1917. An icon signed by each member of the

13. Ibid., 34.

royal family was placed in the coffin. Czar Nicholas, who had returned from the front to pay his last respects to his family's spiritual friend, was there with Alexandra and their children.

The next day, the Czar writes in his diary, he took "a walk in the dark."[14] We can only guess what Nicholas's thoughts must have been as he trudged the frozen grounds of the Winter Palace. No doubt he recalled Rasputin's prophecy that the fate of Russia, of the future Czar, and of the royal family were inextricably entwined with the *staretz*, and that they would suffer a violent death soon after his own savage demise. Now that Rasputin had been slain as he had foretold, how much longer before the prophecy would be completely fulfilled? What would become of the *Czarovich*, the future heir to the throne? Who would restore Alexey to health after his bleeding episodes? The military disasters that were debilitating Russia seemed inconsequential before the prospect of an Empire deprived of its imperial family.

Darkness pervaded the House of Romanov. Nicholas spent most of his time comforting the grieving Alexandra. They had isolated themselves from affairs of State. For the following two months the empire remained in uneasy suspense. Even though those close to the Czar warned of the rising discontent among the populace and urged the Czar to reform the government by extending the powers of the Duma, Nicholas continued to intone his monotonous formulas: the autocracy must never be relaxed, the people loved him, the unrest was but temporary, the war was nearly over and things would improve. Then he would withdraw into his melancholy stupor. The monarchy had effectively abrogated its power.

By March, strikes were frequent and widespread in many cities of Russia, but in Petrograd the situation had become desperate. The Czar was prevented from returning to the front because of the hostile demonstrations sporadically erupting in various parts of the city. On March 12, over three hundred thousand workers went on strike and a huge mob roamed Petrograd storming public buildings and attacking officials. Troops refused to fire on the starving popu-

14. Carroll, 35.

lace and many of them deserted to join the people in their violent demonstrations. Gaining force, this human wave inundated the Tauride Palace where an illegal Duma was still meeting. They quickly established the Soviet (Praesidium) of Workers' and Soldiers' Deputies. Soon soviets were set up in other cities. The Duma had assumed full authority over Russia. Three days later, Czar Nicholas II abdicated in favor of his brother, Grand Duke Michael, who in turn abdicated the next day.

The entire royal family was exiled to Siberia, where in July of the following year they would be sentenced to death. In the village of Ekaterinburg near the Urals, Nicholas II, Alexandra, their four daughters, and Alexey would all be gunned down in a basement by a village commissar and his guards. Their seven bodies would be dismembered, burned, macerated in acid, and finally discarded into a mine shaft, thereby meeting the violent fate predicted by Rasputin some twenty years before.

Rasputin's body was not to remain in hallowed ground. In the early morning of March 23, 1917, his coffin was exhumed from its grave in the Imperial Park and taken by soldiers to a clearing in the forest where a huge pyre had been erected. So repulsed were they by this malevolent fiend that they were afraid to touch his corpse. They prized the body out of the coffin with sticks, doused it with gasoline, and set it ablaze, leaving its ashes to be scattered by the icy wind.

With the Czarist regime ended and the Russian army in disarray, Germany could afford to transfer much-needed troops to the Western Front. Seizing its opportunity, the German High Command assisted a number of Bolshevik exiles in returning to Russia to foment unrest and to sabotage Russia's war effort from within. Among these was Vladimir Ilyich Ulyanov, whose Bolshevik Party name was Lenin. He arrived in Petrograd on April 16, 1917, accompanied by a Polish Marxist named Leon Trotsky. They were met by a number of leaders from the Bolshevik Party, principal among whom was Joseph Stalin. Lenin said to Stalin:

> Come, we shall form an alliance. The Provisional Government must be overthrown, and we shall overthrow it when the masses

are with us! I guarantee they will be with us very soon, because we shall promise them everything they can demand from a victorious revolution. Will you join me?[15]

Soon Imperial Russia would die. From its corpse a new Russia would grow. Caught up in the throes of a global war, the world had no inkling of the revolutionary storm looming on the horizon. Even those countries only collaterally involved in the war were otherwise embroiled in their own internal conflicts.

Not least among these countries was Portugal. It too was undergoing a transformation from a monarchy to a republic. Like Russia, Portugal suffered from internal problems brought on by the Industrial Revolution and the Marxist doctrines parasitic upon it. There were the same growth of radicalism, rotation of political leaders, corruption, and resistance to reform and popular education. Syndicalists, socialists, and anarchists capitalized on the discontent incited by burdensome taxation and despotic legislation.

At the beginning of the century, Carlos I was the reigning King of Portugal. He was the nephew of Peter V (1853–1861), who had married into the Hohenzollern family in an attempt to form a political alliance that would heal the ravages his country endured during the Napoleonic Wars. Carlos's father, Luis I, was Peter's brother. He acceded to the throne upon his brother's sudden death from cholera. Luis I had inherited a country that was just beginning to recover from the Napoleonic invasions as well as the civil wars, political upheavals, and economic hardships that often accompany such military intrusions. His rule was a facsimile of the severity and rigidity that characterized the European dynasties of the time. As a result of this inflexibility, the country's economic recovery was frustrated by a number of bungled financial deals with Germany, leading to the loss of several Portuguese colonies to Germany and Britain. When Carlos I succeeded his father in 1889, he began to rule Portugal with the same autocratic intransigence that had character-

15. Ibid., 66.

ized his father's reign, which only served to feed the growing republican movement.

Like Nicholas II, Carlos tried to placate the republican forces with vain legislative libations that only fomented the discontent. A bungling official by the name of Joao Franco, a well-known monarchist sympathizer, came to be suspected of illegally transferring public revenues to the King. This incited a rebellion which culminated in the assassination of King Carlos and his son and heir, Crown Prince Luis Felipe, on February 1, 1908.

He was succeeded by Manoel II, who was unable to bring unity to the country. The general election of 1910 produced republican majorities in the governments of Lisbon and Oporto. In October, one of these republican representatives was murdered by an extremist. A general uprising against the monarchy ensued. Armed civilians, soldiers, and seamen led the insurrection. The army and navy seized Lisbon. King Manoel II fled the country, eventually seeking sanctuary in England, where he lived in exile in Twickenham until his death in 1932, at which time his body was returned to Portugal.

The first republican elections ever held in Portugal took place on June 19, 1911. A constitution was installed on August 20, and the new president, Manoel Arriaga, took office four days later. Under newly-elected Democratic Party leader Afonso Augusto da Costa, a series of anti-clerical laws was enacted. By the Law of Separation (of church and state), religious orders were expelled, their property confiscated, and Church moneys appropriated. Several Churches were seized as military barracks or animal stables, and monasteries and convents were converted to government buildings or administrative institutions. Holy days were abolished to be replaced with work days. Many priests and religious were arrested, accused of having supported the government. In major cities such as Lisbon and Oporto, religious celebrations of all kinds were forbidden. Minister of Justice Alfonso Costa announced that the Catholic religion could be extinguished in Portugal within just two generations.[16]

The First World War brought an opportunity for Portugal to attempt to recoup its territorial losses to Germany and Britain.

16. John de Marchi, *Fatima: The Full Story*, 30.

Seeking territorial favors from Britain, Portugal declared its adhesion to the English alliance on August 7, 1914, and on November 23 committed itself to military operations against Germany. In September 1915, an armed expedition was dispatched to reinforce their colonies in Africa, resulting in fighting in Mozambique, Tanganyika, Southern Angola, and German South-West Africa. An attempted naval blockade by German ships was seized off the coast of Portugal in February, 1916. Portugal also sent expeditionary forces to the Western Front.

> With the outbreak and continuance of the First World War, the condition of the country became steadily worse. Things were in an unhappy condition when Salazar took over the helm of the ship of State. The financial situation was deplorable; there was a monstrous debt and payments were in arrears; there were obligations unfulfilled, debts unpaid and a chronic deficit. The country which in other times "had given worlds to the world," had fallen into moral and material despair. "Portugal had forgotten God," said the Holy Father, "but God had not forgotten Portugal." Help was at hand.[17]

That help was to come through three small shepherd children who lived in the tiny village of Aljustrel, some three quarters of a mile south of Fatima, high in the remote hill country of the Serra da Aire.

17. Ibid., 31.

The little shepherds of Fatima (left to right):
Lucia dos Santos (age 10), Francisco Marto (age 9),
and Jacinta Marto (age 7).

The Annunciation

I N THE SPRING OF 1916, the Battle of Verdun was raging. Czar
Nicholas II was away at the Russian front, and Rasputin was
approaching the pinnacle of his powers. Portugal had successfully broken the German blockade and had entered the war in
Africa. But for three Portuguese shepherd children tending their
flocks on the windy slopes of the Loca do Cabeço, the war was a distant rumor and it was yet another day for filling up with singing and
dancing.

They had brought their sheep from the tiny hamlet of Aljustrel,
perched atop a mountain of the Serra da Aire in central Portugal.
The farming village of Aljustrel comprised only two rows of whitewashed stone cottages lying on either side of a single, winding lane.
Lucia, the oldest of these three children, came from one of these
farming families. Her father, Antonio dos Santos, was of moderate
means, owning several plots of land scattered about the parish of
Leiria-Fatima. Nicknamed "Abobora" or "pumpkin" because of the
main crop he cultivated, he was a sociable man who preferred "con-
viviality to Mass and wine rather than work."[1] As Lucia remembers:
"my father had fallen into bad company, and let his weakness get
the better of him; this meant the loss of some of our property."[2] The

---

1. William Thomas Walsh, *Our Lady of Fatima*, 2.
2. Sister Maria Lucia of the Immaculate Heart in Fr. Louis Kondor (ed.), *Fatima in Lucia's Own Words*, 64. Also see 99–100, note 20, where Fr. Louis Kondor, Vice Postulator of the Cause, Fatima, states that: "Even if it is true that he [Abobora] liked his wine, he must not be regarded as an alcoholic. As to his religious duties, it is certain that he did not fulfil them in the parish of Fatima for some years as he did not get along with the priest." Hereafter referred to as Lucia's *Memoirs*, this remains the principle primary source for information about the events at Fatima. Other primary sources consulted include interviews recorded in Fr. Antonio Maria Martins and Fr. Robert J. Fox, *Documents on Fatima*. The fullest and most informative chronicle is that by John de Marchi (see Bibliography).

task of looking after the family fell upon Lucia's mother, Maria Rosa, a hard-working, rather stern, but devout, Catholic. She cared for the family with an affectionate diligence and with sincere religious convictions. These she firmly implanted in her seven children through frequent family devotions, readings from the Scriptures and the lives of the saints, and regular participation in the annual cycle of holy feasts. Lucia reflects:

> My mother was in much demand thereabouts as a nurse. In cases of minor ills, people came to our house to seek her advice, but when the sick person was unable to go out, they asked my mother to go to their homes. She often spent entire days there, and even nights. If the illness was prolonged, or the sick person's condition required it, she occasionally sent my sisters to stay by the patient's bedside at night, to give the family a chance to get some rest. Whenever the sick person was the mother of a young family, or some one who could not stand the noise of children, my mother brought the little ones to our house and charged me with keeping them occupied.[3]

Lucia was the youngest of seven children. Born on 22 March, 1907, she was a robust, active, and responsible girl who at an early age was entrusted with the flocks. She was quite intelligent, possessing an excellent memory which revealed itself fairly early during her catechism classes. In fact, Lucia had learned her catechism so well that, on the recommendation of a Jesuit missionary from Lisbon, the local prior agreed to proceed with her confirmation when she was only six years old. (The customary age for confirmation was nine or ten.) However, she had not yet been taught how to read or write and remained illiterate until she was twelve years old. Lucia loved to dress up, especially for the fiestas, when she would appear in her gold chains, large earrings, beads, and shawl, which she decorated with feathers. She was very affectionate, fond of games, and extremely popular with the other children in the village. She could often be found sitting on the porch with a dozen children around her, listening intently as she related to them the stories her mother

3. Lucia, *Memoirs*, 58.

had taught her. Her sister, Maria dos Anjos, provides the following impression of Lucia:

> We loved her because she was so intelligent and affectionate. Even when she was older, when she came home with the flock, she used to run and sit on her mother's lap and be cuddled and kissed. We, the elder ones, used to tease her and say: "Here comes the cuddler!" And we would even get cross with her. But she always did it again the next day. When my first baby was born you should have seen her! She came home from the Serra, shut up the sheep and ran as fast as her legs would carry her to my house, which was just in front of my mother's. She clutched at the baby and covered it with kisses, not at all like the people round here.
>
> She loved children and they adored her. Sometimes they would collect in our yard, a dozen or so, and she would be quite happy decorating the little ones with flowers and leaves. She would make little processions with saints, arranging flowers and thrones and sing hymns to Our Lady as if she were in church. I can still remember the ones she liked best. (Here Maria dos Anjos hummed a well-known Portuguese hymn to Our Lady.) And she would end up by giving the "blessing." She knew how to look after children and the mothers used to leave them in our house when they went out to work. When I was at my weaving and my sister Carolina at her dressmaking, we used to keep an eye on them but when Lucia was there, even when she was quite tiny, we didn't have to bother.[4]

Two of these children, who later became her constant companions, were Francisco and Jacinta. They were Lucia's first cousins by her father's sister, Olimpia, and Olimpia's second husband, Manuel Marto. Lucia's aunt had two children by her first husband before he died and seven by her second husband. Francisco and Jacinta were respectively the sixth and seventh of those children born to Tia (Aunt) Olimpia and Ti (Uncle) Marto.

Ti Marto was "a man of exceptional character, who would command instant respect anywhere."[5] He carried himself with the dignity of a hard-working peasant who had also seen something of the world, having been a soldier in Africa. He treated everyone as his

---

4. John de Marchi, *Fatima: The Full Story*, 32.
5. Walsh, 12.

equal, accorded due respect to dignitaries, but with no servility. Unlike his brother-in-law, Antonio, he never cared for gaming or carousing. He worked hard, paid his debts, and saved his money. He was devoted to his family and was kind but firm with his children.

His wife, Olimpia, was much thinner than her sister-in-law. Neither was she as sturdy: in fact she was rather pale. However, her wiry appearance belied a remarkably strong constitution for a woman who had borne nine children. She was energetic and good-humored. Although she had a firm faith, she was content with much less religion than would satisfy a Maria Rosa. But it was the decent minimum for a woman living in a faithfully religious community like Aljustrel.

Their youngest son, Francisco, was born on June 11, 1908. He did not resemble his cousin, Lucia, in any respect. He had finer features and a straighter physique. His face was small and round. He had fair hair, dark eyes, a small thin mouth, and a well-formed chin. A generally amiable and independent boy, he was described by Lucia as "quiet and submissive."

> I recall how, one day, he came to my house and was delighted to show me a handkerchief with a picture of Our Lady of Nazaré on it, which someone had brought him from the seaside. All the children gathered round him to admire it. The handkerchief was passed from hand to hand, and in a few minutes it disappeared. We looked for it, but it was nowhere to be found. A little later, I found it myself in another small boy's pocket. I wanted to take it away from him, but he insisted that it was his own, and that someone had brought him one from the beach as well. To put an end to the quarrel, Francisco then went up to him and said: "Let him have it! What does a handkerchief matter to me?" My own opinion is that, if he had lived to manhood, his greatest defect would have been his attitude of "never mind."[6]

Francisco was anything but a coward. He would boldly explore unknown parts of the Serra on the darkest or foggiest night; or he would catch wild rabbits or foxes, making pets of them. He played with lizards and snakes, which he would bring right into the house,

6. Lucia, *Memoirs*, 120.

much to the distress of his terrified mother. He also had a mischievous sense of humor, often playing practical jokes on his brothers and sisters. Ti Marto recalls one evening when Francisco's elder brother John was snoring by the fire with his mouth wide open: "[Francisco] picked up a chip of wood and would have put it straight into his brother's mouth if I had not prevented him!"[7] Yet he could also display a highly developed sense of moral rectitude and strength of will, as his mother, Olimpia relates:

> One day as he was going out with the sheep, I told him to take them to Teresa's ground which isn't here but near the village. And he said at once: "No, I don't want to do that!" I was just going to give him a slap when he turned to me and said very seriously: "Mother, are you teaching me to steal?" I felt mad with anger and took him by the arm and pushed him outside. But he didn't go to Oiteiro! Not till the next day, after asking permission from his godmother, who said that he and Lucia might always go there.[8]

On another occasion, Francisco's moral conscience and his sensitivity for animals were mutually reinforced when he confronted a boy who had captured a young bird. He pressed the boy to release the bird, but when he refused, he offered the boy his only penny to set the bird free.

Francisco loved music and spent many hours playing his reed pipes, either by himself or for Lucia and Jacinta, who would sing and dance to the many tunes he could play. His poetic sense betrayed a natural tendency towards contemplation, especially for the works of nature. He and his sister used to debate which of the two "lamps" in the sky were the loveliest, the sun or the moon.

> "No lamp is as beautiful as Our Lord's," he used to remark to Jacinta, who much preferred Our Lady's lamp because, as she explained, "it doesn't hurt our eyes." Enraptured, he watched the sun's rays glinting on the window panes of the homes in the neighbouring villages, or glistening in the drops of water which spangled the trees and furze bushes of the serra, making them shine

7. de Marchi, 37.
8. Ibid., 38.

like so many stars; in his eyes these were a thousand times more beautiful than the Angels' lamps.[9]

Completely opposite to Francisco was his sister, Jacinta. Although similar to him in appearance—"the same round face and regular features, the small mouth, fine lips and well-proportioned body"[10]—the straight line of her brows and well-spaced, sparkling eyes suggested a brighter intelligence and a more stubborn spirit. The youngest of the family, Jacinta was born March 11, 1910. "Seven months after the girl was born," Ti Marto was fond of saying, "Portugal came under the Republic, and after another period of seven— seven years—Our Lady appeared." Being the youngest, she was, of course, the smallest of the children in our story. However, she had the strongest character of the three. Her heroic tenacity in the face of the sufferings she was about to endure establishes this beyond doubt. But even before that, one could perceive flashes of her strong will. For example, from the first moment she learned to pray, she made up her mind to say "Hail Mary, full of graces," instead of "full of grace," and no one could ever induce her to use the proper singular form.[11]

Jacinta was the darling of the Marto family and was overindulged by her brothers and sisters to such an extent that she became somewhat spoiled. She loved to get her own way among the children and pouted when she did not. If the other children did not accede to her wish to play the game she wanted to play, she would stamp off to a corner to sulk. Lucia and the other children referred to this quirk as "tethering the donkey." She was also possessive. Her favorite game was "buttons," and Jacinta, who usually won, would refuse to give them up. Lucia, minus her dress buttons, often had to face a row from her mother. Jacinta's intention was to hang on to them so that she would not have to risk losing her own buttons next time.

However, there were many qualities that she had in common with her brother, Francisco. She shared his sincerity and love of truth, as Maria dos Anjos affirms:

9. *Memoirs*, 120.
10. de Marchi, 39.
11. Walsh, 14.

One day, the children were playing a game of "forfeits" in the sitting-room. Jacinta was sentenced to give a kiss to my brother Manuel who was writing at a table. She protested, saying that she would rather kiss the crucifix on the wall. As the others agreed she took down the crucifix and did so. When I came in I saw the crucifix on the ground and the children gathered round it. I scolded them all, telling them that if they could not leave things alone they had better go and play outside. Jacinta owned up at once and said that it had been her fault and promised not to touch anything again.[12]

She also shared Francisco's fondness for nature, especially for the tiny lambs, which she deftly carried on her shoulders in imitation of a picture she had seen of the "Good Shepherd." She had a special name for each one: "Dove" and "Star" and "Beauty" and "Snow." "Jacinta loved to hold the little white lambs tightly in her arms, sitting with them on her lap, fondling them, kissing them, and carrying them home at night on her shoulders, so that they wouldn't get tired."[13] Jacinta, whose name means "hyacinth," also loved flowers which she collected to adorn her hair or to weave into garlands for Lucia. And we have already noted how she adored the nightly lamp of Our Lady because of its soft light.

Like Francisco, Jacinta was gifted musically. She was always singing and composing songs usually about the beauty of the Serra or about Mary. She would listen enchantedly as the echo of her singing returned to her from across the valley. "The name which echoed best, says Lucia, was Maria. Jacinta sometimes said a whole Ave Maria, but only beginning the second part of the prayer when 'Maria' had ceased echoing."[14]

Like most of the children of the Serra, Lucia, Francisco, and Jacinta grew up in a world that had not learned to separate religion from everyday life. The stories, songs, and dances they enjoyed, even the festivals and holidays, all had religious themes. Thus, in a sense one could say that they were not distinctively religious. For

12. de Marchi, 41.
13. *Memoirs*, 28.
14. de Marchi, 41.

them there was only living: Jesus, Mary, and the saints, Masses, festivals, and devotions were but essential elements of their daily round. This does not mean that the children took these things for granted. On the contrary, they reveled in the marvelous stories and colorful pageants. But these things were so much a part of their life that faith was second nature to them. They inhaled them with the crisp mountain air and drank them with the sparkling water. As a result they manifested a simple wisdom for things "religious" which was often quite charming.

For example, Jacinta had her own name for the Eucharistic host. She called it the "hidden Jesus," betraying at her young age her simple grasp of the mystery of the Real Presence of Christ in the Sacred Host. This was her way of understanding the mystery that Jesus was substantially present in the bread, but hidden under the accidental appearance of its elements. Needless to say, she still had some difficulty with the concept: "How is it that so many people receive the little Hidden Jesus at the same time?" she asked Lucia one day. "Is there one small piece for each person?" "Not at all!" counseled Lucia, drawing upon all her wisdom. "Don't you see that there are many Hosts, and that there is a Child Jesus in every one of them!"[15] She then supported her explanation by alluding to the story of the multiplication of the loaves and fishes. About the passion and death of Our Lord, Jacinta would say: "Poor little Lord! Poor, poor Our Lord! I am never going to commit another sin, if it makes you suffer so much!"

These three happy children were constantly playing in each other's company. Therefore, when it became time for nine-year-old Lucia to share her family responsibilities by shepherding their flocks, Francisco (nearly eight) and Jacinta (only just six) desperately wanted to go with her. They begged Olimpia to let them go, but Olimpia refused to allow such young children to remain exposed so long in the countryside. Jacinta characteristically gave her mother no rest on the matter, beseeching her every single morning to allow her to set out with Lucia. Even Francisco, otherwise so passive, joined in the pleading: "When he persisted in plead-

---

15. *Memoirs*, 27.

ing with his mother to let him take care of the flock and therefore come along with me," Lucia points out, "it was more to please Jacinta than anything else, for she much preferred Francisco's company to that of her brother John." Olimpia continued to withhold her permission, responding with a curt "No." And Francisco would murmur, "It's all the same with me. It is Jacinta who feels badly about it."[16] After many such episodes, Olimpia, mindful of how responsible Lucia was and noting the approach of warmer weather, finally agreed to allow them to accompany Lucia on the pastures of the open Serra.

A typical day for these children would begin with "a breakfast of vegetable or rice soup with a little olive oil and a piece of home-made bread."[17] Olimpia would pack them a simple lunch of bread, olives, and sardines or dried fish, loosening the sheep from the corral while they finished their breakfast. Happily the children would herd the sheep to join up with those of Lucia.

After combining their flocks, Lucia selected the day's pasture, which would either be common wasteland or a property which belonged to a member of the family. Sometimes they would pasture at Fatima, other times at Moita. Their favorite place was called Cabeço (the head). It was a rocky hill overlooking the village, abounding in trees and shrubs and fodder for the flocks. "Here the family owned a little olive grove, where the olive and pine trees and the great stones afforded a pleasant shade to the children in the heat of summer, as well as being an excellent place for games."[18] They would heartily indulge in uninterrupted play, letting the sheep fend for themselves. For at this time in the Loca do Cabeço the various herbs, flowers, and grasses, nourished by the spring rains, had sprouted among the rocks and stones and provided excellent pasture for their sheep.

Lucia's leadership and intelligence fitted her for being the chief games organizer. One of her former companions has left a description:

16. *Memoirs*, 120.
17. de Marchi, 43.
18. Ibid.

Lucia was very amusing. She had a way of getting the best out of us so that we liked to be with her. She was also very intelligent and could dance and sing and taught us to do the same. We always obeyed her. We spent hours and hours dancing and singing and sometimes forgot to eat. As well as the hymns we used to sing in church I remember one to Our Lady of Mount Carmel which I still sing as I go about my work and which my children have already learned. . . . We sang folk songs, too, which I can't remember now, and the little boys used to play their pipes while we danced.[19]

These songs were often accompanied by Francisco on his pipes. One of the folk songs they enjoyed singing is given by Lucia:[20]

> In this life everything sings,
> And who sings better than I?
> The shepherdess out on the serra,
> Or the maid a-washing in the stream!

> There's the merry chirp of the goldfinch
> That comes to awaken me,
> As soon as the sun arises,
> The brambles come alive with his song.

> The screech owl cries at night
> Seeking to frighten me,
> The girl in the moonlight sings
> As she gladly shucks the corn.

> The nightingale in the meadow
> Spends the whole day long in song,
> The turtle dove sings in the wood,
> Even the cart squeaks out a song!

> The serra is a rock-strewn garden
> Smiling happily all the day long,
> Sparkling with gleaming dew drops
> That glisten on the mountain side!

So it went on, day after joyful day among the simple shepherd children on the Serra da Aire. The warm midday sun directly over-

19. Ibid., 44.
20. *Memoirs*, 125.

52

head would announce their lunch break and the lengthening shadows of evening would direct them home. Supper was followed by nighttime devotions, and, the final Rosary having been offered up, the sleepy, carefree children would rest soundly on their fragrant mattresses of maize, grateful for another day of salutary delight.

However, this untroubled time of innocent play was about to be brought to a sudden end. It was around the spring of 1916, as we have mentioned. Lucia had left her former companions to join her sheep with those of Francisco and Jacinta. "To avoid going to the serra with all the other shepherds, we arranged to pasture our flocks on properties belonging to my uncle and parents."[21] One day they set out for land at the bottom of the Cabeço, facing eastwards. It was called Chousa Velha. They arrived about midmorning when it began to drizzle with a very fine, misty rain.

Loco do Cabeço as it was when the children played.

The children sought shelter within a hollow among some rocks. Looking out, they could see the village, their parents' home, and several nearby hamlets. Soon the sky began to clear. Eager to begin their playtime, the children quickly ate their lunch and said their Rosary. They had their own abbreviated form for the Rosary which consisted of saying the first two words of each of the prayers: "Our

21. *Memoirs*, 61.

Father, Hail Mary, Hail Mary… Glory Be." There, it was done, now they could commence playing.

They had barely started their game of "pebbles" when they saw at a distance above the trees which spread towards the east "a light, whiter than snow, in the form of a young man, transparent, and brighter than crystal pierced by the rays of the sun," as Lucia later described it.[22] As he approached, they could distinguish his features: the young man was about fourteen or fifteen years old and indescribably beautiful. Lucia takes up the story:

> We were surprised, absorbed, and struck dumb with amazement. On reaching us he said:
>
> "Do not be afraid. I am the Angel of Peace. Pray with me."
>
> Kneeling on the ground, he bowed down until his forehead touched the earth. Led by a supernatural impulse, we did the same, and repeated the words which we heard him say:
>
> "My God, I believe, I adore, I hope, and I love You! I ask pardon of You for those who do not believe, do not adore, do not hope, and do not love You!"
>
> Having repeated these words three times, he rose and said:
>
> "Pray thus. The Hearts of Jesus and Mary are attentive to the voice of your supplications." Then he disappeared.
>
> The supernatural atmosphere which enveloped us was so intense, that we were for a long time scarcely aware of our own existence, remaining in the same posture in which he had left us, and continually repeating the same prayer. The presence of God made itself felt so intimately and so intensely that we did not even venture to speak to one another. Next day, we were still immersed in this spiritual atmosphere, which only gradually began to disappear.

The sense of secrecy which imposed itself upon the three was such that it hardly needed Lucia's enjoining the children not to speak of the incident. In fact, they never mentioned it. It was first made public much later in 1937 when Lucia, in obedience to her Bishop, wrote it down in her second collection of memoirs. Yet even though the children never otherwise mentioned the angel, there is

---

22. *Memoirs*, 150.

existing testimony from one of the nuns in the Asile of Vilar that Lucia recounted the prayers of the angel to her as early as 1921, but without mentioning the supernatural circumstances.[23]

Time passed, the impression left by the angel began to wane somewhat, and the children soon returned to their pastimes as before. Nevertheless the angelic vision had left an imprint upon their activities. For it was related in an interview made some four years later that Francisco in imitation of the angel would often take the role of a priest pretending to offer the Sacrament to the children. He would make a little altar from the surrounding stones and, using the white portions of bread from their packed lunches, would cut tiny slices in the form of the Sacred Host and, having recited the words of the angel, would offer them to the other two who received them with great respect. As with many children who in play will rehearse those events that are most significant to them, so the games of these three innocents have thus preserved for us a record of their experience.[24]

As the heat of summer enveloped them, it became too hot to leave the sheep exposed on the sun-baked Serra. The children would return home at noon only to venture out with their flock in the cool of the evening. One day while they were taking their siesta under some shady trees by a well at the bottom of Lucia's garden, suddenly the same angel was standing beside them.

> "What are you doing?" he asked. "Pray! Pray very much! The Hearts of Jesus and Mary have designs of mercy on you. Offer prayers and sacrifices constantly to the Most High."
>
> "How are we to make sacrifices?" I asked.
>
> "Make of everything you can a sacrifice, and offer it to God as an act of reparation for the sins by which He is offended, and in supplication for the conversion of sinners. You will thus draw down peace upon your country. I am its Guardian Angel, the Angel of

---

23. Francis Johnston, *Fatima: The Great Sign*, 26.

24. In an interview given during 1921–1925 between Dom Jose Pedro da Silva, Bishop of Leiria-Fatima, and Dina Magalhaes Pereira, later Sister of the Congregation of Saint Dorothy, who knew Lucia personally. Recorded in Fernando Leite, *Francisco de Fatima*, 41–42.

Portugal. Above all, accept and bear with submission, the suffering which the Lord will send you."[25]

A pattern was beginning to emerge that was to continue through all the apparitions. All three children were given the vision; but only Lucia and Jacinta could hear what was said, and only Lucia ventured to speak. Thus, Francisco immediately asked what was said by the angel. "Didn't you hear?" Lucia asked Francisco.

"No. I could see that he was talking to you. I heard what you said to him; but what he said to you, I don't know."

However, the "power of the supernatural," as Lucia called it, made it difficult for her to think very clearly, so she advised him to ask Jacinta or herself the next day. Addressing his sister, he said: "Jacinta, you tell me what the angel said." But she too could not bring herself to indulge in conversation.

"I'll tell you tomorrow. Today I can't talk about it."

The next day, as soon as he saw Lucia, Francisco asked her about the words of the angel. Lucia repeated the words of the first and second apparitions, but Francisco was full of questions. "Who is the Most High? What is the meaning of: the Hearts of Jesus and Mary are attentive to the voice of your supplications?" Lucia struggled to explain as best she could, but Francisco would interrupt with even more questions.

Finally, Jacinta interrupted: "Listen! We shouldn't talk much about these things." Jacinta could not understand it, but something about the angel rendered her unable to talk or sing or play. "I haven't strength enough for anything."

A transformation was beginning to overtake the children. They began to devote many hours to prayer. Daily they would "offer to the Lord all that mortified us, without, however, seeking out other forms of mortification and penance, except that we remained for hours on end with our foreheads touching the ground, repeating the prayer the Angel had taught us."[26] The great themes of Fatima were beginning to emerge: prayer and reparation. The children were being initiated into the mystery of intercessory prayer.

25. *Memoirs*, 152.
26. Ibid.

The Annunciation

Imperceptibly, summer turned to autumn. The season for olives was ending as the days drew in and the rains cooled the air. The time of siestas was over and the shepherd children resumed their little treks to the pastures. It was late September or early October when the children were herding their sheep from an olive grove called Pregueira on the cabeço. They had just completed their lunch and had decided to go to a place called Lapa on the other side of the hill. There they stopped to pray among the rocks. Having offered up a Rosary, they began to prostrate themselves in order to repeat the prayer the angel had taught them when an extraordinary light shone upon them. The angel had appeared before them for the third and last time. He was holding in his hands a chalice into which blood was dripping from a host floating above. Leaving these suspended in the air, the angel then prostrated himself on the ground and repeated the following prayer three times:

> Most Holy Trinity, Father, Son and Holy Spirit, I adore You profoundly, and I offer You the most precious Body, Blood, Soul and Divinity of Jesus Christ, present in all the tabernacles of the world, in reparation for the outrages, sacrileges and indifference with which He Himself is offended. And, through the infinite merits of His most Sacred Heart, and the Immaculate Heart of Mary, I beg of You the conversion of poor sinners.[27]

The angel arose and took the chalice and the host in his hands. He gave the host to Lucia, but to Francisco and Jacinta, who had not received their first Communion, he gave the chalice. As he did so he said: "Take and drink the Body and Blood of Jesus Christ, horribly outraged by ungrateful men. Repair their crimes and console your God." Prostrating himself on the ground once more, he invited the children to repeat with him three more times the Eucharistic prayer, "Most Holy Trinity..." Then he vanished.

The children, impelled by the spiritual power that overwhelmed them, continued prostrating themselves and repeating this prayer over and over. Like St. Paul they were transported to such spiritual heights that they did not know whether they were in the body or

---

27. Ibid.

out of it (2 Cor. 12:2). They felt the force of God's presence so intensely that they were utterly absorbed by it. With their bodily senses suspended, they felt as if their individuality had been annihilated. Even for some days after, they drifted through their daily tasks as though impelled by that same spirit. Lucia recalls that "the peace and happiness which we felt were great, but wholly interior, for our souls were completely immersed in God." The experience was so intense that their diminutive bodies were left physically exhausted. These symptoms—constant awareness of God, the "sleep" of the senses, wounds of joy and love, and physical exhaustion—are familiar to those Christian saints who have scaled the heights of prayer.

> In the prayer of simple union all the interior faculties of the soul are centred on God alone; only the external senses are still free. But in the prayer of conforming union God captivates even the external senses, with the result that the soul is totally divinised, so to speak, and prepared by God to move to the full and final commitment of the transforming union. . . . In the prayer of conforming union, therefore, the soul loses the use of its external senses, either partially or totally, because all the interior faculties are absorbed in God and the senses are alienated from their proper natural functioning. It is with difficulty that the soul turns its attention to external activity, though it knows that sometimes it must leave "God for God" in performing its duties or services of charity for others.[28]

Heaven had chosen these children for something and prepared them for it by giving them Holy Communion and passive purification of the senses, thereby bringing them to a stage where they could willingly undergo the intercessory reparations that the angel had asked them to perform. The angel had left, having fulfilled his mission of cleansing and reconciliation. The children from this time onward would lead lives of extreme sanctity and devotion. This by itself would be a wonderful confirmation of the experience, for "which of you by anxious thought can add one cubit to his stature?" (Mt. 6:27)

After several days when the children had again recovered their

---

28. Jordan Aumann, *Spiritual Theology*, 344–45.

composure, Francisco, who did not hear the locutions, asked the others:

"The Angel gave you Holy Communion, but what was it that he gave to Jacinta and me?"

"It was Holy Communion, too," replied Jacinta, with inexpressible joy. "Didn't you see that it was the Blood that fell from the Host?"

"I felt that God was within me, but I did not know how!"

Then he and his sister spontaneously fell to the ground and prayed repeatedly, "Most Holy Trinity…"

Here we have a wonderful confirmation of what Jacinta liked to call the "Hidden Jesus"—the mystery of the Real Presence of Christ in the Eucharist. The children were shown the blood of Christ dripping from the host into the chalice. Yet even though none of the trio received Communion under both kinds, each understood that they were partaking of the very Person of Jesus Christ. They realized that His Presence is whole and entire in either form of the Eucharist.

Was this communion physical or was it a spiritual experience? In a later interrogation by Bishop Dom Jose Pedro da Silva, Lucia was asked:

"When [you] received communion from the hand of the Angel, did you feel, in the mouth, the *physical* contact of the Sacred Species, such as today when you communicate?"

"Yes."

"Do you remember having swallowed the Sacred Host?"

"Yes."

"The Angel of Peace… the Angel of Portugal… are they two or only one?"

"I do not know: He seemed to me to be always the same one."

"In the second apparition, could there have been some difference… in aspect… apparel?"

"I do not remember noticing any difference."[29]

We might also reflect upon the meaning of the prayers the angel taught the children. The first prayer was: "My God, I believe, I adore, I hope, and I love You! I ask pardon of You for those who do

---

29. Recorded in Fernando Leite, *Francisco de Fatima*, 40–41 (italics in original).

not believe, do not adore, do not hope, and do not love You!" This prayer emphasizes the responsibility and duty towards others that proper devotion to God should evoke. To love God is to be concerned for others (Mt. 22:37–38) especially for their spiritual welfare (Mt. 6:33; Lk. 10:42; Ro. 14:17). Such concern leads naturally to a desire to pray for others. And the words of the angel clearly indicate those who are especially in need of such intercession: those who withhold belief in God, or lack the faith to place their hope and trust in Him, or do not render to God heartfelt adoration and worship, or do not manifest their love for Him. Here are found the theological virtues of faith, hope, and adoring love that Paul places at the heart of Christian devotion. Moreover, the intensity and expansiveness of our love for God give us such a profound sense of his majesty and radiance that we desire to see such adoration and worship offered to Him by all His creatures. He is worthy of no less. Hence the prayer. Hence the prostration of the angel.

The second prayer is even more sublime and richer theologically:

Most Holy Trinity, Father, Son and Holy Spirit, I adore You profoundly, and I offer You the most precious Body, Blood, Soul and Divinity of Jesus Christ, present in all the tabernacles of the world, in reparation for the outrages, sacrileges and indifference with which He Himself is offended. And, through the infinite merits of His most Sacred Heart, and the Immaculate Heart of Mary, I beg of You the conversion of poor sinners.[30]

Firstly, we have the clear affirmation of the Divine Trinity: God the Father, God the Son, and God the Holy Spirit. We have a separate acknowledgment of the divinity of Jesus Christ as well. Indeed, the entire prayer is suffused with the incarnation. For the Whole Christ is also present in the Eucharistic elements housed in all the tabernacles throughout the world.

That God is a Trinity should be apparent to any self-reflexive person. For we who are self-aware sense the subjective and objective phases of our own souls. There is that in us which is aware, the "I," and that of which we are aware, the "me." The self-reflective process

30. *Memoirs*, 152.

contains both the intention to reflect and the object of that reflection. These are distinguishable phases arising within us when we reflect on ourselves. Once we understand this—that within our consciousness there is a willing agent that intends to reflect as well as the object of that reflection—it is easy to see that any self-aware being will, in some analogous manner, manifest this internal dialogue. Moreover, we also express ourselves—act, think, and feel—out of this internal dialogue. We may even say that our character—our projected image, our personality, our very self-expression—proceeds from these self-reflexive phases of our souls. We are an image of the Trinity: subject-object (Principle and Logos) and the character or spirit they both express.

If this is so for us, it is assuredly true for God, who is, among so many other wonderful attributes, also self-aware. Ever since the Cappadocian Fathers—Basil the Great, Gregory Nazianzus, Gregory of Nyssa—we have understood the Trinity in this way. It was St. Basil the Great (c. 330–339) who first grasped the three Persons of the Trinity in terms of their internal relationships.

The Father is unbegotten and, therefore, absolute Subject of His Being. This means that the Father has no beginning and is His own principle of Being. God the Father is an eternal, underived Substance in whom there is nothing accidental—His Being is absolutely necessary in and of itself alone (Ex. 3:14).

The Son is eternally begotten of the Father. He also is without beginning, but is eternally conceived from the self-awareness of the Father as a real, complete, and perfectly expressed image of the Father, full of majesty and excellence. From the moment God reflects upon Himself as object, He is also the Subject of that reflexive activity. And this is an eternal activity, because there never is a moment when the all-knowing God is not thoroughly transparent to Himself (Mt. 11:27; Jn. 1:18; Col. 2:3; 1 Tim. 6:16; 1 Jn. 1:5).

The third Person of the Trinity is the life, breath, or Spirit of truth and love shared by the Father with the Son, and by the Son with the Father. The essential characteristic of the Holy Spirit is spiration (Jn. 20:22). He is breathed forth from the Father and from the Son as the expression of their eternal and indissoluble complaisance. He is the blissful communion of the Father with the Son (Jn. 16:13–15).

Thus, we can conceive of the life of the Trinity as an everlasting self-reflexive and expressive activity sharing in one eternal Substance: one God, eternally self-aware, omniscient, continually creative; one all consuming, overflowing reservoir of love, mercy, and justice; Father, Logos, and Spirit; three Persons, one God, of infinite majesty and worth.

We also note, in the angel's prayer, mention of the Sacred Heart of Jesus and the Immaculate Heart of Mary. We have already touched upon the heart of Mary when we saw that it is the seat of the theological, cardinal, and religious virtues that Mary manifested in her earthly pilgrimage. We also noted that these virtues were derivative in nature, i.e., they were bestowed upon her by the merits and grace of Christ. Thus, they flow from the Heart of Jesus. What is this Sacred Heart?

Devotion to the Heart of Jesus has its origins in the substantial (hypostatic) union of the Divine and human natures of Jesus Christ. We understand from sacred tradition that "the Word (Logos) became flesh and dwelt among us full of grace and truth" (Jn. 1:14). That is to say, the Second Person of the Trinity (the Wisdom of the Father) assumed human flesh and was born of a virgin of Nazareth, living a life among humankind.

Therefore, because of the incarnation, there is a mutual immanence (circumincession) of the Divine nature in the human (Jn. 10:30; 14:10–11; 17:21), so that whatever we may concretely say of the Divine Logos we may also say of the human Jesus. Moreover, since Jesus's human will was so completely obedient to the Divine will (Lk. 22:42; Jn. 5:30; 6:38), we may also speak of the hypostatic or substantial union of the Divine and human wills in Jesus Christ.[31] In other words, Christ's human nature conforms with the Divine nature: their natures are in perfect accord.

We have noted that in the Scriptural tradition the heart is the locus of the affections. Therefore, because of this union, the heart of Jesus becomes the locus of the Divine affections also, especially Christ's divine redeeming love for human beings. Moreover, when we consider Christ's passion and suffering, particularly the spear

---

31. Cf. St. Thomas, *Summa Theologica*, III. Q.18, Art. 1, reply obj. 4.

thrust into His heart, the Heart of Jesus comes to represent the seat of sorrow, of Divine Pity, for suffering and wayward humanity. That is why, in the vision given to Catherine Labouré, she beheld the Sacred Heart of Jesus surrounded and pierced by a crown of thorns, a crown woven for Him by uncaring and egocentric human beings. Since Christ's redeeming love is manifested so poignantly and essentially in His passion and crucifixion and in the Holy Eucharist, so the veneration of the Heart means veneration of the redemptive suffering of Our Lord. As we shall soon see, this devotion has its practical aspect. But for the moment we need only comprehend that the "infinite merits of the Sacred Heart of Jesus" refers to this seat of suffering, passionate sorrow which yearns for the repentance of indifferent, even blasphemous humanity.

We also address at this point the difficulty some have had with the angel's offering up of the Divinity of Jesus Christ to the Trinity. How, some ask, can the Divinity be offered up to itself? How can God sacrifice to God? Yet, we have seen that it is an essential principle of the incarnation that whatever can be asserted concretely of the Divine Son may also be affirmed of Jesus in His humanity. Because the two natures are intimately united in Jesus, but without confusion, then whatever Jesus suffers in his humanity is appropriated by His Divine Person. The Son assumed human flesh and all that it suffered, and offered it to the Father, through and in the Divinity of the Person of the Son. Thus it is perfectly admissible to assert that on the cross Jesus offered up His Divinity to the Triune God, for He is both Priest and Victim (Heb. 1:5–13; 5:1–10).

Clearly, the theology of these annunciations to the little children is lofty. It is certain that little children of nine, eight, and six years of age could not fully comprehend its significance, in spite of the graces given to them. Yet that meaning is there all the same, and will be reinforced by those heavenly messages yet to come to them.

But the children did comprehend the central import of the message. The manifestations of the angel had made such a profound impression upon these tiny innocents that they began to spend many hours in their parish church prostrated upon the floor, endlessly repeating these sublime prayers. They undertook to fast, not only from food and drink, but from play and rest, in order to offer reparation in intercession for others (Ro. 12:1; 2 Cor. 12:15; Col. 1:24; 2 Tim. 1:8; 2:10; 1 Pet. 2:5; Jas. 5:16). They would crawl around the interior of the church on their knees in penance.[32] They shed bitter tears for the sorrow-stricken Heart of Jesus. The angel's message was having its desired effect: the children were being made ready for the appearances and message of the Mother of God the following spring. For what was about to be entrusted to the tender souls of these young children would have grave consequences for the entire world.

32. Fr. Robert J. Fox, *Fatima Today*, 18–19.

The Visitation

APART FROM THE THREE CHILDREN, no one knew of the appearances of the angel the previous year. These little ones had been so marked by the intensity of the experience that an instinctive reserve surrounded and safeguarded its intimacy. Also, the children were constantly in one another's company, so that when they were on their own they were assumed to be playing together. No one realized the frequency of their devotions, nor were they aware of the fervency of their penance.

Life that year was becoming so increasingly difficult for Maria Rosa that she was too preoccupied to have noticed the change in her youngest daughter. Her two eldest daughters, Maria and Teresa, were married, and were no longer able to help the family. Antonio Abobora was becoming more shiftless. Consequently, property had to be sold to meet the debts that had begun to mount because of his drinking and because of the loss of income from the neglected farm. Maria Rosa was forced to send Gloria and Carolina to work as servants in order to bring in some income, while she attempted to earn a little extra through nursing, in addition to everything else she had to do.

Besides this, the war had now come to the village. Every day one heard of someone leaving for the Western Front. Among these was Lucia's elder brother, Manuel, who jumped at the opportunity to escape from the drudgery of farm work. After all, his father, Antonio, shirked the responsibility, so why should he have to bear it? One evening Manuel came home with the news that he had enlisted and would soon be leaving once he passed the physical. With her four eldest girls away, with her husband habitually late while he lingered in a wine shop for yet another *copozinho,* and with their property and income rapidly diminishing, Manuel's announcement came as the final blow. That evening as she looked around the remaining three members of the family—young Antonio, Lucia, and Manuel, who was about to be sent to war—this otherwise resilient woman broke down: "My God, where has the joy of our home gone?" And dropping her head onto the rude table beside her, she wept bitterly, until Manuel and his sister succumbed also. "It was one of the saddest scenes I have ever witnessed," wrote Lucia.[1]

From that time on, Maria Rosa's health steadily worsened. She became so debilitated that Gloria had to forgo her employment to take care of the family. Doctors were of little help in those days, and Maria Rosa continued to suffer. Carolina was called back home to help. Finally, Manuel's godfather promised to obtain a military exemption. He had a word with the doctor responsible for Manuel's medical examination. "And thus the good Lord deigned to grant my mother this relief" (from having to send Manuel off to battle). It was only after some weeks that Maria Rosa began to recover physically. However, she was never able to shake off her bitterness until much later, when she finally came to accept the reality of the coming events.

The Marto family, too, had to struggle with the bitterness of war. One of their sons had gone to the front. Rumors came back that he was killed in action. The rumors turned out to be false, but for some weeks the entire Marto family was desolate. Francisco and Jacinta added their tears to those of Lucia. They were beginning to realize the substance of the angel's words: "Above all, accept and bear with submission the suffering which the Lord will send you," for they would offer up even these sufferings for the "conversion of poor sinners." They were going on to maturity, learning to live the Christ-like life of loving self-sacrifice.

> For his sake I have suffered the loss of all things, and count them as refuse, in order that I may gain Christ and be found in him, not having a righteousness of my own, based on law, but that which is through faith in Christ, the righteousness from God that depends on faith; that I may know him and the power of his resurrection, and may share his sufferings, becoming like him in his death, that if possible I may attain the resurrection from the dead. Not that I have already obtained this or am already perfect; but I press on to

1. *Memoirs*, 64.

make it my own, because Christ Jesus has made me his own. (Phil. 3:8–12)

By the time spring came, Maria Rosa's health had improved and the family's life had stabilized somewhat. With the arrival of May, everyone in the parish of Leiria-Fatima was preparing for the Feast of the Ascension. The thirteenth of the month was the Sunday before the Feast, and the family went to Mass as usual. It was a fine Sunday, and Ti Marto needed to obtain a pig for slaughter, so he hitched up his cart and, together with Olimpia, went to Batalha, where the family could hear Mass at the beautiful cathedral there and then do their shopping in the local Sunday markets. Leaving Jacinta and Francisco to attend Mass in Fatima with Lucia's family, they departed.

> God preserve us (said Senhora Olimpia vehemently) from letting Sunday go by without Mass. We always went, children and all as soon as they were of an age to understand. Sometimes we had to go to other villages quite a distance off, but whatever the weather, rain or fine, I never remember missing Mass even when I had the children at the breast. I used to get up early and leave everything to my husband, who went to the later Mass. We never took the toddlers to church because they don't hear Mass or allow you to either. You think you're taking a little angel and it turns out to be a little devil![2]

After the Mass the children returned home, collected their lunch bags, and set off with their flocks to their pasture for the day. Since it was a delightfully warm day, Lucia and her two cousins felt like going further afield. Lucia selected a small property that still remained within their parents' possession some two and a half kilometers distant. It was located in a vast hollow in the ground known as the Cova da Iria, which was so seldom used that it was often overgrown with grasses and flowering shrubs. The Cova resembled a huge bowl that formed a natural amphitheater. One side was bordered by a road and a dry stone wall, while the other sides descended gently into valleys quilted with numerous small hold-

2. de Marchi, 50.

ings. The basin floor of the Cova itself was covered with a thick foliage of olive trees and sundry evergreens, many of them belonging to the holm (holly) oak family. Two types of holm oak were prevalent in these parts: the larger *carrasqueira,* which offered fine shade, and the smaller *azinheira,* which only grew one to two meters high.

The name Cova da Iria is, like many of the names around Fatima, of Muslim origin. (Fatima itself is the name of Muhammad's daughter.) Iria, Ourem, Santarem, Leiria, all come from the name of a Portuguese saint, Irene or Iria. The legend has it that in the seventh century a young Moorish girl named Iria was placed by her uncle, the Abbot Celio, in the care of her two aunts, who were Benedictine nuns. While still a child, she consecrated her virginity to God. However, her rejection of a marriage proposal from an ardent suitor eventually led to disaster. The young Britaldo, unable to accept the spurning of his marriage proposal, had his man-at-arms slay her with his sword and throw her body into the River Nabao, which flowed into the Tagus. According to legend, the Abbot had a dream in which he learned of his niece's fate. He followed the river downstream, looking for his niece. When he came to the spot near Santarem, the river Tagus receded, exposing the body of Iria. The body could not be extricated and was eventually covered by the returning river. Later, King Denis erected a monument to St. Iria in what is now called Santarem. Such legends were part of popular folklore in the hill country of the Serra.

The children arrived at the Cova at about lunch time. After taking lunch, they had the idea of making a house out of a thicket of furze by closing off its opening with a wall. They were absorbed in the task of shifting some heavy stones to the spot and heaving them onto one another, when suddenly there was a flash of light, but no thunder. Fearing that the flash betokened a threatening thunderstorm, Lucia advised her cousins to herd the sheep home. They were hurrying the sheep in the direction of a large holm oak, southwest of where they had been playing, when another flash of light rooted them to the spot. Aware of the danger of standing next to a large tree in a lightning storm, they scampered off toward the east. They had only gone a few steps when, just as they were approaching a small holm oak, they stopped abruptly, astonished by what they

The Visitation

saw. There on top of the prickly *azinheira* they saw a globe of light, and in its center stood a beautiful Lady dressed all in white.

> She was more brilliant than the sun, and radiated a light more clear and intense than a crystal glass filled with sparkling water, when the rays of the burning sun shine through it.[3]

The children were only a few feet from her. Her face was indescribably beautiful, "not sad, not happy, but serious." The palms of her hands were held together in a gesture of prayer, with a Rosary suspended from her right hand. Her garments were made of the same white light: a simple tunic fell to her feet, over which was draped a mantle that covered her head and fell to the same length. Its edge was tinged with a still more luminous light, glittering like gold. A brilliant star shone from its hem. Neither her hair nor her ears were visible under the mantle, and her facial features were too dazzling to behold. A radiant aura surrounded her and extended outwards for over a meter, its shimmering penumbra just embracing the children in its soft luminescence. Gently, she spoke to the surprised children.

"Do not be afraid. I will do you no harm."

Feeling her courage return, Lucia asked the Lady where she came from.

"I am from heaven," the Lady responded, pointing upwards.

"What do you want of me?" asked Lucia.

"I have come to ask you to come here for six months in succession, on the thirteenth day of the month, at this same hour. Later on, I will tell you who I am and what I want. Afterwards, I will return here yet a seventh time."

Naturally, the little child's attention eagerly seized upon the word *heaven*.

"Shall I go to heaven, too?"

"Yes, you will."

"And Jacinta?"

"She will go also."

"And Francisco?"

---

3. Lucia, *Memoirs*, 156.

69

She paused and looked closely at Francisco. "He will go there too, but he must say many Rosaries."

Then Lucia recalled two girls who had recently died. They were close friends who used to come to her sister to learn to weave.

"Is Maria das Neves in heaven?"

"Yes she is."

"And Amelia?"

"She will be in purgatory until the end of the world." At this, Lucia began to cry. Reassuringly the Lady continued to speak, implying that Amelia's fate was only conditional.

"Are you willing to offer yourselves to God and bear all the sufferings He wills to send you, as an act of reparation for the sins by which He is offended, and of supplication for the conversion of sinners?"

Lucia, speaking for all three, consented.

"Then you will have much to suffer, but the grace of God will be your comfort."

> As she pronounced these words (Lucia explains), Our Lady opened her hands for the first time, communicating to us a light so intense that, as it streamed from her hands, its rays penetrated our hearts and the innermost depths of our souls, making us see ourselves in God, Who was that light, more clearly than we see ourselves in the best of mirrors. Then, moved by an interior impulse that was also communicated to us, we fell on our knees, repeating in our hearts: "O most Holy Trinity, I adore You! My God, my God, I love You in the most Blessed Sacrament!"[4]

After a few moments, when the children had finished the prayer and their attention had returned, the Lady spoke once more.

"Pray the Rosary every day, in order to obtain peace for the world, and the end of the war."

With that, she began to rise serenely, ascending towards the east. Her radiant aura "seemed to open up a path before her in the firmament" until she disappeared into the blue vault of sky.

The children remained spellbound, their eyes fixed upon the

---

4. *Memoirs*, 158.

point in space where the vision had vanished. After a short while they regained their composure. Lucia later recalls that the spiritual state they experienced with this Lady was, in one very important respect, different from that which they endured with the angel. They felt the same intimate joy, peace and happiness, but instead of the physical prostration, they enjoyed "expansive ease of movement"; instead of the annihilation of the senses, they expressed "joyful exultation"; instead of the enforced silence, they manifested "communicative enthusiasm."

The remainder of the day was spent remembering and savoring the exquisite details of the beautiful Lady and her promise to return to them. Lucia remained pensive. The Lady had foretold further suffering and Lucia, having already endured so much bitterness in her family, fully appreciated what that foreshadowed.

Jacinta, on the other hand, was entirely enraptured by it all. "*Ai, que Senhora tao bonita!* Oh, such a lovely Lady," she would sigh over and over. And Francisco was overjoyed at the expectation that he would be going to heaven. Making the sign of the cross, he exclaimed: "Oh, my dear Our Lady! I'll say as many Rosaries as you want!"

"Oh, what a lovely Lady!" Jacinta sighed again.

"I can see what will happen. You'll end up saying that to somebody else," Lucia remarked.

"No, I won't," promised Jacinta, "don't worry. *Ai, que Senhora tao bonita!*" Her ebullient manner and shining face betrayed the fragility of her promise.

Lucia could not entirely share her cousins' innocent enthusiasm. She was not only pensive about the prospect of what was in store for them, but sad for her friend Amelia, who, as the Lady from heaven had attested, was in purgatory.

Lucia was sad because her childlike understanding of purgatory was imperfect. Indeed, the Old Testament authors themselves had only a hazy understanding of the afterlife. For them, after death the soul descended into an unseen world of virtual reality. This "place of shades" was called Sheol and it had many planes of existence. Some levels were destructive and punitive (Deut. 32:22; Ps. 116:3). Others were less so (Ez. 31:16, 32:21, 27). It was not necessarily a permanent abode (Ps. 16:10; Ps. 86:13). And in some cases, human beings could be summoned from this realm of the dead, as was the eminent prophet Samuel (1 Sam. 28:3–19.) An intertestamental book, 2 Maccabees, even speaks of an "expiatory sacrifice offered for the dead so that they might be released from their sin" (12:45).

In the New Testament, a tripartite distinction was made in the afterworld. There was heaven, of course. But there were also Gehenna and Hades. Old translations of the Scriptures did not distinguish between the latter two, rendering both Gehenna and Hades as *hell*. However, some modern translations judiciously make this distinction by translating Gehenna as *hell* and leaving *Hades* untranslated. It is important that this differentiation be made, for the two terms are variously applied. The term hell (*Gehenna*) is associated with damnation and eternal destruction (Mt. 5:22, 29–30, 10:28; 18:9; 23:33; Mk. 9:43, 45, 47; Lk. 12:5), while *Hades* never is. *Hades* is sometimes simply rendered as death (Mt. 16:18) or contrasted with heaven (Mt. 11:23; Lk. 10:15). It is a place of torment (Lk. 16:23) but, unlike hell, Hades is not permanent (Acts 2: 27; 31; Rev. 1:18; 20:13) and will one day be destroyed (Rev. 20:14). In fact, there is even a fourth term applied to the afterlife, *Tartarus*, meaning a netherworld (Limbo?) like that of Sheol (2 Pet. 2:4).

Clearly, therefore, the Biblical tradition contained a progressive reflection upon the afterlife. This tendency continued in the Church, especially when it was noted that the Scriptures implied a period of purification after death (1 Cor. 3:12-15) in order to bring imperfect souls to the state of holiness without which no one can behold God (Heb. 12:14; Rev. 19:7–8). The early Latin fathers (St. Cyprian, St. Clement, St. Augustine) recognized that there must be a process, however instantaneous, which brings a person from the state of imperfection at death to the perfection necessary to withstand the beatific vision of God. The term *purgatory* was applied to that process of glorification which takes place in heaven (Rom. 8:30). This is precisely what the concept of purgatory emphasizes: namely, that Divine love which burns like a refining fire in the presence of which each soul is entirely renewed (Zech.13:9; Mal. 3:2; Is. 48:10). It reminds us of the purity and holiness of God and of the perfection He requires of us before we can stand before Him. His love for us is so great that He cannot rest until we are rendered quintessentially holy.

> I see that God is in such perfect conformity with the soul, that when He beholds it in the purity wherein it was created by His Divine Majesty He imparts a certain attractive impulse of His burning love, enough to annihilate it, though it be immortal; and in this way so transforms the soul into Himself (its God) that it sees in itself nothing but God, who goes on thus attracting and inflaming it, until He has brought it to that state of existence whence it came forth—that is the spotless purity wherein it was created.... It sees in the Divine light how considerate, and with what unfailing providence, God is ever leading it to its full perfection, and that he does it all through pure love; it finds itself stopped by sin, and unable to follow the heavenly attraction ... and this sense of the grievousness of being kept from beholding the Divine light, coupled with that instinctive longing which would fain be without hindrance to follow the enticing look— these two things, I say, make up the pains of the souls in purgatory.[5]

For sure, young Lucia could not understand this properly. She was thinking of purgatory in a materialistic, rather than in a spiritual, sense.

As far as the statement that Amelia was to remain in purgatory until the end of the world is concerned, this must be understood as conditionally applied, as the next utterance of the Lady makes clear. Moreover, there is no time in eternity. "Until the end of the world" means "until the day of judgment." What happens to souls from the time of death until that day is not obvious in Scripture.

We are also approaching a deeper appreciation of the concept of reparation. We shall have more to say on this. For the time being, we simply observe that the purification that the children underwent in the presence of the angel, the suffering they have yet to endure, the need for us to offer intercession for those who are lost, and the notion that we have yet to be purified after this life, are themes which consistently point to a Divine economy of justice and restitu-

---

5. St. Catherine of Genoa, *Treatise on Purgatory*, cp. ix.

tion at work in the cosmos. It is this mystery that lies at the heart of Fatima.

It is no wonder then that Lucia was so pensive. She had much to absorb even at her tender age. For the rest of the day she was silent and subdued. After her evening devotions with her family she quietly went to bed.

Such was not the case with Jacinta. She was so excited by what had happened at the Cova that she could not wait for her parents to return from the Sunday market at Batalha. The entire Marto family (with the exception of the boy, who was at war) were there waiting also. Even an uncle by marriage, Antonio da Silva, had dropped in for supper. As evening approached, the older girls had placed a huge kettle of potato and cabbage soup on the hearth. The aroma of warm, baked bread pervaded the house. But Jacinta could not remain still. Bursting with the news she would run again and again outside to the gate to watch for their approach. Eventually the sound of a mule cart on the cobbled road signaled their return. Jacinta streaked outside. She could scarcely contain herself while Manuel Marto struggled to extricate the pig from the wagon. "But at the sight of Olimpia's kindly and ready smile, the child ran to clasp her about the knees."[6]

"Mother, I saw Our Lady today at Cova da Iria!"

"I believe you, child! Oh, yes, you are such a good saint that you see Our Lady!" With that she swept into the house.

"But I *saw* her," insisted Jacinta, following after.

Senhora Marto takes up the narrative confirming Lucia's version of the incident.

> Then she told me what had happened, of the lightning and their fear because of it ... of the light ... and the beautiful lady surrounded by light so dazzling, you could hardly look at it ... of the Rosary which they were to say every day. But I didn't believe anything she was saying and hardly listened to her. I told her she must have taken leave of her senses to think that Our Lady had appeared to her!
>
> After that I went to get some food for the pig. My husband had

6. Walsh, 54.

stayed in the corral to see if it was getting on with the other animals. When we had finished seeing to the animals we went back to the house. My Manuel sat down by the hearth and began to eat his supper. His brother-in-law, Antonio da Silva, happened to be there too, and all my children as far as I can remember, all eight of them. Then I said to Jacinta:

"Tell us that story about Our Lady in the Cova da Iria."

And she told us what happened with the greatest simplicity. There had been a most beautiful lady ... dressed in white with a gold cord hanging from her neck to her waist. Her head was covered with a mantle, whiter than milk, and fell to her feet. It was edged with gold and was so beautiful ... her hands had been joined, so. . . . And my little girl got up off the stool and stood with her hands folded on the level of her chest in imitation of the vision.

She said: "The lady held a Rosary in her hand; a beautiful Rosary shining like the stars, and a crucifix that shone. . . . She spoke with Lucia a great deal but not with me, or Francisco. I heard all what she said. Oh, Mother, we must say the Rosary every day; the lady said this to Lucia. She said too, that she would take us all to Heaven, and other things which I can't remember, but which Lucia knows. When she went back to Heaven the doors seemed to shut so quickly that I thought her feet would get caught. . . ."[7]

Throughout Jacinta's story Francisco was nodding approval and interjecting details. His sisters were listening intently to Jacinta, but the other brothers began to taunt her. Olimpia, too, continued to ridicule Jacinta's implied presumption of sainthood, while Antonio da Silva pointed out that, if the children had seen a beautiful Lady dressed in white, it could be no one other than the Blessed Virgin. Manuel Marto, however, was more reflective:

From the beginning of the world, Our Lady has been appearing, at different times and in different ways. These have been the important things. If there had not been such things the world would be even worse than it is. The power of God is very great. We do not understand everything, but let God's Will be done.[8]

7. de Marchi, 55–56.
8. Ibid., 56.

Later on Ti Marto would recall:

> From the beginning I somehow felt that the children were speaking the truth. Yes, I think I believed from the first. It seemed to me extraordinary because the children had no instruction whatever about such things, at least hardly anything. If they had not been helped by Providence how could they have said such things! And if they were lying? But I knew so well that Francisco and Jacinta never lied.[9]

Thus, on that Sunday evening in the middle of May, Manuel Marto became the first to believe in the apparitions of Fatima. The next day, Olimpia, no doubt encouraged by Manuel's favorable response, had begun telling the story to the neighbors. It was not long before the news spread throughout the village right up to the door of Maria Rosa. A neighbor had recounted the gossip to Lucia's sister, Maria dos Anjos, who relates this conversation.[10]

"Lucia, I heard you saw Our Lady in the Cova da Iria. Is it true?"

"Who told you?" gasped Lucia.

"The neighbors are saying that Jacinta came out with it to Olimpia."

Lucia reflected for some time and replied that she had told Jacinta many times not to tell. Maria asked why she had admonished her so. And Lucia answered that it was because she was not sure it was Our Lady, although she was a beautiful Lady. Then Maria asked what the Lady said.

"That she wanted us to go for six months running, to the Cova da Iria and that she would tell us later what she wanted."

"Didn't you ask her who she was?"

"I asked her where she came from and she said: 'I come from heaven.'" After that Lucia resumed her characteristic silence.

Maria dos Anjos was disturbed by what she felt was the emergence of a tendency towards invention in Lucia. She immediately reported the incident to her mother. Antonio, her father, was there at the time. He dismissed the entire story as "women's tales," and

9. Ibid.
10. Ibid., 57.

with that set out for the fields. Maria Rosa, on the other hand, was furious. "This was all I needed for my old age!" she lamented bitterly. "To think that I always brought my children up to speak the truth! And now this one brings me a whopper like this!"[11] Maria Rosa, who had become bitter because of her circumstances, was predisposed to expect bad news in everything. Also, she was very devoted to the Church and would not believe in any such tales until the Church itself gave its approval. She knew of the legends and folklores (such as that of St. Iria) that were often confused by the locals with authentic tradition, and she knew that these were seldom approved by the Church. Until the Church authorities pronounced favorably on these apparitions, Maria Rosa would refuse to accept them.

It was a heartbroken and intimidated Lucia who met with her cousins that day. As they drove their flocks to the pastures, Jacinta began to cry pitifully.

"I won't tell anyone ever again," Jacinta promised, not realizing that it was too late.

"I've already told," added Francisco, accusing himself instead of Jacinta. "I said that the Lady promised to take us to heaven. When they asked me if that was true I couldn't lie! Forgive me, Lucia, I won't ever tell anyone anything more!"

The delight of the vision was spoiled, and the moroseness that enveloped the pair was too much for Lucia to bear. Feeling sorry for Jacinta, she said encouragingly, "Jacinta, come and play."

"I don't want to play today."

"Why?"

"Because I am thinking how the Lady told us to say the Rosary and make sacrifices for the conversion of sinners. Now when we say the Rosary we must say the whole thing and not shorten it like we used to. And how shall we make sacrifices?"

Francisco suggested they could give their lunch to the sheep. They did so, but later realized that it would be more pleasing to the Lady if they gave it instead to the poor children from Moita who

11. Walsh, 57.

begged their bread from door to door. This they continued to do daily. By mid-afternoon, they would become unbearably hungry. One day, Francisco picked some acorns. However, they were too palatable to be eaten sacrificially, so Jacinta found some that were less ripe and more bitter. Lucia remembers that "our only nourishment consisted of pine cones, and little berries about the size of an olive which grow on the roots of yellow bell-flowers, as well as blackberries, mushrooms, and some other things we found on the roots of pine trees—I cannot remember now what these were called. If there was fruit available on the land belonging to our parents, we used to eat that."[12]

One hot day they were in a pasture generously lent to them by a neighbor. At midday they became very thirsty, so Lucia approached the neighbor to ask her for some water. The little old lady gave her a pitcher of water and some bread. Lucia ran back to her companions, who were resting in the shade of an oak tree. She offered the pitcher to Francisco, who refused, saying that he wanted to make a sacrifice for sinners.

"You have a drink, Jacinta," Lucia said, passing the pitcher to her.

"But I want to offer this sacrifice for sinners, too."

Lucia poured the water into a hollow of a rock for the sheep. However, the sun that day was scorching, which, combined with the lack of food, caused Jacinta to succumb to a headache. The shrill singing of the crickets and grasshoppers, along with the croaking of the frogs in the neighboring marsh, created an unbearable din. Jacinta, weakened by hunger and thirst, and almost desperate with the noise, beseeched Lucia with her natural simplicity: "Tell the crickets and the frogs to keep quiet! I have such a headache."

"But don't you want to suffer this for sinners?" asked Francisco. And the stricken little girl, replied: "Yes, I do. Let them sing."

In the meantime, the news of the apparition had spread to the surrounding villages. Maria Rosa was doing her best to quash the rumors. She felt ashamed and guilty that she had raised a daughter who was the source of deceptions that were misleading so many

---

12. *Memoirs*, 31–32.

decent people. Maria Rosa, who had been esteemed in the village for her sobriety and uprightness, now had to face the *tuts* and sidelong glances of her neighbors. "If you do not admit this was a lie," she admonished Lucia one day, "I will lock you up in a dark room where you will never see the light of the sun again!" She would alternate threats with caresses in an effort to effect an admission of falsehood from Lucia. One day, she chased Lucia out of the house, beating her with the end of a broom. But Lucia only continued to affirm her story, or else remained mute.

Outside the house, Lucia's treatment was no better. Neighbors would wag their fingers at her, remarking "If she were my child..." Others would stop to scold her. One old woman even kicked out at her while she was walking along. Children would gather around to ridicule her saying, "Hey, Lucia, is Our Lady going to walk over the roofs today?"

The situation became so ugly that Maria Rosa decided to take Lucia to the parish priest, whose authority might bring Lucia to confess her errors and repent of her contrariness or, at the very least, dissuade her from going to the Cova. "When you get there," said her mother, "go down on your knees and confess that you have lied and ask pardon, do you understand? You can explain it how you like; either you undeceive all these people or else I'll shut you in a dark room! My children have never told lies, and now I have this sort of thing with the youngest of you. If it was some little thing it would not matter so much, but a lie of this sort, taking in all those people!"

"But, Mother, how can I say that I did not see, when I did see?" Her mother became silent, disarmed by her tearful earnestness.

"Just you listen to me!" she said at last as they approached the priest's apartment. "What I want is that you should tell the truth. If you saw, say so! But if you did not see, admit that you lied."

Silently they climbed the stairs to the priest's study. Father Manuel Marques Ferreira received them with kindness and, as Lucia relates, with affection. He questioned Lucia seriously, but courteously, at great length, and with various stratagems to test the consistency of her story. However, he could not deviate her from her position, nor could he uncover any inconsistency. Shrugging his shoulders, he advised Maria Rosa: "Let them go if they persist, and see what happens. Then bring them to me and I will question them further. We will get to the bottom of this yet!"

Rev. Fr. Manuel Marques Ferreira,
parish priest at Fatima, 1914–1919

Immaculate Heart

THE 13th OF JUNE is the Feast of St. Anthony of Padua, the patron saint of Portugal. He was born in Lisbon on August 15, 1195. When he was fifteen years old, he entered the Augustinian monastic order, but in 1220 went to Assisi to join the new order under St. Francis (d. 1226). He spent the remainder of his life teaching theology at Bologna, Toulouse, Montpellier, and Padua. He is chiefly noted for his charismatic preaching, particularly on Marian devotion. One of his teachings confirms, in true Augustinian fashion, what we have already said about Mary: "The Blessed Virgin, the throne of glory of the most high from the beginning, that is, from the foundation of the world, was predestined as Mother of God in the sanctifying power of the Spirit. . . . Because of the honor due to the Lord . . . the glorious Virgin was prepared (*praeventa*) and filled with a singular grace that she should have as the fruit of her womb the One whom she had from the outset as Lord of the Universe."[1] His devotional homilies also speak of Mary as a source of hope through her example, her intercession, and her Motherhood. He died in Padua on June 13, 1231. Since his canonization in the following year by Gregory IX, his festival has been annually celebrated on the thirteenth of June throughout Portugal as well as in Padua. It is appropriate, then, that the Mother of God should choose this date for her second visitation to the little shepherds.

In 1917, the Feast of St. Anthony fell on a Wednesday. The shepherd children of Aljustrel always arose extra early that day in order to bring the sheep back by nine o'clock. This would give them plenty of time to make themselves ready in order to attend the *Missa Cantata* at ten. After the Mass was sung, a procession would form. Wagons decorated with branches, flowers, and pennants, draped with colorful fabrics and filled with cooked meats, vegetables, olives,

---

1. Quoted in O'Carroll, *Theotokos*, 34.

cheeses, and fruit, would follow the procession. The colorful pageant would pass several times around the church, finally stopping at the portico where the priest gave his blessing. After the procession, the wagons would form a corral. The sound of ringing bells announced the time of almsgiving, and some 500 of the poor from the surrounding villages would gather around the wagons to receive donations of food. Then came music, dancing, and, of course, wine.

Our three shepherd children, like all the children of the parish of Fatima adored the "festas." This was just what their parents were counting on to divert them from all this nonsense about apparitions of Mary at the Cova da Iria. Lucia's sister, Maria dos Anjos, once again leaves us with this attestation:

> Our mother knew well that Lucia adored the festa, and hoped that the whole story of the Cova da Iria would pass away with it. "It's a good thing we're having St. Anthony tomorrow," she said. "We mustn't say anything to her about the Cova da Iria, but only talk about the festa, and then, tomorrow she will have forgotten all about the other thing. Perhaps it is our fault for talking about it so much." We were careful to do as she said, but Lucia hardly said anything and took no notice at all of our plans. From time to time she reminded us: "But tomorrow I'm going to the Cova da Iria; that is what the Lady said."[2]

Similarly, at the Marto house neither Francisco nor Jacinta could keep quiet about the promised visitation. They were so full of joy and expectation that they wanted their mother to share in their happiness. Jacinta, in her simplicity, could not understand why Olimpia refused to accept what to the little girl was such an apparent reality. After all, she had seen the Lady and heard her speak with as much apparency as she was sharing with her own mother at that moment.

"Oh, mother, do come with us tomorrow to the Cova da Iria to see Our Lady!"

"What Lady, you silly girl? . . . Tomorrow we are going to St. Anthony. Don't you want to see the Feast? And hear the music and the sermon and the fireworks?"

2. de Marchi, 62.

"But mother, Our Lady comes to the Cova da Iria!"

"I am certainly not going there; it isn't true that Our Lady appears to you."

"But she does, and she said she would come again, and so she will!"

Here we have the innocent acceptance of a child. The beautiful lady that Jacinta had been contemplating and dreaming of during the last month was returning as she had promised. As far as Jacinta was concerned, this was a fact. What saint or feast could compare with her splendor? For the past month the children had been expressing their devotion to this Lady, unbeknown to their parents, and were they going to disappoint her now?

"Don't you want to go to St. Anthony?"

"St. Anthony's no good."

"Why?"

"Because that Lady is much, much nicer. I'm going to the Cova and so are the others, although we would go to St. Anthony if the Lady told us to."

Ti Marto, having overheard this conversation, was in a dilemma about what to do.

> Then I had an idea. There was a fair next day at Pedreira and I'd go there and buy some oxen. "Look, wife," I said to my Olimpia, "tomorrow we won't have any festas or anything else either. We'll go to the fair to buy oxen and when we get back this affair of the children will be finished with. What a business it is to be sure!"[3]

Jacinta awoke on the Feast of St. Anthony full of expectation. She jumped out of bed and ran to her parents' room only to find it empty. Then her eldest brother told her that her parents had gone to Pedreira and would not return until evening. At first, she was disappointed that they would not see the beautiful Lady. Then she had a thought. She ran to awaken Francisco, explaining that they were free to go to the Cova after all! While Francisco dressed, Jacinta went to loose the sheep, and when he was ready they hurried off,

---

3. Ibid., 62.

eating their breakfast of bread and cheese on the way. Soon they met up with Lucia.

They decided to take the sheep to Valinhos near the Cabeço, as it was closer and would give them more time to get ready to go to the Cova later. However, they were only in the fields for a short time when Lucia's brother, Antonio, came running across the fields to say that there were several people waiting at her house desiring to speak with her. Not suspecting anything, she left her brother in charge of the sheep and returned home only to be accosted by a horde of curious men and women. The news had spread all over the mountain, bringing people from villages as far as thirty kilometers away. Excusing herself by telling them that she had to go to eight-o'clock Mass, Lucia managed to escape from their endless questioning.

When she returned home, the strangers were still waiting for her in the shade of some of the fig trees in her garden. She took refuge inside the house. But her mother and her sisters "persisted in their contemptuous attitude," Lucia recalls, "and this cut me to the heart, and was indeed as hurtful to me as insults."[4] At eleven o'clock, she went to find her cousins, who by then had fed their sheep and returned home to change into nicer clothes. Together they left for the Cova with the impertinent strangers trooping after.

On that day, Lucia was overwhelmed with bitterness. She understood the aversion her mother held about lying. From the cradle Maria Rosa had instilled into her children a horror of lying, and she would chastise severely any of her children who told an untruth. Lucia's sisters had inherited this from their mother and would side with her against Lucia. All around Lucia was an atmosphere of scorn and contempt. "Then I would remember the old days," she writes, "and ask myself: 'Where is all that affection now, that my family had for me just a short while ago?'"

She wept as she walked while Jacinta attempted to comfort her by pointing out that these were the sufferings Our Lady had warned them about the first time she came. "That is why you are suffering, so that you can make reparation to Him and convert sinners."

4. *Memoirs*, 67.

However, as if she were a gift of mercy sent from heaven, a woman arrived from the village of Moita who would not only come to believe in the apparitions, but would be the first to offer constant and faithful support to Lucia and her cousins. She was Senhora Maria dos Santos Carreira, later known as Maria da Capelinha (Maria of the Chapel). Her tireless work in collecting money for a chapel at the Cova in honor of the Lady would earn her this name. She had heard of the apparitions from her husband, who had been working with Lucia's father Antonio.

> It was two or three days after the first apparitions when my husband, who had been with Lucia's father, said: "Have you heard, wife, that Antonio Abobora says that Our Lady appeared in the Cova da Iria to one of his children—the youngest—and also to two of his sister Olimpia's children, the one who is married to Ti Marto, and that Our Lady spoke to them and promised to go back there every month till October?" And I said to him: "Yes, and I have got to find out whether it's true or not. And if it is I want to go there and see. But where is the Cova da Iria?" I asked him. As a matter of fact it's very near where we lived at Moita, hardly ten minutes' walk from our house... My man told me whereabouts it was; and then said: "Do you want to go? Don't be silly! Do you think you'll see her, too?" Then he said nothing more so I knew he would let me go, and I myself was quite determined to go there on the thirteenth of June.[5]

"Their son, John, was a cripple, hunch-backed, with knees that crossed and knocked together as he walked."[6] Maria of the Chapel desperately clutched at the thought that if the apparitions were genuine, the Blessed Lady's intercession might cure her seventeen-year-old son. She joined in the small group of about fifty people who had assembled around the three children as they stood near the *azinheira*. Among them were fourteen children from Lucia's confirmation class, as well as a pious lady from Boleiros who began reading from a prayer book. The quizzical strangers who had travelled from distant villages were now devouring the lunches they had brought.

---

5. de Marchi, 61–62. She told the same thing to Walsh, 66.
6. Walsh, ibid.

"Will Our Lady delay much longer?" Maria da Capelinha inquired of Lucia.

And Lucia, hearing for the first time a supportive voice, answered reassuringly, "No, Senhora, not very long." The children from Lucia's confirmation class enticed Jacinta to play. But Lucia told them that the Lady would soon be coming.

Then they all began repeating the Rosary. As soon as they had finished five decades, Lucia saw the light approaching from the east. She jumped up immediately and cried out "Jacinta, Our Lady must be coming: there's the lightning." They ran closer to the *azinheira* and knelt down, the crowd forming around them. There on the holm oak was the Lady, appearing just as she had in May. Maria da Capelinha vividly recounts the details of the scene:

> We knelt down on the rocks and stones. Lucia lifted up her hands as if she were praying and I heard her say, "Your Worship told me to come here, please say what you want of me." Then we began to hear something like a tiny little voice, but we could not hear what it was saying. It was rather like the buzzing of a bee![7]

What they were unable to hear has been revealed by Lucia:[8]

"I wish you to come here on the thirteenth of next month, to pray the Rosary every day, and to learn to read. Later, I will tell you what I want."

Lucia then asked for the cure of a certain sick person.

"If he is converted, he will be cured during the year."

And then moved by the bitterness that she was experiencing, Lucia asked:

"I would like to ask you to take us to heaven."

"Yes, I will take Jacinta and Francisco soon. But you are to stay here some time longer. Jesus wishes to make use of you to make me known and loved. He wants to establish in the world devotion to my Immaculate Heart."

"Am I to stay here alone?" Lucia asked sadly.

"No, my daughter. Are you suffering a great deal? Do not lose

---

7. de Marchi, 66.
8. *Memoirs*, 160–61.

heart. I will never forsake you. My Immaculate Heart will be your refuge and the way that will lead you to God."

With these words, she opened her hands for the second time, transmitting to them the rays of that same penetrating light that had been communicated to them on her previous visitation.

> We saw ourselves in this light, as it were, immersed in God. Jacinta and Francisco seemed to be in that part of the light which rose towards heaven, and I in that which was poured out on the earth. In front of the palm of Our Lady's hand was a heart encircled by thorns which pierced it. We understood that this was the Immaculate Heart of Mary, outraged by the sins of humanity, and seeking reparation.[9]

In this ethereal tableau, Lucia, Francisco, and Jacinta were receiving symbolically what had already been communicated to them verbally. The vehicle of this message was not words but light. The "true light that enlightens every person" (Jn. 1:9; 1 Jn. 1:5) surrounded them, interpenetrated them, and revealed to them the meaning of the words already spoken by the angel and by the Lady.

Francisco and Jacinta were immersed in the light that streamed to heaven, confirming what the Lady had said: "I will take Jacinta and Francisco soon." However, Lucia remained in the light that bathed the ground. She had a task to perform and would have to wait "some time longer" upon the earth in order to make the Lady known and loved throughout the world. Moreover, it was the Lord Jesus himself who desired that Lucia let this light shine in the world. This is why the Lady told her she must learn to read and say the Rosary every day.

The essential message, which Lucia was given the heavenly mandate to promote, was the message of devotion to the Immaculate Heart of Mary: devotion not merely to her image or her virtues but, much more deeply and genuinely, to her very Heart. The heart of Mary, as we have already seen, is portrayed in Sacred Scripture as the seat of Mary's reflection upon those truths revealed to her by the angel Gabriel, the Holy Spirit (through Elizabeth, Simeon, Anna,

---

9. *Memoirs*, 161.

and Mary's own Magnificat), as well as the life, death, and resurrection of her Son and Lord. And Mary "kept all these things in her heart" (Lk. 2:51). It is also the source of those graces bestowed upon her at her conception, when she was predestined by the Father before the foundation of the world to be the Mother of God. Finally, Mary's Heart is the locus of the reception of the Holy Spirit at Pentecost.

How then are we to understand this devotion? Certainly we can try to imitate her tender and gracious virtues, yet those blessed virtues are the virtues of our glorious Lord. Therefore, it seems almost redundant for Jesus to promote this devotion, since such devotion could be fulfilled directly by imitating Him. Of course, there is a fundamental difference between Mother and Son: Mary is a created being and does not share in Christ's Divinity in the substantial sense we have already described. She is a creature like us, although endowed with a most especial privilege and, through the merits of her Son, preserved in an immaculate state of grace. We would certainly not go wrong in imitating her virtues, any more than we would go wrong if we imitated Paul, who in turn, imitated Christ (1 Cor. 4:16, 11:1). But if we are to imitate Paul, how much more should we imitate Mary who is full of grace! And if we devote ourselves to imitating Mary, will not this imitation direct us to Christ, upon whom she constantly meditated in her heart? Will not Mary always glorify her Son and lead her spiritual children to Him? Will not her soul constantly "magnify the Lord" (Lk. 1:46) and instruct us to "do whatever He tells you"? (Jn. 2:5). Thus, imitation of this humble servant of the Lord will be efficacious insofar as she will most certainly guide us toward her Son.

However, no matter how correct these teachings may be, they are not the central message of Fatima. Fatima has something much simpler to relate. For at Fatima Mary gives us a simple daily path. The secret of this path is the Rosary—that chaplet, garland, or crown of rosebuds, that liturgy of prayer and contemplation, that analogue of Mary's reflective and Immaculate Heart.

This June 13th appearance at Fatima is hardly the first time that the Blessed Virgin appeared to mankind with the Rosary. She had it in hand when she first visited our three shepherd children the previous month. Fifty-nine years earlier, when she appeared to Bernadette Soubirous at Lourdes, she prayed the Rosary along with her, only remaining silent at the recitation of the "Hail Mary". But the history of the Rosary is older still. According to a tradition promulgated by Alan de la Roche, the Rosary goes back to St. Dominic, who received it from Our Lady in 1214 as a device for defeating the Albigensian heresy (from Albi in France). This heresy, also known as Catharism, developed in the eleventh century from the old Manichaean dualistic belief in two gods, one of spirit and one of matter, whose dialectical struggle formed the universe. The Albigensians set their religion up as an alternative to Christianity, proclaiming themselves the true harbingers of world unity. They denied the Divinity of Christ, His resurrection, the sanctity of marriage, and the value of private property. Matter, and therefore the body, was evil and had to be purged (*catharsis*) of all emotion.

St. Dominic, a contemporary of Ss. Anthony and Francis and the founder of the Dominican order, seeing that the gravity of the people's sins was fertile ground for these heresies, retreated to a forest near Toulouse, where he prayed incessantly for three days and nights, begging for guidance on how to check its proliferation. Tradition has it that Our Lady appeared, instructing him to promote the Rosary as the weapon against this heresy. St. Dominic's earnest preaching and indefatigable travels, as well as his poverty, simplicity, and austerity, helped promote this devotion and the piety which ensued. This increase in piety and sanctity among the populace helped to check the essential immorality implicit in the heresy, leaving it with no ground to take root.

It is doubtful that Dominic invented the Rosary, since its origins can be traced back even further than his time; the Rosary prayers that he handed on were different from those used later. A Rosary resembling its present form was not established until the sixteenth century. However, there is no reason to doubt that St. Dominic was an enthusiastic promoter of the use of the Rosary; and it may be he was stimulated in this by a vision or, at least, by his fervent devotion to the Virgin Mary.

Thus, the long tradition of the Rosary is closely connected with Marian devotion—an association made still more explicit by the events at Lourdes. Now, at Fatima, the Rosary is associated with Mary's Heart.

The reason for this is obvious when we recall the nature of Mary's Heart as the seat of her reflection upon the events unfolding around her and realize that the Rosary is constructed so as to require of its faithful devotee that same reflective practice. We have, in the Rosary prayers, teachings of profound depth and Scriptural orthodoxy. One only has to pause to reflect upon the teachings contained in these recitations to see the truths they reveal—the sublime truths which Jesus has asked us to reflect upon. Furthermore, the incidents from the life of Jesus which he shared with His Mother contain lessons of important virtues and verities for living the Christian life. As one kneels before the Holy Trinity, fingers the buds of the Rosary, recites the prayers, and meditates on the virtues and teachings contained in the mysteries, one becomes involved in the prayer physically, mentally, and spiritually. One's entire being becomes directed to God in this devotion. Its unity of expression and intent focuses one's entire attention within one's own heart where the Presence of Christ's Spirit dwells in those devoted to Him. There follows the gentle transformation of the heart that the Lord requires of us all. Out of this renewed heart will flow those virtues of meekness, patience, and loving self-sacrifice which glorify God and draw others to His Kingdom.

Thus, the regular practice of the Rosary is, by its very form, an imitation of the Immaculate Heart of Mary, since it is an analogue of that reflective and obedient Heart which was so consecrated to her Son and Lord. By devoting oneself to the Immaculate Heart of Mary in this way, one becomes devoted to the Sacred Heart of Jesus, increasingly drawn into the heart of His life and virtue, becoming more like Him through contemplating His truth and growing more centered in His Word. The establishment and growth of such a devotion would spread a holiness throughout the world that, by its example and strength, would defeat the resurgence of the Albigensian heresy that has engulfed the world today.

This heresy reappeared in another form during the middle of the nineteenth century. It was the century of utopian revolutionary movements under such reformers as Saint-Simon, Proudhon, and

Blanc. It was also the century in which Karl Marx and Friedrich Engels worked out their dialectical materialism. The year 1848 saw the publication of the *Communist Manifesto,* in which Marx and Engels reduced all social and economic woes to a class struggle between owners and non-owners of the means of production. The family was to be abolished, and the Communist Party was to become an alternative savior to Christ. The *Manifesto* was also historicist, arguing that history developed according to its own (materialist) laws, and that since all problems were material—not spiritual—in cause, they required only material (socio-economic) solutions. There was no God and, therefore, no immutable truth. All moral values were relative to the state that determined them, so that only political correctness mattered. Since there was no Providence to direct history, the future was entirely in human hands. Finally, the *Manifesto* promoted the utopian belief that through human praxis *alone* history would find its fulfillment in universal peace and social justice.

These were the "errors" that Marxism was to bequeath to the world. Every one of these ideas has penetrated to form the consciousness of present-day Western thought. Like a virus, it has infected the thinking of many a theologian and even found unquestioning acceptance among the clergy and religious in the Church.

To trace all the historical connections to Fatima would implicate us in a maze of events and ideologies requiring a much wider examination of history. It would include the abortive mid-nineteenth century revolutions in Russia, Denmark, Prussia, Austria-Hungary, France, Spain, and Italy, which only served to strengthen the power of Napoleon III, the Hapsburgs, the Hohenzollerns, and the Romanovs. We would have to trace the rise of irreligion since the so-called "Enlightenment."

Fortunately, all of that is not necessary. It is enough merely to recognize that Lucia, Francisco, and Jacinta were living at a time when these "errors" were about to find an entire nation's advocacy and a world already prepared and waiting for its new rationalist "messiah." Our Blessed Mother had come to intercede for the Church as she had done with Juan Diego against the human sacrifices of the Aztecs, with St. Dominic against the Albigensians, and with Melanie, Maximin and St. Bernadette against nineteenth-century liberalism. Now she had given the little shepherds of Fatima the weapon against the coming tribulation that threatened to overwhelm the Church.

However, only Lucia was to remain on earth to spread the devotion: her two cousins would soon be taken. Lucia would be alone, but not abandoned. "Don't lose heart. I will never forsake you. My Immaculate Heart will be your refuge and the way that will lead you to God."

After the children had been bathed in the Light of the Presence of God, the Lady left them. Her ascent from the tree sounded (to Maria of the Chapel) rather like a fireworks rocket, in the distance, streaking upwards. Lucia jumped to her feet and, with her arm stretched out, cried: "Look, there she goes! There she goes!" Maria da Capelinha describes the Lady's departure.

> We saw nothing except a little cloud a few inches from the tree which rose very slowly and went backwards, towards the east, until we could see it no more. Some people said: "I can still see it; it's still there…" until at last no one could see it any more. The children stayed, silently looking in that direction until at last Lucia said: "There, now we can't see her any more. She has gone back into Heaven, the doors are shut!" We then turned towards the miraculous tree and what was our admiration and surprise to see that the shoots at the top, which had been standing upright before, were now all bent towards the east, as if someone had stood upon them.[10]

Reverently, they began picking twigs and leaves from the miraculous bush, but Lucia told them to take them from the bottom branches untouched by the Lady. Senhora Maria also collected some sprigs of rosemary as a souvenir. A member of the group from the distant villages suggested they recite a Litany. This they did, slowly and pensively. Late in the afternoon, the small band of pilgrims began to make their separate ways homeward, praying the Rosary as they went.

10. de Marchi, 68.

The Number of the Beast

THE CHILDREN HAD BEEN constantly hounded by questioning people wherever they went. At home, family members were just as relentless. The children adopted the tactic of responding with the bare minimum of information: "She is a very beautiful Lady, more lovely than any ever seen. She desires the Rosary to be said every day and the performance of penance for poor sinners. She will come back every month until October, when she will say who she is and what she wants." About the devotion to her Immaculate Heart, they would say nothing. "It's a secret," they replied.

Then there were the taunts and impertinences of disbelievers:

"Lucia, did the Lady appear on the top of the tree?"

"So, Jacinta, Our Lady didn't say anything to you this time?"

"Well, Francisco, why are you still here and not in heaven?"

Such irreverence toward the beautiful Lady lacerated their hearts. They yearned to share with others the loveliness of the vision and the majesty of her expression, but the flippancy and churlishness of these people were insulting to the Lady and a real martyrdom for the children. Soon the trio became quite adept at recognizing from a distance these obnoxious people and straightway avoided them. When importunate strangers accosted them in the street, asking if they knew where the visionaries lived, the shepherd children would direct them to their homes while they headed in the opposite direction. If such people called to the house while they were there, the children would hide under the bed, in the attic, behind the well, anywhere where they could avoid those condescending questions and fawning grins.

The children found themselves increasingly isolated from the world. It was only with each other that they could relax and revel in the wonder of what they had seen and heard. Of course, poor Francisco still did not hear what the Lady said and was dependent upon the others for enlightenment. His questions, too, were endless. On the day of the second apparition, as they were going home, he asked Lucia a question.

"Why did Our Lady have a Heart in her hand, spreading out over the world that great light which is God? You were with Our Lady in the light that went down towards the earth, and Jacinta was with me in the light which rose towards heaven!"

"That is because you and Jacinta will soon go to heaven," Lucia replied, "while I, with the Immaculate Heart of Mary, will remain for some time longer on earth."

"How many years longer will you stay here?" asked Francisco.

"I don't know. Plenty (*bastantes*)."

"Was it Our Lady who said so?"

"Yes, and I also saw it in the light that she shone into our hearts."

"That's how it was," added Jacinta, "I saw it too."

Then Francisco remarked: "These people were so happy just because you told them that Our Lady wants the Rosary said, and that you are to learn to read! How would they feel if they only knew what she showed to us in God, in her Immaculate Heart, in that great light! But this is a secret; it is better that no one should know it."

They all agreed that the revelation about the Immaculate Heart must remain a secret. However, Francisco was ecstatic at the prospect of going to heaven. "I am going to heaven soon! Jacinta and I are going to heaven soon! Heaven! Heaven!"

His enthusiasm infected Jacinta who eagerly joined in the refrain. When they arrived home that evening, they burst into their house and found to their delight that their mother and father had already returned home from the fair at Pedreira, rather pleased with the two fat oxen they had purchased. The rest of the family had also returned from the festivities in Fatima. Everyone was in high spirits, sharing the excitement of the day's events. The happy household was a crescendo of frivolous chatter. The door suddenly swung wide open and there stood two breathless and jubilant children.

"We saw the Lady again, Mother!" squealed Jacinta, "and she told me that I am going to heaven soon!"

94

"Nonsense! What Lady?" teased Olimpia.

"The beautiful Lady. She came again today."

"Was the Lady as beautiful as So-and-so?" asked one family member.

"Oh, much, much more beautiful."

"More beautiful than the statue in the church with her mantle covered in stars?" echoed another, referring to the sculpture of St. Quiteria in St. Anthony's church.

"No! Much prettier."

"As lovely as Our Lady of the Rosary?"

"More beautiful still!"

They continued to tease her with references to saint after saint until an exasperated Jacinta declared the beauty of the Lady of the Cova to be beyond comparison with anyone on earth. With that, she turned reticent. When they asked her what the beautiful Lady said, Jacinta resorted to their customary formula: "We must say the Rosary, and go again every month until October."

"Is that all?"

"The rest is a secret."

"Oh a secret! A secret! Tell us the secret!" they all chimed together.

At this point Ti Marto took control. "A secret is a secret and must be kept." Ti Marto was sure that his children were not lying, and it grieved him to see them badgered in this manner. Although he was proud of their integrity and intransigence, still, they were only children, and such teasing could easily get out of hand. He knew that if Jacinta was pushed too far she would "tether the donkey" and nothing would shift her. He would later reminisce on just how reticent Jacinta could be.

I remember very well a time when some ladies came here with a lot of gold ornaments on them.

"Do you like these?" asked one of them, showing Jacinta her bracelets and necklace.

"Yes, I do."

"Would you like them?"

"Yes."

"Then tell us the secret!" and they pretended to be taking off the ornaments. But my little girl was very upset and cried out:

"Don't, don't, I can't tell you anything! I couldn't tell you the secret even if you gave me the whole world!"[1]

Ti Marto never asked the children to tell him the secret. But the rest of the family were not so considerate. Their endless prying sometimes had a pitiless intent that was bewilderingly hurtful for the young children. For Lucia, however, the ordeal was much more overt and pernicious. Maria Rosa refused to countenance a single detail of the story. As far as she was concerned, the apparition was a malicious lie and her daughter had succumbed to some evil influence. And this time it was worse: Lucia had bewitched and enticed fifty innocent people into making a troublesome journey just to witness her brazen theatrics. Maria Rosa's holy ire was smoldering on the verge of eruption. She reached her limit when Lucia requested she be allowed to go to school to learn to read as the Lady desired. (In those days village girls did not attend school.)

"School, indeed! A lot it matters to Our Lady whether the likes of you can read and write!"

For the next few days, all she could hear was gossip about the apparitions. Maria Rosa found it impossible to carry on her normal affairs. When she at last received notification from Father Ferreira that he wanted to interview the children, she was relieved that he was going to take the burden of worry from her shoulders. The parish priest had permitted the children to go to the Cova on the 13 June so that he could interview them later. Maria Rosa had welcomed the good Father's instruction to bring Lucia before him as soon as possible after the apparition.

"Tomorrow, we are going to Mass, first thing in the morning. Then you are going to the Reverend Father's house. Just let him compel you to tell the truth, no matter how he does it; let him punish you; let him do whatever he likes with you, just so long as he forces you to admit that you have lied; and then I will be satisfied."

Antonio dos Santos in turn passed the message to Manuel Marto who describes what happened:

1. de Marchi, 70.

96

I went as I had been asked, in good faith. "Reverend Father," I said, "my brother-in-law told me to come here with the children but I came to speak with you first to find out what we had better do." Then he said: "I'm sick and tired of this. First it's one thing and then another!" I kept quite calm and said: "Does your Reverence want the truth or not?" And he: "I've never heard such things in my life. And everyone else seems to know more than I do." He was obviously annoyed and said crossly: "If you want to bring them, bring them, and if you don't want to, don't. Do as you please." "Then I shall do what I think is right and that is to come," I answered. We then went out on the veranda and when I was leaving for home and was half-way down the steps, he said to me again: "This is your responsibility; bring them or not, as you please." At the bottom of the steps I turned round and said: "Your Reverence, I shall bring them because I think it is the right thing to do and not because I want to make trouble."[2]

Lucia's sisters again sided with their mother and invented various threats to frighten Lucia about the impending interview. A distraught Lucia fled to her cousins' house. She told Francisco and Jacinta that her mother was taking her to the priest and described the awful things her mother and her sisters said the priest was going to do to her. Jacinta replied: "We're going also. The Reverend Father told our mother to take us there too, but she hasn't said any of those things to us. Never mind if they beat us, we will suffer for love of Our Lord and for sinners."

Early next morning Maria Rosa and Lucia set out for Fatima after having stopped at the Marto house to pick up the two cousins.[3] Then they silently made their way to Fatima. They attended early Mass at St. Anthony's and crossed the field to the rectory. The

2. Ibid., 71.

3. Ti Marto recalls that Jacinta went with them, and he thinks Francisco also went along. He had promised the priest he would bring both of them. This is likely, since there is evidence of Francisco's consoling Lucia afterwards. And of course, Francisco was very protective towards Jacinta. Walsh, however, has Lucia attending after Jacinta and Francisco, and Lucia's own memoirs do not mention the presence of the cousins at the rectory. They do, however, mention that Maria Rosa stopped at the Marto house on the way. The evidence indicates that all three children were interviewed that day, and that the Marto children were interviewed first.

priest's sister greeted them pleasantly and invited them to wait upon a bench. All the while Maria Rosa had remained mute and the children too were subdued by her austere and rigid demeanor. After a short wait, they were taken in to the priest. Manuel Marto gives an account of what happened.

> It was Maria Rosa who took the little girls and, I think, Francisco as well. When they came back she came to see me and said: "I have taken my Lucia and Jacinta to see Fr. Ferreira. He asked Jacinta questions but she would not answer him a word." Then he said to her: "You don't seem to know anything; sit down there or run away if you like." Jacinta took out her Rosary and started to say it, while Fr. Ferreira began to question Lucia, who answered well. From time to time Jacinta got up and told Lucia to be sure and explain things properly. At that (continues Ti Marto) my sister-in-law was a bit surprised, and Fr. Ferreira said rather crossly to Jacinta: "When I was asking you questions you did not know anything and would not say a word, and now it's the other way about."[4]

The priest was dissatisfied with the proceedings. He had questioned the children minutely and compared details. He could find no reason to doubt the sincerity of the children's story, but neither could he find anything that would convince him that the Blessed Virgin had come to visit the children. The children had not told him about the Immaculate Heart devotion or the Divine light. Their answers only corresponded to their usual formula, with descriptions of the Lady. The priest reasoned that Our Lady would not have come from heaven just to instruct people to say the Rosary every day, especially since this custom was already well established in the parish. He also recalled that at Lourdes Bernadette was told to inform the priest about the Lady's messages, and, similarly, at Guadalupe, La Salette, and Paris. But the reticence of the children about the establishment of devotion to the Immaculate Heart left the priest wondering about the import of the Lady's visitations. Then again, at Guadalupe there was the tilma, at Paris the Miraculous Medal, and at Lourdes there was the sign of the healing spring. And did not Our Lord, himself, perform many signs and wonders?

4. de Marchi, 72.

In the absence of any firm evidence, the Father Ferreira could only conclude:

"It doesn't seem to me like a revelation from heaven. It is usual in such cases for Our Lord to tell the souls to whom He makes such communications to give their confessor or parish priest an account of what has happened. But this child, on the contrary, keeps it to herself as far as she can. This may also be a deceit of the devil. We shall see. The future will indicate what we have to think about it."

For Father Ferreira, what was missing in the Lady's revelation were, on the one hand, theological content of an orthodox nature and of a heavenly grandeur and, on the other, a confirming sign. He was perfectly aware that Jesus had warned that in the end time "false Christs and false prophets will arise and show great signs and wonders, so as to lead astray, if possible, even the elect" (Mt. 24:24). Of course, this saying was in the context of the coming of Christ in judgment, which was not what the Lady had implied. Even so, the implication was clear that "the coming of the lawless one by the activity of Satan will be with all power and with pretended signs and wonders" which would deceive those who "refused to love the truth" (2 Thess. 2:9–10). Thus, the hallmark for "testing the spirits" (1 Jn. 4:1) was the truth revealed by the agent, not merely the presence of signs and wonders. The fundamental test that a Spirit is of God is the confession of Jesus Christ (1 Jn. 4:2). Given that the children had not related to him any such sacred confession from the Lady, the good Father was reluctant to acknowledge any heavenly agent behind the messages. There was a real possibility, in the mind of the priest, that the devil was behind the events, using them to deceive the people by stirring up unhealthy enthusiasm or worse. The priest was fully aware of the liberalism that was infecting Portugal at that time. He knew that the end result of such false doctrines would be the promotion of immorality and irreligion. Perhaps this was another manifestation of that same demonic infestation.

However, there is no doubt that the Father was familiar with Jesus's admonishment of the Pharisees who attributed Jesus's signs and wonders to Beelzebul (Mt. 12:22–32). It would seem unlikely that Satan would encourage people to say the Rosary. Why would the devil want people to pray the Lord's Prayer, recite a creed as incarnational and Trinitarian as the Apostle's Creed, glorify the Trinity in the Doxology, or utter the Angelic Salutation? Would the devil work against his own intentions in this way? "Every kingdom divided against itself is laid waste, and no city or house divided against itself will stand" (Mt. 12:25). Therefore, no demon would encourage such a devotion unless it were a ruse to entice people to flock to the Cova. Even Satan can disguise himself as an angel of light (2 Cor. 11:14). Eventually, his malicious and malignant intention would betray itself and mislead a gullible populace into believing false doctrines or even performing immoral acts. But what if it were a visitation from heaven? Then the priest might be found to be opposing God! (Acts 5:39).

Thus, there were only three possible outcomes. If the agents were human, then this movement, like so many others in history, would eventually fail (Acts 5:38). If the agent were Satanic, it would most assuredly reveal its malevolent nature (Mt. 7:15–17; 12:33–35). But if it were from God it would proclaim the glory of Christ and work to further His Kingdom—nothing could oppose it. Therefore, Father Ferreira let the youngsters go to the Cova to see what would transpire. Meanwhile, the Church would remain aloof from the entire affair.

However, the damage had been done. Lucia had heard the priest's opinion, that the devil might be behind the whole business, and it deeply disturbed her. Disillusionment and gloom overpowered her. She was plunged into a darkness of spirit that gave rise to intense anxiety and heartache.

> How much this reflection made me suffer, only God knows, for He alone can penetrate our inmost heart. I began then to have doubts as to whether these manifestations might be from the devil, who was seeking by these means to make me lose my soul. As I heard people say that the devil always brings conflict and disorder, I began to think that, truly, ever since I had started seeing these things, our home was no longer the same, for joy and peace had fled. What anguish I felt![5]

5. *Memoirs*, 69.

She unburdened her distress to her cousins. And Jacinta responded very firmly and directly:

"No, it's not the devil! Not at all! They say the devil is very ugly and that he is down under the ground in hell. But that Lady is so beautiful, and we saw her go up to heaven!"

Jacinta, who loved flowers, lambs, and the glories of nature, pointed in her simple way to the essential beauty of the vision.

She knew that all good things come from God. In her innocence she could not suspect that evil can sometimes disguise itself with light. "Beauty is truth, truth beauty," Keats once said, and that was all that young Jacinta could "know of life, and all she needed to know." Jacinta understood the benevolent beauty that comes from God, and the malignant ugliness that characterizes the demonic.

Still, Lucia was not convinced. She was so befuddled by her love for her mother and family and the ill treatment she was receiving from them—by the ugliness of what had transpired after the visions and the loveliness of the Lady—that she unwillingly saw an escape from all her turmoil. All she had to do was to declare that she had been deceived by the devil. How malicious and insidious he could be! She had not deliberately lied, after all. Here was a way back into the affections of her family. No longer would she have to make sacrifices. She could put an end to the entire affair. She began to wonder whether she ought to admit to the devil's influence and confess the falsity of the messages.

"Don't do that," exclaimed Francisco, the moralist. "Don't you see that now you are going to lie, and to lie is a sin?"

This only increased her anguish. She started to suffer from nightmares in which she was being mocked by the devil as he clutched at her, dragging her down into hell. Often she would scream out in the night. At other times she was too terrified to sleep. Her only recourse was to seek some solitary spot where she could abandon herself to her tears. Even the companionship of her cousins became burdensome to her. She began to hide from them despite their constant callings.

"The poor children! At times, they would search for me, calling out my name and receiving no answer, but I was there all the while, hidden right close to them in some corner where they never thought of looking."[6]

However, there were moments when her anguish would subside, and Lucia found she could pray with her cousins. On some of these occasions they were supported by the presence of Maria of the Chapel, who suddenly started coming to the Cova to pray with the children. She also began to beautify the place as well as she could, in spite of a recurrent illness.

She would decorate the tree with carnations and clear away the stones and weeds from around it.

> At home I felt as if I had no strength, but when I got [to the Cova] I felt quite another person. I began to clean up a bit round the tree, and make a little clearing. I took away the gorse and prickles and cut paths with a pruning saw. I took away some of the stones and hung a silk ribbon on one of the branches of the tree. It was I who put the first flowers there! [7]

This dear lady's faith was a comfort to Lucia, but she could not eject from her mind the persistent impression that the apparitions of the Lady were demonic in origin. As the thirteenth of July approached, her mother would reinforce that very thought: "The devil will be there for sure," Maria Rosa would say. She did not say this out of malice toward her daughter, but out of a sense of obedience to the Church. For she believed Lucia was committing a mortal sin. And had not Father Ferreira said as much? Until the priest gave his blessing to the apparitions, Maria Rosa felt duty bound to obey him and to guide her daughter accordingly. Lucia's sisters, of course, were only obeying their mother. The upshot of this opposition was that Lucia decided she would definitely not be going to the Cova on the thirteenth of July. She had had enough. While people were already arriving from surrounding areas and, this time, more distant villages and towns, Lucia went straight to her cousins' house to tell them of her firm decision.

6. *Memoirs*, 69.
7. de Marchi, 74.

"How can you think it was the devil," Francisco wondered. "Did you not see Our Lady and Our Lord in that great light? And how can we go without you, if you are the one who has to talk?"

"We shall go, anyway," put in Jacinta. The Lady told us to. *I* will speak to her," Jacinta decided. Then she broke down and cried.

"Why are you crying?" Lucia asked.

"Because you don't want to go."

"No, I am not going. Listen, if the Lady asks for me, tell her I am not coming, because I am afraid it may be the devil."

Then Lucia ran off to hide behind some bramble bushes in a neighbor's property a little to the east of their well. Her mother assumed she was playing with some village children. When she came home that night she received another scolding.

"A fine little plaster saint you are, to be sure! All the time you have left from minding the sheep, you do nothing but play, and what is more you have to do it in such a way that nobody can find you."

Later Francisco ran to her house and called her out to the old threshing floor, venturing one last rebuttal to turn her around.

"Look, aren't you going tomorrow?"

"I am not going. I told you I am not going back there any more."

"Don't you see it can't be the devil? God is already sad enough over so many sins, and now if you do not go, He will be even sadder. Come on, say you'll go."

Francisco had stumbled upon an irrefutable argument. Had not the Lady said that Jesus's Heart is sorrowful because of the sins and indifference of humanity? The devil would not be sorrowful over such disobedience: he would relish it. Therefore, it could not be the devil at the Cova. Moreover, to disobey the Lady's request to attend the next visitation would add to the sum of disobedience in the world. This would only make Jesus more sorrowful. But it would gladden the black heart of any demon. Therefore, to stay away is evil, to go is not. Given the original assertions, the conclusion follows naturally. A masterly argument! Surely this would convince Lucia.

"I tell you I am not going!" Lucia declared. "It's no use asking me."

With that, she retreated abruptly to her house. Maria Rosa was relieved at Lucia's reluctance to return to the Cova. Her relief turned to joyful satisfaction when early the next morning she found Lucia still determined not to take the sheep back to that place.

Meanwhile, Francisco had returned home dejectedly. He spent the rest of the night in tearful prayer, beseeching Our Lady to make Lucia go the next day to the Cova da Iria.[8] The next morning as the moment approached for Lucia to collect the sheep, she suddenly felt an irresistible force well up inside her that compelled her to go to the Cova. All her doubts and apprehensions dissolved, to be replaced by an inner assurance. The exhilaration of her newly restored faith propelled her out of the door and down the road to the home of the Marto children. Entering the house to see if they were still there, she found Jacinta and Francisco kneeling by their beds, weeping profusely.

"Aren't you going then?" invited Lucia.

"Not without you! We don't dare. Come. Oh, come!"

"Yes, I will come," Lucia replied.

Their tear-stained faces lit up with joy. "Vamos!" they said and, with lightened hearts, off they went along the familiar winding paths to meet with the beautiful Lady of the Cova.

The middle of July in Portugal can be stiflingly hot, particularly in the sun-parched Serra da Aire when the midday sun blazes directly overhead. This is the time for siestas, not for tramping along a dusty road to be jostled and harangued by crowds of people. For the news had circulated all over the Serra and beyond that the Queen of Heaven had again come to earth to visit little children. On this occasion the lanes and fields were overflowing with pilgrims— some 3000 hopeful souls. Many of them had come from distant villages and had set off several days before. They had been sleeping under the stars for many nights. Some had brought food with them, others bought or begged for it along the way, while some of the more pious undertook the penance of fasting.

Among these hopeful was Maria of the Chapel, who had come from Moita with her incredulous husband, her daughters, and her crippled son, John, who sat himself upon a stone waiting for a cure. She had asked Lucia several days earlier to request from the Lady a

8. *Memoirs*, 127.

cure for her son. Also from Moita was one José Alves, who fervently believed in the genuineness of the apparitions. In fact, he had had an earlier altercation with Father Ferreira on that very issue. He had told the Prior of Fatima to his face that his hypothesis of diabolical agencies was sheer nonsense. Who ever heard of the devil inciting people to pray?

Olimpia was also there with Maria Rosa, whom she had convinced that the children's safety was at risk if it all turned out to be a lie. "We must go after them," Olimpia insisted, "or we may never see our children again. Anything might happen, they might even be killed!" The two women concealed their identity by throwing their overskirts over their heads and sneaking along the back roads to the Cova. To protect against any evil entities that might be lingering in the area, each armed herself with a holy candle and a supply of matches. When they arrived at the Cova, they secreted themselves behind some rocks and peered out at the scene, apprehensive of what might occur.

Ti Marto, who was convinced of the sincerity of his children, was more open. He followed the little visionaries right up to the holm oak.

> What a crowd of people there was! I couldn't see the children but there was a sort of clump of people in the road and I judged they must be there in front. I thought at first that I would stay behind but in the end I couldn't resist trying to get near to them. But how? That was the question! There was such a crush. At one moment, two men, one from Ramila and the other from here, made a barrier round the children so that they wouldn't be so crushed, and then seeing me there they pulled me by the arm saying: "Here is the father, let him through!" And so I got to my Jacinta. Lucia was kneeling a little way off saying the Rosary which the people were answering aloud. When it was finished she got up so quickly that it seemed as if she were pulled up. She looked to the east and then cried out: "Shut up your umbrellas (used for the sun) Our Lady is coming!" I looked as hard as I could but could see nothing at first. And then I saw what looked like a little greyish cloud resting on the oak tree, and the sun's heat lessened and there was a delicious fresh breeze. It hardly seemed like the height of summer. The people were so silent you could have heard a pin drop. And then I

began to hear a sound, a little buzzing rather like a mosquito in an empty bottle. I couldn't hear any words! I think talking on the telephone must sound like that though I have never done it! What is it?—I said to myself. Is it near or far away? All this was for me a great proof of the miracle.[9]

Lucia had seen the flash of light as before. The radiant Lady from heaven had descended upon the *azinheira* and was smiling at them. Then Lucia, absorbed into the intimacy of the vision and enraptured by the loveliness of the Lady, felt all her loneliness, anguish, and confusion dissolve in the peaceful light that pervaded their souls. Lucia felt her aching heart mend as she abandoned herself to the consoling Presence. She was immersed in the healing warmth of an infinite love.

"Lucia, speak. Our Lady is talking to you," urged Jacinta, rousing her from her contemplative bliss.

"What do you want of me?" asked Lucia, as before.

"I want you to come here on the thirteenth of next month, to continue to pray the Rosary every day in honor of Our Lady of the Rosary, in order to obtain peace for the world and the end of the war, because only she can help you."

Then, wanting everyone who doubted to share her assurance, Lucia asked the Lady to say who she was and to perform a miracle so that everyone would believe.

"Continue to come here every month. In October, I will tell you who I am and what I want, and I will perform a miracle for all to see and believe."

Lucia then recalled the many requests that had been confided to her. The Lady replied she would cure some but not others. One of these requests was for Maria da Capelinha's crippled son. She was told that he would not be cured, but that his livelihood would be assured, if he said his Rosary every day. (He later became sacristan of the Chapel of the Apparitions.) Then the Lady's countenance became grave.

"Make sacrifices for sinners and say often, especially whenever you make a sacrifice: O Jesus, it is for love of You, for the conversion

9. de Marchi, 76.

of sinners, and in reparation for the sins committed against the Immaculate Heart of Mary."

As Our Lady spoke these words, (Lucia recalls) she opened her hands once more, as she had done during the two previous months. The rays of light seemed to penetrate the earth, and we saw, as it were, a sea of fire. Plunged in this fire were demons and souls in human form, like transparent burning embers, all blackened or burnished bronze, floating about in the conflagration, now raised into the air by the flames that issued from within themselves together with great clouds of smoke, now falling back on every side like sparks in huge fires, without weight or equilibrium, amid shrieks and groans of pain and despair, which horrified us and made us tremble with fear. The demons could be distinguished by their terrifying and repellent likeness to frightful and unknown animals, black and transparent like burning coals.[10]

At this moment, Ti Marto relates that Lucia gasped for breath, turned as pale as death, and cried out in terror, calling upon Our Lady. The terrified children looked up imploring the Lady for help. Tenderly and sadly she spoke to them.

"You have seen hell where the souls of poor sinners go. To save them, God wishes to establish in the world devotion to my Immaculate Heart. If what I say to you is done, many souls will be saved and there will be peace. The war is going to end, but if men do not cease to offend God another worse one will begin during the reign of Pius XI. When you see a night lit by a strange, unknown light, know that this is the great sign given you by God that He is about to punish the world for its crimes, by means of war, famine, and persecutions of the Church and of the Holy Father.

"To prevent this, I shall come to ask for the consecration of Russia to my Immaculate Heart, and the Communion of Reparation on the First Saturdays. If my requests are heeded, Russia will be converted, and there will be peace; if not, she will spread her errors throughout the world, causing wars and persecutions of the Church. The good will be martyred, the Holy Father will have much to suffer, various nations will be annihilated. In the end, my

10. *Memoirs,* 104, 162.

Immaculate Heart will triumph. The Holy Father will consecrate Russia to me, and she will be converted, and a period of peace will be granted to the world. In Portugal, the dogma of the Faith will always be preserved. [Here follows the third secret.] Do not tell this [the third secret] to anybody. Francisco, yes, you may tell him.

"When you pray the Rosary, say after each mystery: O my Jesus, forgive us, save us from the fire of hell. Lead all souls to heaven, especially those who are most in need."

The Lady had now revealed all three secrets to the children. The first secret is the chastisement which God will inflict upon us because of our sins. In this world: war, famine, persecution of the Holy Father, and the Church. In the next: the reality of hell for those who die refusing to repent of their sins. The second secret is devotion to the Immaculate Heart of Mary in reparation for sin and the eventual conversion of Russia after a period of apostasy. And there was also a third secret which the children were admonished never to tell anyone.

The children dutifully kept silent about all three secrets. The first two were never publicly disclosed until Lucia's third memoir, written in August, 1941, when in obedience to a letter from her Bishop, Dom Jose Alves Correia da Silva, Lucia revealed the first two secrets. The third secret was first written down at the end of 1943, again at a behest made by Bishop da Silva the previous June. Lucia notified him that it was ready in a card, which she sent in the beginning of January. It was enclosed in a sealed envelope and delivered to Bishop da Silva on June, 1944. The envelope was then taken unopened to the Bishop's palace in Leiria, where it was placed in safekeeping.[11]

This last point is significant, since confirmation of the genuineness of the apparitions is not to be sought in the revelation of various prophecies. That confirmation was to be given in a miracle which the Lady from heaven said would occur in the presence of the

---

11. Manuel Vilas-Boas et al., *Fatima: Os Lugares da Profecia*, 53. The envelope containing the secret remained there for thirteen years until it was taken to what is now the *Congregation for the Doctrine of the Faith*. It was read by Pope John XXIII in an Italian translation in August 1959, by Paul VI in June 1963, and by John Paul II in November 1980 when its contents were also made known to then Cardinal Ratzinger (Benedict XVI). See Fernando Leite, *Francisco de Fatima*, 71.

people on the following October. This helps us to understand why the fulfillment of the prophecies was never made the basis for Episcopal approval of belief in the Fatima events (given on 13 October, 1930 before the prophecies were even known). As St. Paul points out, prophecies are for believers, not for unbelievers (1 Cor. 14:22). It is for this reason that the persons concerned remained silent about the prophecies until after the events occurred.[12] As Lucia states in her third memoir:

> It may be, Your Excellency, that some people think that I should have made known all this some time ago, because they consider that it would have been twice as valuable years before hand. This would have been the case if God had willed to present me to the world as prophetess. But I believe that God had no such intention, when He made known these things to me. If that had been the case, I think that, in 1917, when He ordered me to keep silence, and this order was confirmed by those who represented Him, He would, on the contrary, have ordered me to speak. I consider then, Your Excellency, that God willed only to make use of me to remind the world that it is necessary to avoid sin, and to make reparation to an offended God, by means of prayer and sacrifice.[13]

Many Fatima scholars feel that the prophecy concerning the war is in two parts: the first part concerns the outbreak of a war and the second those punishments of the world to be heralded by a strange light. There is some support for this opinion, for as early as 1919 Jacinta remarked to Mother Godinho from her sick bed in the hospital at Lisbon: "If people do not amend their lives, Our Lady will send the world a punishment worse than anything it has known before, and it will come first to Spain."[14] The Spanish Civil War erupted in July 1936 during the reign of Pius XI (February 6, 1922–

---

12. There is evidence that Lucia knew about these prophecies as early as June 1929. To her confessor Fr. Francisco Rodrigues and in a letter to Fr. Jose Bernardo Goncalves, she told of the consecration of Russia and of the coming war, as well as of the light that would signal the beginning of a period of persecution. This information was transmitted to the Bishop of Leiria and he, in turn, conveyed it to Pope Pius XI (de Marchi, 249).
13. *Memoirs,* 110-11.
14. de Marchi, 78, n. 3.

February 10, 1939) and lasted until the outbreak of the Second World War.

The second part concerns a strange light which would herald a period of wars, famines, and persecutions of the Church. The strange light on 25 January, 1938 (an *aurora borealis* which lit up the skies over Europe and, atypically, extended as far south as Portugal and the Vatican)[15] and the beginnings of the Second World War two months later—when Germany invaded Austria (March, 1938) and the Sudetenland of northeast Czechoslovakia (September, 1938), followed by the invasion of Albania (March, 1939) and, finally, Poland (September, 1939)—augured a period of wars and famines of an extent and brutality never before experienced. It also saw the beginning of a period of heresy and perversity that threatened to destroy the very structure of society, which in turn led to many vicious attacks on the Church. This period would see priests and religious martyred in South America, Spain, China, Cambodia, Africa, and Russia. The Church itself would be infiltrated by these "errors" and would tragically play its role in spreading false doctrines and in encouraging immorality.

All of this was inaugurated before Lucia wrote her third set of memoirs. It is interesting to note that Lucia did not give the invasion of Poland as the actual beginning of the war, especially since she was writing after that invasion had become the officially accepted engagement. She did not attempt to adjust the prophecy to fit the opinions of historians.

We make these points about the subordinate role of the prophecies because there has grown up among some Fatima devotees an apocalyptic emphasis that is not explicit in the Fatima message. On the contrary, the main thrust of this message is the establishment in the world of devotion to Mary's Immaculate Heart. We have already

---

15. Auroras are caused by sunspot activity which sends out a stream of radiation to interact with the earth's magnetic field near the poles. This aurora occurred when there was no sunspot activity whatsoever. Nor was it confined to the polar regions. It extended over an area of 500,000 square kilometres with a vertical extent of 400 kilometres. It was accompanied by an eerie noise "similar to the sound of burning grass and brush." See Dr. Carl Stoermer, *Die Naturwissenschaften,* 26 (30), September 8, 1938, 633–38.

explained the nature of this devotion and how it is desired by Jesus Christ Himself. We only want to emphasize here that Russia's apostasy was, as it were, the crucible for determining the truth of that message. Once Russia had been consecrated to Mary's Immaculate Heart, *it would recover its faith*. We shall tell the story of that consecration by a Pope (who will have much to suffer), the content of the third secret, and the resulting conversion of Russia later. At this juncture, we merely want to emphasize that this conversion is only an intermediate objective to the establishment of this devotion. The reason Russia would not be converted before being consecrated to the Immaculate Heart of Mary by the Pope in concert with the college of Bishops is that such a step would necessarily involve overcoming the ecclesiastical timidity or personal skepticism of some contemporary Bishops. In other words, it would require a return to a resolute orthodoxy on their part. It is this devotion that Jesus proposes in countering the irreligion that has developed since the Enlightenment.

This is also the reason that the revelation of the prophecies would be delayed. Time had to be given for the worldwide spread of the "errors" out of Russia, so that the conversion of Russia as a direct result of this devotion would be a testimony to its genuineness. It would reveal who is sovereign and Lord of the nations (Ps. 22:28; 44:2) and who really determines the course of history (Dan. 4:17, 25, 32). In the end, the Immaculate Heart of Mary would triumph, ushering in a "period" of peace upon the earth.

A deeper reason for the development of this devotion will be made apparent in the next visitation from the Lady—reparation. The need for reparation has already been alluded to a number of times by the angel and by the Blessed Lady. It is mentioned again in this message when the Lady tells the children, "Make sacrifices for sinners and say often, especially whenever you make a sacrifice: O Jesus, it is for love of You, for the conversion of sinners, and in reparation for the sins committed against the Immaculate Heart of Mary." She also tells them that she will come again (sometime after the October miracle) to ask for the "Communion of reparation." Meanwhile, the children are instructed to add to each decade of the Rosary the prayer, "O my Jesus, forgive us, save us from the fire of hell. Lead all souls to heaven, especially those who are most in need." Again we see the intrinsic relationship between the Rosary, which, in its meditations and teachings imitates the reflective and Immaculate Heart of Mary, and the need for reparation for others. What is emphasized here is the necessity of this devotion in converting human beings to God. The confirmation of its potency will be the conversion of an apostate Russia. Our Lady of Fatima has begun to paint a composition of exquisite beauty and depth.

And then the Lady finished her discourse. After a moment's silence, Lucia asked if there was anything more she desired of her. The Lady replied that nothing more was required that day. Then, as before, she began to ascend towards the east, until she disappeared in the immensity of space. Ti Marto continues:

> We heard a large clap of thunder and the little arch which had been put up to hang the two lanterns on, trembled as if in an earthquake. Lucia, who was still kneeling, got up so quickly that her skirts ballooned round her and pointing to the sky she cried out: "There she goes, there she goes!" And then after a moment or two: "Now you cannot see her anymore." All this was for me a great proof.[16]

The children, who were already markedly disturbed by the vision of hell, were then nearly suffocated by the mob that immediately thronged about them.

"What did she look like? Is it the Blessed Virgin? Will she come again? What did she say? Why do you look so sad?"

"It's a secret," Lucia murmured. "It's a secret."

"Good or bad?"

"Good for some, for others bad."

"And you won't tell us."

"No, I mustn't."

From their hiding place behind the rocks, Olimpia and Maria Rosa clutched themselves in terror. They could see their children being trampled to death. "Ah, Maria Rosa, their killing our children!" Olimpia shrieked.

---

16. de Marchi, 79.

However, Manuel Marto, seeing the throng and also frightened lest his children be crushed, pushed his way into the crowd and gathered up the beleaguered Jacinta into his arms. Placing his hat on her head to protect it from the blazing sun, he carried her out of the crowd. After him came an enormous man, Dr. Carlos Mendes (a lawyer from Torres Novas) who scooped up Lucia, and another man who rescued Francisco. All the while, they were followed by stragglers still hounding them with questions. But Lucia and Francisco kept saying, "It's a secret. It's a secret."

Someone offered them a lift home in an automobile. Ti Marto agreed that this method of transportation was best under the circumstances, and the children had their first ride in a horseless carriage.

After this apparition, the children became even firmer in their commitment. Lucia lost all those doubts that had been assailing her. The terrors of hell and the ugliness of the demons contrasted with the sweetness and intimacy of that penetrating light, assured her that this lovely Lady could not be the devil. Jacinta, too, had been radically affected by the vision of hell. She would begin to express a compelling desire to sacrifice all she could to save people from its horrors. Upon Francisco, however, that vision made the least impression, although it had a marked effect. Rather, it was the light of God that struck him the most deeply. He would come to spend much of his time consoling Jesus, whose Heart was so sorrowful because of the indifference of human beings to the love that he so freely offered. By now, all three children had become stronger spiritually, which was just as well, because they were about to undergo an ordeal that would call upon every ounce of spiritual strength.

Photograph showing the children outside the church in the parish of Fatima, not long after they received the vision of hell.

Baptism by Fire

A S A RESULT OF THE THIRD APPARITION, the lives of the shepherd children were about to become entangled with the secular powers shaping the political climate of Portugal. Although no one knew of the prophecies concerning Russia, dark forces sympathetic to its nascent ideology were gathering against the children. The anti-clerical *O Seculo*, the principal daily newspaper of Lisbon, printed a sardonically twisted account on July 21, under the heading, *A Message From Heaven—Commercial Speculation?*[1] The Church was accused by the revolutionary press of inventing the entire affair to recover the prestige it had lost in the Revolution of 1910. Liberals entertained fanciful conjectures of psychosis, epilepsy, and hysteria. In the media and in the streets, it seemed as though the apparitions had succeeded only in unleashing a revitalized and acrimonious attack against the Church.

Speculation about the secrets was also intense and was spreading rapidly throughout Portugal. Consequently, crowds of the curious and the hopeful swarmed into Aljustrel, seeking the children and their families in order to pry the secret from them. The otherwise insignificant oak tree became a place of pilgrimage where many came to kneel, to leave little gifts and icons, and to offer up the Rosary. On the way home, they would ply the children with petitions for cures, blessings, and guidance from the Lady when she next appeared. However, not all were motivated by faith. Neither were they all simple folk.

> Ladies came (says Ti Marto), goodness knows where from, well dressed and all. People went all over the place as they liked until one felt quite ashamed. Ugh . . . weren't they curious. What they wanted was to get hold of the secret. They would take Jacinta on

---

1. Walsh, 84.

their knees and worry her with questions. But she just answered as she wanted to! That secret . . . you could not get it out of her with a corkscrew! They tried offering presents and pleading with her but it was time wasted for them and for us, with our work and even our meals disturbed. . . . Fine gentlemen came too, just to make fun of simple folk who could not read or write. . . . And what questions they asked! It was a shame some times. Such as if Our Lady kept sheep, and goats, and eats cheese, things which even ignorant people do not ask.[2]

Of course, Manuel Marto was now firmly convinced of the authenticity of the apparitions. Olimpia, however, was still doubtful, and all this pressure and harassment was becoming too stressful. One day she turned on Jacinta and uncharacteristically slapped her across the face saying: "They all go to the Cova da Iria because of you."

"We don't ask them to go," Jacinta protested sobbingly. "If they want to go, they go. If not, they can stay at home."

Priests were no less troublesome. They were perfectly aware of the damage to the reputation and credibility of the Church that could be inflicted by deception. Over the last two millennia, the Church had developed a detailed strategy for inquiring into such matters. Hundreds of questions, designed to uncover the least inconsistency or inaccuracy, had been devised. Scriptural traditions, theological principles, and moral precepts were all brought to bear to test the truth of such messages. Armed with these criteria, clerics could unmask any deception with an exactitude that would never occur to an unbeliever.

After a couple of such grueling encounters with clerics from Torres Novas and Santarem, the children quickly learned to avoid them. The mere glimpse of a black soutane heading toward them was enough to send the children tumbling over a wall or ducking behind some brambles. Their habit of avoiding priests was yet another cause for complaint on the part of the parish priest, Father Ferreira. But these rigorous examinations were too much for the children. "When we saw a priest coming, we always escaped if we

2. de Marchi, 85.

could," wrote Lucia much later. "Whenever we found ourselves in the presence of a priest, we prepared ourselves to offer to God one of our greatest sacrifices!"

Fortunately, not all their encounters with priests were so taxing. One day, Father Cruz travelled all the way from Lisbon to see them. He was the Jesuit Priest who had once intervened to obtain Lucia's early communion. The words he had spoken to her on that day—"My daughter, your soul is the temple of the Holy Spirit. Keep it always pure"—still lived in Lucia's memory four years later. Now here he was, once again desiring to see his young communicant and to discover the truth of the rumors he had heard. He was prematurely aged and was bent almost double, but, having questioned the shepherds to his satisfaction, he still requested that the children take him to the site of the apparitions. "On the way," Lucia recalls, "we walked on either side of His Reverence, who was riding a donkey so small that his feet almost touched the ground." As they traveled, he taught them a series of spontaneous prayers, two of which became special favorites of Jacinta's: "O my Jesus, I love You!" and "Sweet Heart of Mary, be my salvation!"[3] From henceforth he would be one of their staunchest ecclesial allies.

The severest of these trials came from Lucia's family, but this time they had real justification. The hordes of people trampling across their fields were ruining their crops. By this stage, the family had become extremely poor, having only a few plots of ground left. The steady traffic of pedestrians and donkeys had destroyed what little produce they had managed to grow. Antonio Abobora, who had once shrugged off the entire affair as "women's tales," was now explosively hostile. "Thousands of feet had packed the soil so hard that there was no sense cultivating it anymore; horses had eaten or trampled his cabbages, beans and potato vines; all his labor had been wasted. Antonio grumbled and fumed, and drank more copinhos than ever."[4] The source of their livelihood had been ravaged. Maria Rosa was beside herself: "When you want something to

3. *Memoirs*, 39.
4. Walsh, 87.

eat," she snapped at Lucia, "you had better ask Our Lady." Then her sisters added: "You can have whatever comes from the Cova da Iria." During these days Lucia, too terrified to ask her for even a crust of bread, often went to bed hungry.

This time, the effect of all this rancor upon Lucia was different. She was no longer assailed by doubt: her faith became stronger, and she could seek solace in prayer and in the companionship of her cousins, from whom she no longer needed to hide. Yet even among all the beauty of the Cabeço and the hills around the Cova da Iria, or even with the glad camaraderie of her beloved Jacinta and Francisco, she could find no real peace. Their conversations comprised a darker, more urgent content. The terrifying reality of hell had burned itself into their imaginations. One day they were out together at the Cabeço with the flocks. Jacinta, who could not put out of her mind the finality and enormity of the prospect of eternal punishment, sat down puzzled on a stone and said:

"That Lady said that many souls go to hell. What is hell, then?"

"You saw. It is like a big deep pit of wild beasts, with an enormous fire in it, and that is where people go who commit sins and do not confess them. They stay there and burn forever," Lucia explained, drawing upon the knowledge given her by her mother.

"And they never get out of there again?"

"No!"

"Not even after many, many years?"

"No! Hell never ends."

"And heaven? It never ends either?"

"Whoever goes to heaven, never leaves it again!"

"And whoever goes to hell, never leaves it either?"

"They are eternal, don't you see! They never end."

Jacinta paused awhile to reflect on the concept of endless time. She found it quite baffling. Then later she asked.

"But listen! Doesn't hell end after many, many, *many* years? And those people burning in hell, don't they ever die? And don't they turn into ashes? And if people pray very much for sinners, won't Our Lord get them out of there? And if they make sacrifices as well? Poor sinners! We have to pray and make many sacrifices for them! But how good that Lady is! She has already promised to take us to heaven!"

None of the children could understand the nature of the vision that had been given to them. But they did grasp that it was not a pleasant prospect, that it was freely chosen, and that it was endless and final. Once, Lucia asked Jacinta what she was thinking of, and she replied: "Of that war that is going to come, and of so many people who are going to die and go to hell. What a pity there must be a war and they must go to hell because they won't stop sinning!"

But more importantly, they understood the responsibility they had towards those who were lost. Again Jacinta:

"Ah, Hell, Hell! How sorry I am for the souls who go to hell! And the people down there, burning alive, like wood in the fire!" Then, shuddering, she knelt down, joined her hands, and recited the prayer taught them by the Blessed Lady: "O my Jesus! Forgive us, save us from the fire of hell, and lead all souls to heaven, especially those who are most in need."

Jacinta would spend many hours kneeling and repeating this supplication over and over. Occasionally, she would rouse herself "like someone awaking from sleep" and call out to Lucia or Francisco. "Are you praying with me? We must pray very hard to save souls from hell. So many go there! So many!" At other times she would ask why the Lady did not show hell to sinners. If only they knew what was in store for them, she thought, surely it would convince them to stop their sinful ways. Then she wondered just what were the sins that sent people there.

"I don't know," replied Lucia. "Perhaps the sin of not going to Mass on Sunday, of stealing, of saying ugly words, of cursing, and of swearing."

"So for just one word, then, people can go to hell?"

"Well, it is a sin!"

"But it wouldn't be hard for them to keep quiet and to go to Mass."

Such was their simple doctrine. If something was a sin, as Lucia said, then its commission was an act of disobedience whether one was knowledgeable or not, or free to choose or not. They could not have grasped the principle of freely and knowingly choosing to rebel against the will of God that constitutes the basis of all sin (Jas. 4:17). Yet they understood the concept of obedience well enough.

Francisco, who was a boy of few words, spent long hours in solitary prayer. He would quietly wander off from the others by himself. When he was missed, the two children would search for him, only to discover him hidden behind a wall or a clump of blackberry bushes, prostrate with his face to the ground, deep in prayer. It would take no slight effort to rouse him. Then he would stir, look up as though he had just come from a distant world, and, finally, acknowledge the children.

Lucia would ask him, "Francisco, why don't you tell me to pray with you, and Jacinta, too?"

"I prefer praying by myself so that I can think and console Our Lord, Who is so sad."

"Which do you like better: to console Our Lord or to convert sinners so that no more souls will go to hell?"

"I would rather console Our Lord. Didn't you notice how sad Our Lady was last month, when she said that people must not offend Our Lord any more, for He is already much offended? I would like to console Our Lord, and after that, convert sinners so that they won't offend Him any more."

What Francisco thought or felt, in his consolation towards the Lord Jesus, will never be known for certain. We do know that after the vision of hell he remarked: "We were on fire in that light which is God, and yet we were not burnt! What is God? We could never put it into words. Yes, that is something indeed which we could never express. But what a pity it is that He is so sad! If only I could console Him!"[5] On this basis, it would be reasonable to affirm that Francisco's special grace was affective prayer. His pity and compassion for the sorrowful Heart of Jesus would draw him deeply into silent but impassioned communion with Him and with His agony for the Church. In the depth, silence, and absorption of Francisco's prayerful state, his desire to console his beloved Jesus expressed itself through suffering in sympathy with his Lord. Francisco was

5. *Memoirs*, 127.

able to identify with his Lord in His sufferings for His body on earth, the Church, thereby displaying the full meaning of the mystery of the body of Christ: "Now I rejoice in my sufferings for your sake, and in my flesh I complete what is lacking in Christ's afflictions for the sake of his body, that is, the Church" (Col. 1:24).

Jacinta's grace in prayer seemed to be that of supplication and penance, while Francisco's tended towards adoration and worship. Yet each in his and her own way was living a life of authentic intercession for others by realizing in the depths of their hearts the meaning of St. Paul's injunction: "present your bodies as a living sacrifice, holy, and acceptable to God, which is your spiritual worship" (Rom. 12:1). They were conforming their hearts to the reflective and Immaculate Heart of Mary and thereby uniting with the suffering, sorrowful, and Sacred Heart of Jesus.

The two Marto children took very seriously the apostolate that had befallen them. Jacinta had an influence on all who came in contact with her. Her family, who had hitherto neglected their devotions somewhat, began to pray the Rosary daily as a direct result of Jacinta's example. Strangers, passing the fields where the children were pasturing their sheep, would hear a thin, high voice uttering prayers such as those that Father Cruz had taught her. "Jesus, I love you!" and "Immaculate Heart of Mary, save the poor sinners!" would come floating on the wind, across the fields, and into the consciences of passersby. Jacinta would even be found teaching other little children how to pray the Rosary and to accept with gladness the daily sacrifices they must make for others.

Francisco, who was more subdued, was, nevertheless, the little moralist. However, he would not rebuke anyone that he saw doing something improper. He would simply withdraw from them. When asked why he turned aside, he answered: "Because you were not good" or "Because I do not want to play here any more." It was he, more than Jacinta, who reminded the others of their duty to pray. For the children had not entirely ceased playing, singing, and dancing among the flowers and grasses on the *campos*. But at intervals, Francisco would recall them to their devotions, stressing the exemplary life to which the Lady had called them. He would point out how they had been singled out by the Lady to live a life of prayer.

Adults would comment upon how salutary it was just to be in Francisco's presence.

"I don't know what it is about Francisco, but it feels so good to be here with him," a visitor once remarked.

"It's a mystery one cannot fathom!" another agreed.

Lucia, of course, was called to a different apostolate. Her ministry was to remain behind on earth and to spread the message of devotion to the Immaculate Heart of Our Lady. Her penances were not self-imposed, as were those of her cousins. Rather, Lucia's sufferings were imposed upon her from without, mainly by her family and by her neighbors. While her two cousins hardly experienced these persecutions, they would more than make up for that through their impending deaths. For the Lady had foretold that they would soon be taken to heaven.

This, too, had darkened their camaraderie. Lucia knew that one day in the near future she would be alone, facing a disbelieving world without her dear companions to console her. Sometimes Francisco would find her weeping because of this. He would comfort her by promising to pray for her while he was in heaven. But more often than not, the loss was too heartbreaking for the three of them, and then they would all seek refuge in one another's embrace, tearfully kissing and consoling each other behind the well at the bottom of Lucia's garden.

Behind this pageantry of innocence and suffering, consolation and heartache, darker forces were mobilizing. As if directed by some unseen malefactor, they bore down upon the three unlettered shepherd children with a single-minded intent. A few days before the thirteenth of August, while all of Portugal was wondering if there would be another visitation at the Cova da Iria, both Ti Marto and Antonio Abobora received notification from the Administrator (Mayor) of the Council of Ourem, which governed the district of Aljustrel and Fatima. He had ordered that the "ones who disturbed the peace so notoriously" be presented at the town hall of that city for a trial, at the hour of twelve noon on Saturday, August 11, 1917.[6]

6. Walsh, 94.

Baptism by Fire

Arturo de Oliveira Santos was the Administrator of the Council of Ourem at that time. By trade a blacksmith and by outlook an idealist and a materialist, he was a man of little culture and even less compassion. He named his blacksmith's forge the Forge of Progress and three of his children Democracy, Republic, and Liberty. At the age of twenty-six, he joined the Grand Orient Lodge at Leiria and, with the aid of his Masonic friends, rose rapidly in the anti-clerical government that had established itself after the 1910 Revolution. He repaid their help by founding in Ourem yet another Masonic Lodge, quickly becoming its President. He was bitterly anti-Catholic and scoffed at anything suggestive of the miraculous or of Divine intervention.

Administrator Santos was typical of those crass, untalented people who manage to float rapidly to the top in authoritarian systems. He was a master of the art of servile smiles and brisk handshakes which, in a society that fed off praise and flattery, took him, at the age of just thirty-three, to the Presidency of the town's Administration and of the Chamber, and Deputy Judge of Commerce.

> In short, he had become a sort of republican Czar of the whole district, including Fatima and Aljustrel. Fewer and fewer went to Mass and to the sacraments; there were more divorces, not so many children; and when he arrested six priests and held them incommunicado for eight days, the leading Catholic laymen in the Council and the Chamber were so busy making profitable compromises that they did not have time to protest loudly enough to be heard. To the blacksmith and his friends the fight for progress and enlightenment, as they preferred to describe their conflict with the Church, was all but won.[7]

Therefore, when it came to his attention that an invisible woman was seen by shepherd children near a village in his jurisdiction, and that three thousand people had been assembling there without his official approval, he was determined to stamp it out. Such mysticism and fanaticism belonged to the Middle Ages, not to his enlightened times. Was not science the savior of humanity? Did not the Socialists hold the solution to our political and economic woes?

7. Ibid., 97.

Were we not on the verge of a new world order? Certainly, he was not going to allow a superstitious peasantry to dismantle all that his administration had accomplished. Under pressure of the Masonic and liberal presses, who had called for repressive action against this resurgence of mysticism, Santos was determined to react swiftly and ruthlessly.

While most people in the region feared this man, there was one who responded to his orders without the slightest trace of nervousness. When Manuel Marto received the order to appear before Santos, he reacted in his characteristic phlegmatic manner. "There is no sense in taking such young children before a court of that kind," he said. "Besides, it's three leagues, and that's too far for them to walk. And they don't know how to ride a beast. I'm not going to do it. And I will go over and tell the Administrator why." Olimpia agreed with him. Ti Marto continues:

> My brother-in-law received the same summons to appear with his daughter at the Town Hall of Ourem on 11th August at midday. They both came to my house in the morning while I was finishing my breakfast. Then Lucia asked me:
> "Aren't Jacinta and Francisco coming?"
> "What would two small children like them do there! I should think not. . . . I'm going myself to answer for them!"
> Then Lucia ran to Jacinta's room and we heard the latter say:
> "If they kill you, tell them that Francisco and I are the same as you and that we want to be killed, too."
> Then we all three left. On the way Lucia fell three times off her donkey and her father, who was rushing along for fear of the Mayor, went ahead and when I arrived I found them already in the square. I said to him:
> "Is everything all right then?"
> He looked very heated and said: "The door was shut and no one there."
> As it wasn't midday we waited a bit. Then we went back to the Town Hall. Still shut. At last someone came and told us that the Mayor didn't work there any more. Finally we found him and he said to me at once:
> "Where is the child."
> He did not seem to know there were three children and, as he

had ordered me to bring one, I figured that he did not know what he wanted!

"Now, look, sir," I told him, "it's more than three leagues from here to our village and the children couldn't walk all that way, and they are not used to the donkey either." And I wanted to add: "The idea of two children of that age being summonsed!" but I stopped myself in time. Then he became annoyed—much I cared though! After that he began to question Lucia and tried to get the secret out of her. But as usual she would not say a word. At one moment he turned to Antonio and said:

"Do you believe in these things there in Fatima?"

"No, sir," said my brother-in-law, "we think it's all women's stories."

Then I said:

"Here I am your worship and my children say the same as I."

"Do you believe in it then?"

"Yes, I believe what they say!"

They all laughed but it made no difference to me. There were some men who were going to put it all in the papers and at last they let us go. But the Mayor kept on threatening Lucia to the end and said that if she did not tell the secret he would have her killed. As I was leaving I turned round to the Mayor:

"If you send for us we shall have to come as many times as you say, but kindly remember that we have our lives to live."[8]

It was late in the evening when they returned to Aljustrel. Straightway Lucia ran to find her cousins. The two were huddled disconsolately at the well. Seeing Lucia alive, they streaked towards her and embraced her: Jacinta murmured through her tears: "Oh, Lucia, your sister told us that they had killed you!" In her anxiety, she had forgotten the Lady's promise that it was she and her brother who were to go to heaven and that it was Lucia who was to remain behind.

Mayor Santos was furious that an illiterate ten-year-old peasant girl should frustrate and elude him so easily. His orders from his Masonic superiors had been precise and uncompromising. He had been directed to hold the Church to ridicule by exposing the prank-

8. de Marchi, 90.

sters who were perpetrating this facile hoax. Any and all measures must be taken to eliminate this pernicious and backward superstition. He was determined not to fail next time.

On Monday morning, 13 August, as Ti Marto was hoeing a nearby field, he was suddenly called back to the house. When he returned, he saw a crowd of people gathered in front of his doorway. He detoured to the kitchen and, stopping to wash his hands, saw Olimpia seated at the table, looking extremely nervous. Silently she kept nodding in the direction of the sitting room.

"Why such a hurry, I am going there now," Ti Marto said calmly.

Olimpia kept signaling him to hurry. Finally, he entered and found the Administrator standing in the middle of the room and looking very uncomfortable. He was accompanied by a priest. Ti Marto ignored the Mayor and crossed to shake hands with the priest. Then, turning towards the Mayor, he said, "I didn't expect to see you here, sir."

"No, I thought after all I would like to go to see the miracle. Yes, we will all go together, and I will take the children with me in the carriage. We'll see and believe, like St. Thomas." He chuckled nervously and glanced about the room. "Where are the children, by the way? It is getting late. You had better call them."

"There is no need to call them," Ti Marto answered in his matter-of-fact way. "They will be ready, all right, when it is time to go."

At that moment, the three children entered the room with Lucia's father. Mayor Santos turned towards them and pressed them to go with him. The children drew back replying: "It is not necessary, *Senhor*."

"But it will be better that way," Santos said condescendingly. "We can be there in a moment, and no one will bother us on the way. Besides we will have more time to stop at Fatima, at the house of the Prior." Then, turning to Ti Marto: "He wants to ask them some questions, you see."

Unable to think of a suitable riposte, Ti Marto and Antonio Abobora decided they had better go with the children. Francisco climbed into the carriage next to the Administrator, and the girls sat behind. Antonio and Ti Marto followed on foot. It took only a few minutes to get to the rectory at the top of the hill in Fatima. Lucia

126

was the first to be sent in to meet the Prior, who was waiting in his study. His attitude had become belligerent.

"Who taught you to say the things that you are going about saying?" he snapped.

"The Lady whom I saw at the Cova da Iria."

"Anyone who goes about spreading such wicked lies as you do will be judged and will go to hell if they are not true. More and more people are being deceived by you."

"If people who lie go to hell, then I shall not go to hell, because I am not lying and I tell only what I saw and what the Lady told me." Lucia's attitude was now much more confident. "And the people go there because they want to; we do not tell them to go."

"Is it true that the Lady confided to you a secret?"

"Yes, Senhor Prior."

"Tell it, then."

"I cannot tell. But if Your Reverence wants to know it, I will ask the Lady, and if she permits me, I will tell you."

All this time the Administrator was impatiently shuffling in his chair. "Come," he interrupted at last, "these are supernatural matters. Let us be going." With that, he got up and led the children outside into the carriage which had surreptitiously drawn closer to the steps. Bundling the three children into the wagon, they made off at a trot towards the Cova da Iria, leaving Antonio and Ti Marto wondering what was going on. At first, Ti Marto was relieved that the interview was over and that the Administrator appeared to be taking the children to the Cova as promised. But when the carriage arrived at the main road, the horse made a sudden turn in the opposite direction, towards Ourem.

"This isn't the way to the Cova," protested Lucia.

The Mayor calmed the children by explaining that they had an appointment to see a priest in Ourem and then they would all get to travel to the Cova in a shiny automobile which would take them there in plenty of time to see their Lady. Then he threw a rug over the children to hide them from the pilgrims who lined the roadway.

"It had been most cunningly arranged," reflected Ti Marto many years later. "Yes, it was well managed, very clever; and nothing could be done."

Meanwhile, at the Cova da Iria, a crowd of some 6,000 persons were praying and singing hymns, waiting for the children, who never turned up. At about eleven o'clock, Ti Marto came to the Cova and explained why the children were absent. A wave of protest arose and would have led to a riot if suddenly they had not heard a tremendous roll of thunder. Many, realizing that the Cova was the crater of an extinct volcano, feared they would be killed. They thought the devil had manufactured the apparition just to lure them to this precarious place. Maria da Capelinha, who had come early to erect an altar, describes what happened next.

> Everyone began to spread out away from the tree but, of course, no one was killed. After the thunderclap came the flash of lightning, and then we began to see a little cloud, very delicate, very white, which stopped for a few moments over the tree and then rose in the air and disappeared. As we looked around us we noticed the strange thing which we had seen before and were to see in the following months: our faces were reflecting all the colors of the rainbow, pink, red, blue. . . . The trees seemed to be made not of leaves, but of flowers; they seemed to be laden with flowers, each leaf seemed to be a flower. The ground came out in colors and so did our clothes. The lanterns fixed to the arch looked like gold.[9]

The Lady had indicated to them that she had kept her appointment. After these signs ceased, the crowd raised a protest that could be heard in Aljustrel. Some wanted to go to Ourem to protest. "Let's go and beat them all up!" a farmer shouted. "No, let's speak to the priest; it's his fault too!" objected another. Ti Marto tried to calm them down, saying that all of this was in the hands of God, who would punish those responsible. But the crowd was not convinced. Their protestations were so great that Father Ferreira had to issue a proclamation that he was not a party to the subsequent arrest of the children:

> I make this statement on the authority of the parents and for the satisfaction of the 5,000 to 6,000 persons who came many miles

9. Ibid., 93–94.

and with great sacrifice to see and speak with them. I deny this infamous calumny and declare before the whole world that I had nothing to do, directly or indirectly, with this impious and sacrilegious action.[10]

When Olimpia had heard what had happened to her children she ran to her sister-in-law's house.

"What will become of us, Maria Rosa, they have taken our children!"

"It will teach them a lesson if they are lying, and if they are not, then Our Lady will look after them!"

"You have only one," whimpered Olimpia, "but we, we have our two, and they are only babies."

The children had been locked in a room in the Administrator's house. He had counted on their becoming frightened and intimidated by their confinement. Soon the clocks began to chime the hour of noon. The children began to exchange worried glances.

"Perhaps Our Lady is going to appear to us here!" Francisco replied hopefully. But when the time went by with no sign of her coming, Jacinta began to cry. Then he said: "Our Lady must be sad because we didn't go to the Cova da Iria, and she won't appear to us any more, will she?"

"I don't know, I think she will understand," Lucia said.

They spent the rest of the day and all that night locked up in that room without any food or their own warm beds to sleep in and with only each other to depend upon. It was a lonely and fearful time for these young children, who had never before been away from the companionship of their family. They had no idea what horrors awaited them. They could only fear the worst.

The next morning at ten o'clock the Mayor took them to the town hall and subjected them to another grueling interrogation. It was just as unproductive as before. The children would not deny what they had seen and heard; neither would they divulge the secret. The Mayor attempted to bribe them with money and with

10. Ibid., 94, n. 2.

gold chains, but they remained determined in their resolve not to betray their beautiful Lady. Then Santos threatened that if his kindness and fairness had no effect, he would have no other choice but to lock them in a cell with thieves and scoundrels. When they refused to be intimidated, he ordered that they be placed in a cell within the building, admonishing them that, if they still refused to cooperate, he would have them boiled in oil.

The terrified children were thrown into a dingy cell containing a rough-looking group of felons. They ran and huddled in a dark corner of the cell. Jacinta began to cry. Francisco rose to the occasion and tried to comfort his sister, who was bemoaning the fact that she would never see her parents again.

"I want to see my mother," she wailed.

"Don't cry, Jacinta, we can offer this to Jesus for sinners."

Then Francisco knelt on the floor, and the other two, following his example, joined him. The trio held hands and, in the presence of that scurrilous band of fugitives, opened their hearts to Christ: "O my Jesus, this is for love of you, for the conversion of sinners." Then Jacinta added: "And also for the Holy Father and in reparation for sins against the Immaculate Heart of Mary."

There in a lonely cell in a strange town, among discarded desperate men, three little children knelt in supplication, not for themselves, but for just such sinners as were gazing incredulously upon this pitiful scene.

"Don't be afraid, little ones, we won't hurt you," one of the men said reassuringly. Soon all the prisoners were gathered together, questioning the children as to why they were in there.

"The easiest way for you to get out," advised one, "would be to tell the Administrator the secret. It doesn't matter about the Lady."

"But the Lady does not want us to tell it!" said Jacinta candidly.

"What is it to you whether the Lady wants you to or not?"

"Never, I would rather die."

They began to say the Rosary, and the prisoners dutifully joined in. Some of the prisoners were kneeling, others were standing, but all were reciting prayers no doubt left unsaid, since they were children themselves. Francisco, noticing that one of the men still had his hat on, quietly reminded him of it. Sheepishly, the man removed his hat and handed it to Francisco, who gently placed it on a bench beside his own.

By this time, they had all become good friends. The men begged the children to tell them more about the Lady and her messages. One prisoner, who had a harmonium, began to play a tune. They started to sing. One of the men asked the children if they could dance. "I can dance the fandango and the vira," chirped Jacinta. So a large, burly man, who, they had learned, was a thief, lifted Jacinta into his arms and began swinging her around the cell in time to the music. Soon everyone was in an uproar. The cell reverberated with the sounds of shuffling feet, off-key voices, and spirited clapping in time to the tune of a wheezing concertina. This was hardly the intimidation that Mayor Santos had intended for the children.

Suddenly the cell door clanged open. Everyone stopped abruptly and the children gasped, their hearts pounding heavily. An ugly guard had appeared to escort them back to the Administrator. They were thrust into his office, where they were left to confront a furious Arturo Santos. He glared at the children.

"Well?" he growled. "Are you ready to tell me the secret?"

The children stood before him in defiant silence. Santos replied coldly: "Very well. I have tried to save you. But since you will not obey your government, you shall be fried alive in a cauldron of boiling oil." He barked for his guard.

"Is the oil good and hot?"

"Yes, Senhor Administrator."

"Then take this one and throw her in."

The fierce-looking guard grasped the distraught Jacinta and dragged her screaming from the room.

"Jesus... Our Lady... help me..." shrieked the terrified child.

"Tell them nothing!," cried Francisco. "You shall soon be in heaven. It will be all right. Nothing else matters!"

Then she was gone. Francisco sank to his knees and gasped out a Rosary, pleading for courage for his sister. "Holy Mary, Mother of God, pray for us now and in the hour of our death!"

The door opened and the menacing guard returned with a ghoulish grin on his face. "She's fried," he snarled. "Let's have the next one. Or else tell us the secret."

"I cannot, Senhor," stammered Francisco. "I mustn't tell it to any-one."

"Then you must come with me," the guard announced, dropping his heavy hand onto Francisco's shoulder. He dragged Francisco out to share his sister's violent death, leaving Lucia alone with the Administrator.

Lucia was desolate. She remembered that the Lady had foretold her cousin's deaths, but she never imagined they would come with such terrible swiftness or with such heartless cruelty.

"It will be you next," sneered the Administrator, "unless you want to tell me the secret."

"I would rather die," she said with newfound determination.

"Very well, you shall."

The guard returned and ushered her away. Lucia stiffened herself and willingly accompanied him down the long corridor to that dreaded room with the cauldron of boiling oil. She had forgotten the Lady's promise to her. It dawned on her that she would never see her family again. She strengthened herself with the thought that soon she would be reunited with her cousins in heaven and that her sufferings would be over. The guard slowly opened the door to that threatening room. Then he pushed her in and slammed the door behind. There, cringing in the middle of the room, were Jacinta and Francisco, still alive! Immediately, the three were in each other's arms. Radiant with joy, they thanked their beloved Lady of the Cova for their victory. They had passed the test. She would be so pleased with them.

The Mayor did not surrender so easily. The sadistic guard returned and told them they had all been taken there to be boiled together. Their momentary joy turned to terror. They had one last chance to reveal the secret. Again they refused and again the Mayor was defeated. He confined them to the same room as before, where they spent the night. The following morning, one final interrogation fell upon the exhausted children like an anticlimax. Santos was vanquished, and the children, taken by automobile, were released into the hands of Father Ferreira at Fatima. It was the morning of Wednesday, 15 August, 1917, the Feast of the Assumption of Our Lady. Three unlettered children of only ten, nine, and seven years of age had courageously endured two terrifying days and nights without succumbing to the malevolent powers so determined to discredit them. They were reminded of the words of their beautiful Lady:

"Don't lose heart. I will never forsake you. My Immaculate Heart will be your refuge and the way that will lead you to God."

Meanwhile, Ti Marto and Olimpia were frantic with worry. All official avenues of determining what had befallen their children had been closed to them. No one would admit any knowledge of where the children were. Ti Marto believed them to be in Santarem, but lacking a telephone and forced to travel on foot, he had no way of finding out. On the morning of the Feast of the Assumption, the Marto family, along with Lucia's family went to Mass.

After Mass, someone noticed the children standing on the veranda of the presbytery. They were in the company of what Manuel Marto described as "a funny little official, a man who was in the service of the Mayor, who shook and trembled in the most extraordinary way." The crowd was incensed, but Ti Marto got to his children first. He rushed up and hugged Jacinta. The tears of joy pouring down his face "made Jacinta's all wet." Then Francisco and Lucia ran over to him, crying: "Father, Uncle, give us your blessing!" Ti Marto, realizing that the children had passed the inquisition successfully, turned to the petty official and said:

"This might have had a sorry ending, and it's not your fault that it didn't. You wanted them to say they were lying, and you couldn't make them. And even if you had made them, I should have told the truth."

Then, turning to the enraged mob that had assembled, he declared, "Be quiet all of you! Some of you are shouting against the Mayor, some against the priest and the official, but it all comes from lack of faith and is allowed by God."

Mayor Santos showed himself to the crowd, hoping to appease them. But he only enraged them even more. Ti Marto observed some young thugs with bludgeons menacing the Mayor, so, to show them that there were no hard feelings towards him, he decided to accept an invitation from Santos to accompany him to the tavern and to permit him to buy a luncheon of bread, cheese, and wine.

The Administrator, even then, tried to imply that the children had told him the secret. But Ti Marto knew better: "Sure, sure. As they would not tell it to their father and mother, it is natural that they would tell it to you."

Meanwhile, the children had gone to the Cova da Iria to give thanks for the grace to endure the ordeal to which they had been subjected. There they found Maria of the Chapel in a quandary as to what to do with the offerings that the people had begun to leave on the makeshift altar. Lucia said she would ask her Lady about it.

The following Sunday afternoon, Lucia, Francisco, and his brother John were shepherding at a rocky field known as Valinhos. Suddenly, the air became fresher and there was the familiar flash of light. Lucia, aware of the imminent arrival of the Lady and seeing that Jacinta was not there,[11] besought John to run to fetch her. He refused until Francisco offered him a couple of pennies. There was a second flash of light just as Jacinta came running toward them. Suddenly the Lady was there in front of them as before.

"What do you want of me?" Lucia asked in her customary greeting.

"I want you to continue going to the Cova da Iria on the thirteenth, and to continue praying the Rosary every day. In the last month, I will perform a miracle so that all will believe."

"What do you want done with the money that the people leave in the Cova da Iria?"

"Have two biers made. One is to be carried by you and Jacinta and two other girls dressed in white; the other one is to be carried by Francisco and three other boys. The money from the biers is for the festa of Our Lady of the Rosary; and what is left over will help towards the construction of a chapel."

Lucia then asked for the cure of some sick persons; this the Lady agreed to do within the year. Then she became very sad and said: "Pray, pray very much, and make sacrifices for sinners; for many

---

11. According to an interview with Jacinta's brother, John (Joao), Jacinta's mother was treating her for head lice, which she had picked up during her stay in prison.

Valinhos, where Our Lady appeared on 13 August, 1917.

souls go to hell, because no one makes sacrifices for them." Then she ascended and disappeared in her usual manner.

With this last communication, we come to the central message of Fatima: the message of reparation to God for the sins of this world. Now, it is certainly true that Jesus Christ, by his life, passion, and death, has atoned for the sins of the entire world. Therefore, at first blow, it may strike us as rather strange that a vision from heaven should be asking for us to "make sacrifices for sinners; for many souls go to hell, because no one makes sacrifices for them." Has not Jesus Christ made the ultimate sacrifice on behalf of such souls once and for all? (Ro. 6:10; Heb. 9:25–26; 1 Pet. 3:18) How, then, can Our Lady say that there is no one to make sacrifices for sinners? Surely Christ has done this already!

Although Christ has made this-once-and-for-all sacrifice, we are being asked in union with Him (Ro. 8:17) to "complete what is lacking in Christ's afflictions for the sake of his body, that is, the Church" (Col. 1:24). Jesus Christ, "by being made perfect, became the source of eternal salvation to all who obey Him" (Heb. 5:9). Jesus Christ became the great high priest (Heb. 4:14), perfectly fulfilling the law, teaching, forgiving sins, healing, and sanctifying life. He was "holy, blameless, unstained, separated from sinners, exalted above the heavens" (Heb. 7:26). Therefore, He and He alone (1 Tim. 2:5–6) is the unblemished Lamb of God Who takes away the sins of the world (Jn. 1:29) by the perfect offering of His obedient life, atoning suffering, and sacrificial death (Heb. 9:13–14). "For by a single offering He has perfected for all time those who are sanctified" (Heb. 10:14).

Then why are we asked by the Blessed Lady, in perfect harmony with St. Paul, to "gladly spend and be spent" (2 Cor. 12:15); to be poured as a libation" (Phil. 2:17); to "share in suffering for the gospel" (2 Tim. 1:8); and to "endure everything for the sake of the elect, that they also may obtain salvation in Christ Jesus" (2 Tim. 2:10) if Christ has already secured this? Since what she is asking is perfectly Scriptural,[12] it is crucial to understand this urgent plea, which is an essential part of the Christian call.

The clue lies in the phrase "those who are sanctified" in the quote from Heb. 10:14 above. We are asked to endure our sufferings and to offer up sacrifices because of the present state of the Church, which is in tribulation from a world that has lost its way.

Here at Fatima, Our Lady warns of the errors that are infiltrating the Church and distorting its truths, as well as the punishment that will befall those who continue in this defection. In order to correct this, she is calling for the faithful to imitate her reflective and Immaculate Heart by contemplating and conforming themselves to the life and teachings of Jesus Christ. The basis for this devotion is the Rosary, but its fruits must be acts of loving self-sacrifice in reparation for, and in restoration of, a scandalized and persecuted Church.

We are called to complete what is lacking in the sufferings of Christ by proffering our own sacrifices for the sake of his body the Church. For even though Christ has offered up the once-and-for-all, perfect sacrifice, we are still called to follow in his steps. "For to

---

12. See also Mt. 5:11; 10:2; Lk. 21:19; Jn. 15:13, 18–21; Acts 14:22; Ro. 8:17–18, 36; 12:1; Gal. 6:17; Phil. 3:10–11; 2 Thess. 1:4–5; 1 Pet. 2:21; 4:1, 13; 1 Jn. 3:16.

this you have been called, because Christ also suffered for you, leaving you an example, that you should follow in his steps" (1 Pet. 2:21). Our Lord has called us to deny ourselves, take up our cross daily, and follow him (Mt. 16:24; Lk. 9:23). It is here that we come to the seminal mystery of the body of Christ. We shall examine this mystery under two aspects: the sufficiency of our sufferings for the body of Christ and the necessity of our sufferings for the body of Christ.

The first aspect—the sufficiency of our sufferings—can be answered fairly quickly. Scripture notes the inevitability of suffering by those who faithfully follow the Christian path. "Indeed all who desire to live a godly life in Christ Jesus will be persecuted" (2 Tim. 3:12). However, we need only attend to the words of our Lord: "You will be hated by all for my name's sake. But he who endures to the end will be saved" (Mt. 10:22). Anyone who attempts to live a holy life will not conform to this world and, by example, will remind the world of its guilt. For these reasons, the righteous will be despised by those who willfully live according to their own desires and values. These latter will try to justify themselves by inventing dubious philosophies and arbitrary ideologies which they then support with questionable methodologies and fabricated histories (Romans 1:18–23, 28–32). But such contrivances will inevitably fail (1 Cor. 1:18–25; 2:18–20). In short, the righteous person is a contradiction to a dissipated and ruthless world. Therefore, the just will be hated, and they will suffer for Christ's sake.

But God will honor their sufferings for the sake of His Son, who gave his last ounce of suffering for His Church. "Blessed are you when men revile you and persecute you and utter all kinds of evil against you falsely on my account. Rejoice and be glad, for your reward is great in heaven, for so men persecuted the prophets who were before you" (Mt. 5:11–12).

Beloved, do not be surprised at the fiery ordeal which comes upon you to prove you, as though something strange were happening to you. But rejoice in so far as you share Christ's sufferings, that you may also rejoice and be glad when his glory is revealed. If you are reproached for the name of Christ, you are blessed, because the spirit of glory and of God rests upon you. (1 Pet. 4:12–14)

Although suffering is inevitable for the Christian, it is acknowledged as a sacrifice for the sake of the majesty, worth, and glory of the One who chose to suffer on behalf of His Church, as Our Lord declares: "a servant is not greater than his master. If they persecuted me, they will persecute you" (Jn. 15:20). Therefore, through similar afflictions, we are called to share in that same dignity of Christ. It is His dignity that gives worth to our endurance. God is not indifferent to our sighs and groans. "For God is not so unjust as to overlook your work and the love which you showed for his sake in serving the saints." (Heb. 6:10) But since He acknowledges them, He honors them by bestowing upon them the dignity of Christ who has offered up His sufferings for the world. God would not commend to the Church any less dignity than He affords His Son—the Church is, after all, the body of His Son. Christ has elevated *all* suffering to the dignity of the cross (Gal. 6:14). Suffering is a mark of our union with Him (2 Cor. 4:7–12; Gal. 6:17; Phil. 3:10–11). Because our sacrifices are the sufferings of Christ, God accepts them as a sufficient offering for others (2 Tim. 2:11–12; Jas. 5:16; 1 Pet. 2:19; 3:12, 14, 17–18; 4:14; 5:9–10). "I appeal to you therefore, brethren, by the mercies of God, to present your bodies as a living sacrifice, holy and acceptable to God, which is your spiritual worship" (Ro. 12:1). Thus, though suffering is inevitable, it is blessed by God, provided it is endured in unity with Christ (Ro. 8:12–17).

Our sufferings are also necessary for the body of Christ. Recall that the object of our discussion is the injunction, "make sacrifices for sinners; for many souls go to hell, because no one makes sacrifices for them." Mary indicates that the patient acceptance of suffering offered up to God will save souls; otherwise many souls will be condemned.

Why, then, is it necessary that we sacrifice for others in order to save them from condemnation? Again, has Christ not done this already?

The answer to this question of the necessity for sacrifice is to be found in the nature of those sacrifices we are called to make. They are simply the sacrifices of a righteous and holy life, which are offered up in spite of the persecutions and sufferings that inevitably will come our way in a fallen world. They are but the corporal and spiritual works of mercy.[13] "Do not neglect to do good and to share what you have, for such sacrifices are pleasing to God" (Heb. 13:16). As we strive to live lives of holiness, we will endure hardship, loss, and personal pain. The necessity for suffering grows out of its inevitability.

Moreover, without our willingness to obey God in all things, the Church, the body of Christ, would not endure; it would have violated the teachings of Christ by conforming to this world (Ro. 12:2; 1 Jn. 2:15–16). Our refusal to conform will bring hardship upon us, but it is necessary that we endure such afflictions for the sake of Christ and His Church. Therefore, if the Church is to survive and if the Gospel is to be preached, we must be prepared to endure patiently the difficulties that the Lord sends us.

Finally, suffering for others is necessary if we are to emulate the life of Jesus Christ. For this is what He called his Church to do. To accomplish this we only have to unite our everyday crosses with the sufferings of Our Blessed Lord. These crosses become meritorious simply because they participate proportionally in his redemptive work. By accepting our crosses as a form of prayer, we become united with Christ's sacrifice and transform our prayers into a fragrant offering to God. Indeed, our love for Jesus transforms all that we may offer into a prayer of intercession. "Come to him that living stone, rejected by men but in God's sight chosen and precious; and like living stones be yourselves built into a spiritual house, to be a holy priesthood, to offer spiritual sacrifices acceptable to God through Jesus Christ" (1 Pet. 2:4–5).

Therefore, in harmony with the Gospel, Our Lady of Fatima is calling us to sacrifice and to pray for those who have no one to offer sacrifices for them: for the lonely, the oppressed, the naked, and the hungry; for those in error; for the proud, the confused, the willful,

---

13. The corporal works of mercy are: feed the hungry; give drink to the thirsty; clothe the naked; harbor the homeless; visit the sick; ransom the captive; bury the dead. The spiritual works of mercy are: instruct the ignorant; counsel the doubtful; admonish sinners; bear wrongs patiently; forgive offences willingly; comfort the afflicted; pray for the living and the dead.

and the perverse, for all who are lost. By helping others in this way, we live the Gospel. To what else would we expect heaven to call us?

> Humble yourselves therefore under the mighty hand of God, that in due time he may exalt you. Cast all your anxieties on him, for he cares about you. Be sober, be watchful. Your adversary the devil prowls around like a roaring lion, seeking someone to devour. Resist him, firm in your faith, knowing that the same experience of suffering is required of your brotherhood throughout the world. And after you have suffered a little while, the God of all grace, who has called you to his eternal glory in Christ, will himself restore, establish, and strengthen you. To him be the dominion for ever and ever. Amen. (1 Pet. 5:6–11)

In the patio of the Marto's home, 1917.

Penance

THE LAST WORDS OF THE Lady of Fatima penetrated deeply into the hearts of the three children: "Pray, pray very much, and make sacrifices for sinners; for many souls go to hell, because no one makes sacrifices for them." Remembering the prayers of the angel and of the Blessed Lady, as well as the vision of hell and the consequences of sin upon the world, the children began to join their prayers to voluntary acts of penance on behalf of those "poor sinners" who had no one to intercede for them. They understood deeply the need to "pray at all times in the Spirit, with all prayer and supplication . . . with all perseverance, making supplication for all the saints" (Eph. 6:18; cf. Acts 1:14; Ro. 8:26; 1 Tim. 2:1; Lk. 18:14; Jas. 4:9–10; 1 Pet. 5:6). Illiterate though they were, they manifested in their attitude toward prayer that obeisance which moves the Divine Pity:

> Jesus also suffered outside the gate in order to sanctify the people through his own blood. Therefore let us go forth to him outside the camp, and bear the abuse he endured. For here we have no lasting city, but we seek the city which is to come. Through him then let us continually offer up a sacrifice of praise to god, that is, the fruit of lips that acknowledge his name. Do not neglect to do good and to share what you have, for such sacrifices are pleasing to God (Heb. 13:12–16).

Through an inner grace, Lucia, Francisco, and Jacinta realized what it really means to intercede for those in the Church who are so deluded by the world, so blinded by concupiscence, so hardened in their hearts, that they are unable to come to repentance by themselves (Mt. 3:8; Lk. 13:3; Acts 17:30; 26:20). Therefore, these children voluntarily undertook sacrifices on behalf of those who had no one to make sacrifices for them (1 Cor. 5:1–2; 2 Cor. 2:5–10; 7:8–12; Jn. 20:23). For "if one member suffers, all suffer together; if one member is honored, all rejoice together" (1 Cor. 12:26). This is the mystery of the body of Christ.

Meditating unceasingly upon this mystery, the children thought no sacrifice too great, no suffering too painful, no obeisance too beneath them for the sake of the elect: the remnant of God, the light of the world, the Church of Jesus Christ. Day and night, they would offer up prayers and supplications on behalf of the lost. Sensing the urgency of the times that were at hand, they spent hours prostrate on the ground repeating the prayer of the angel: "Oh, my God, I believe, I adore, I hope, and I love you, I ask forgiveness for those who do not believe, nor adore, nor hope, nor love you." In deep mortification of spirit, they recited Rosary after Rosary, remembering to interject after each decade the prayer their sorrowful Lady had taught them: "O my Jesus, forgive us, deliver us from the fire of hell, and take all souls to heaven, especially those who are most in need [of your mercy]."

In their concern for a Church in tribulation, these three would seek out as many ways as they could to offer up sacrifices. They obeyed the words of the angel: "make of everything you can a sacrifice, and offer it to God as an act of reparation for the sins by which He is offended and in supplication for the conversion of sinners." One day, Francisco was suffering from a headache, and Lucia went to comfort him.

"Francisco, do you feel very sick?"

"I do, but I am suffering to console Our Lord."

"Don't forget to make the offering for sinners," Jacinta reminded him.

"Yes. But first I make it to console Our Lord and Our Lady, and then, afterwards, for sinners and for the Holy Father."

On another occasion, Olimpia brought them some grapes to refresh them. However, they immediately gave them to the poor children along the roadside, and acted similarly when figs were given to them.

In their eagerness to help others, they sometimes went to extremes of self-mortification. One day, while they were herding their sheep along the road, Lucia found, lying near her bare feet, a rope which had fallen from a cart. She picked it up, and, while toying with it, noticed that it scratched her arm. "Look, this hurts!" she said to her companions. "We could tie it around our waists and offer this sacrifice to God." Lucia then proceeded to unravel three skeins and distributed two of them to Francisco and Jacinta. Although the skeins irritated, pricked, and chafed their tender skins, the children would not remove them. The three of them wore these makeshift hair shirts day and night. They caused their skins to sweat beneath them, and their unbearable itching deprived them of sleep. But for these fervent innocents, no sacrifice was too intense to make for the sake of unfortunate sinners. They had matured far beyond any residual taint of self-interest. They desired only to glorify God.

These children were no longer content to remain babes in Christ (Heb. 5:13–6:2), but, utterly forgetful of self, chose to accept the disciplines that came their way (Heb. 12:4–11). Constant opposition to the apparitions by the people of the village provided an external source of penance that made the children's self-mortifications virtually unnecessary. A day did not pass without some villager venting his spleen upon one or other of the children. When a village woman from Aljustrel was wont to revile them by accusing them of being liars and impostors, the children, rather than answer back, would retreat to a silent spot to pray and to make penances for her. Eventually, the woman desisted from these calumnies.

Even the endless streams of devout pilgrims, though they meant well, were a source of mortification. The constant questioning of these visitors was a real strain on the children and their families. At least the scoffers did not come knocking on their doors at all hours of the day or night, asking questions, looking for relics, requesting prayers for healing, or simply wanting to touch the children.

Yet there was no shortage of scoffers beyond the village. The liberal press, such as O Mundo, became particularly outspoken in their invective, calling for the wholesale arrest of any who visited the Cova da Iria. Atheistic pamphlets were circulated attacking the superstitious ignoramuses who believed such tales and demanding that the perpetrators of the farce be exposed and severely punished. Anarchist street speakers would, with no small amount of self-contradiction, denounce the Church authorities for permitting these absurdities to grow unchecked. It was astonishing how the mere sight of a quiet procession of pilgrims through their towns threatened the robust ideologies of these "free thinkers."

Yet all this calumny only served to further the cause of Fatima. The people of Portugal had heard of what the Administrator had done to three innocent children, and his actions reverberated against him. To many, his acrimony highlighted the contrast between the hostile nature of the opposition and the pious devotion of the pilgrims. The former appeared angry, resentful, hateful, sardonic, and arrogant; the latter, humble and overflowing with expectation. There was something enchantingly beautiful and spiritually edifying in the stories and messages that were circulating about Fatima, speaking of heavenly solicitude and divine consolation while these secular thinkers spoke of destruction and revolution. Even if the apparitions were illusory, the virtues expressed at Fatima were far more salutary than the poison exuded by the unbelievers. Fatima expressed the Gospel; the freethinkers vain and insubstantial opinions. So the more the secular press fulminated, the more the pious and devout quietly resolved to undertake the long trek through the mountains to Fatima.

By the time the thirteenth of September had arrived, more than twenty thousand people had assembled at the Cova da Iria. Most of these crowds consisted of pious, poorly-shod peasants, many of whom had trudged for leagues across rocky terrain, hoping to catch a glimpse of the wondrous Lady or, more often, to petition on behalf of their loved ones. When they saw Lucia, Francisco, and Jacinta pass by, they shouted out to them: "For the love of God, ask Our Lady to cure my son, who is a cripple!... And to cure mine, who is blind!... To cure mine, who is deaf!... To bring back my husband, my son, who has gone to the war!... to convert a sinner!... To restore my health, as I have tuberculosis!" Lucia tenderly recalls the scene:

> All the afflictions of humanity were assembled there. Some climbed up to the tops of trees and walls to see us go by, and shouted down to us. Saying yes to some, giving a hand to others and helping them up from the dusty ground, we managed to move

forward. . . . Now, when I read in the New Testament about those enchanting scenes of Our Lord's passing through Palestine, I think of those which Our Lord allowed me to witness, while yet a child, on the poor roads and lanes from Aljustrel to Fatima and on to the Cova da Iria. I give thanks to God, offering Him the faith of our good Portuguese people, and I think: "If these people so humbled themselves before three poor children, just because they were mercifully granted the grace to speak to the Mother of God, what would they not do if they saw Our Lord Himself in person before them?"[1]

Then there were the curious, the affluent, the skeptical, and the scornful, who came for no other reason than that they had nothing better to do. They came in their fine cars and fancy clothes, bringing baskets of bread and wine to consume, laughing and jeering at the curious-looking country bumpkins, tattered, worn, misshapen, and hungry, passing before them. *"Botas da serra! Botas da serra!"* "Clodhoppers! Mountain clodhoppers!" they taunted.[2]

Finally, there were also a noticeable number of priests and seminarians there. Among some of these were: Rev. Fr. Manuel Pereira da Silva, curate at Leiria; Mons. Manuel do Carmo Gois; and Mons. Joao Quaresma, Vicar-General of the Diocese of Leiria and later a member of the Canonical Inquiry. The latter leaves the following description of the events:

> At midday there was complete silence. One only heard the murmur of prayers. Suddenly there were sounds of jubilation and voices praising the Blessed Virgin. Arms were raised pointing to something in the sky. "Look, don't you see?". . . "Yes, yes, I do!" Much satisfaction on the part of those who do. There had not been a cloud in the deep blue of the sky and I, too, raised by eyes and scrutinised it in case I should be able to distinguish what the others, more fortunate than I, had already claimed to have seen. With great astonishment I saw, clearly and distinctly, a luminous globe, which moved from the east to the west, gliding slowly and majestically through space. My friend also looked and had the good fortune to enjoy the same unexpected and delightful vision. Suddenly

1. *Memoirs*, 167.
2. Walsh, 125.

the globe, with its extraordinary light, disappeared.

Near us was a little girl dressed like Lucia and more or less the same age. She continued to cry out happily: "I still see it! I still see it! Now it is coming down...!"

After a few minutes, about the duration of the Apparitions, the child began to exclaim again, pointing to the sky: "Now it's going up again!" and she followed the globe with her eyes until it disappeared in the direction of the sun. "What do you think of that globe," I asked my companion, who seemed enthusiastic at what he had seen. "That it was Our Lady," he replied without hesitation.[3]

The Lady from heaven had appeared once again in splendor on the holm oak in the Cova da Iria.

"Continue to pray the Rosary in order to obtain the end of the war. In October, Our Lord will come, as well as Our Lady of Dolors and Our Lady of Carmel. Saint Joseph will appear with the Child Jesus to bless the world. God is pleased with your sacrifices. He does not want you to sleep with the rope on, but only to wear it during the daytime."

After this forecast—that they would see likenesses representing the three sets of mysteries of the Rosary—the apparition of the Lady of Fatima promised to grant some of the petitions which Lucia brought before her. She reaffirmed her promise to perform a miracle in October. Then, as before, she gently ascended towards the east.

Lucia rose, saying, "If you want to see her look over there!" She pointed in the direction the Lady was moving. Thousands of people followed the luminous globe until it finally vanished in the eastern sky. "We felt remarkably happy," commented Mons. Quaresma. "My companion went from group to group in the Cova and afterwards on the road, gathering information. Those he questioned were of all sorts and kinds and of different social standing, but one and all affirmed the reality of the phenomena which we ourselves had witnessed."[4]

3. de Marchi, 112.
4. Ibid., 113. These testimonies are kept at the archives in Fatima. See also Martins & Fox, *Documents on Fatima*, 143 ff.

Another seminarian, who was later to play a significant role in Fatima as Canon Dr. Galamba de Oliveira, left the following account:

> After the apparition, I cannot say the exact moment, I looked up to the sky, perhaps because someone told me to, and I saw, about a meter above the earth, a sort of luminous globe which soon began to descend towards the west and from the horizon went up again towards the sun. . . . Before or after, but certainly on the same day, we—but I don't know if this is true of all those present—began to see a fall of rose petals or snow drops which came from above and disappeared a little way above our heads, so that we could not touch them. I did not see anything else, but it was enough to comfort us and we left with the certainty, like an intuition, that there was the finger of God.[5]

A little later, after the children managed to get off by themselves, Francisco asked Lucia what the Lady had said. When he heard that in the following month he would be granted to see Our Lord, he was overwhelmed with joy. *"Ai que bom!"* "Oh, how good he is! I have only seen Him twice, and I love Him so much!" (Here he refers to the apparitions of June and July, in which he had seen the Lord in the mysterious light communicated to them by the Lady.) From then on, at intervals, he would ask Lucia, "Are there many days left till the thirteenth? I am longing for that day to come, so that I can see Our Lord again." After reflecting for a moment he added: "But listen, will He still be sad? I'm so sorry to see Him sad like that! I offer Him all the sacrifices I can think of. Sometimes, I don't even run away from all those people, just in order to make sacrifices!"

It was during this month that Dr. Carlos Mendes, the large man who had rescued Lucia from the crowd during the July apparition, came to visit. Because of his enormous size, he cast such an imposing figure that Lucia thought he must be a German. (At that time, adults used to frighten children by saying that if they were not good, a great German would come to take them away.) However, he soon put Lucia at her ease. Taking her on his lap, he asked her a number of questions about the apparitions. Then, satisfied with her answers, he asked Maria Rosa's permission to allow Lucia to accom-

5. Fox, 27.

pany him to the Cova da Iria. With this permission granted, Lucia set off alone with the huge lawyer. She remarks that she trembled with fear at finding herself alone with this tall stranger. When they arrived at the holm oak in the Cova, he knelt down and invited Lucia to pray a Rosary with him in order to obtain from Our Lady the favor that a certain young woman would consent to become his wife. Lucia wondered at such a request and wondered still more about the woman he had mentioned: "If she has as much fear of him as I, she will never say yes!" Dr. Mendes leaves us the following impression of these children in a letter to his fiancée, written after a visit to the Marto household.

The little mite (Jacinta) didn't want to come without her cousin (they are inseparable), and her sister had to coax her along. Very tiny, very babyish and shy, she came up to me. I sat down so as to see her better and sat her down on a chest near me. I must tell you, she is a little angel, a darling. She had a red flowered handkerchief on her head, the points tied behind. It was rather torn and old, and her coat was not particularly clean. Her skirt was full and wide in the local manner. Her eyes are very dark and enchantingly vivacious, while her expression is really angelic, so extraordinarily sweet and kind that one is attracted to her, without knowing why. She was so shy and timid.

Francisco arrived. His head was well covered by a cap, he wore a very short jacket, the waistcoat open and showing his shirt and narrow trousers—in fact, a little man in miniature. He has a splendid boyish face and his expression is both lively and manly. He answered my questions with confidence, and then Jacinta, too, began to gain courage. Shortly afterwards Lucia arrived. You cannot imagine Jacinta's joy when she saw her! . . . Lucia is not so impressive to look at. Her expression is lively, but for the rest she is ordinary looking, typical of the region. She, too, was shy to begin with, but I soon put her at her ease, and then they all responded without any embarrassment and satisfied my curiosity.

I questioned the three of them separately. They all say the same thing without any alteration of the story. All three say that a Lady appeared to them but they do not know who she is. After six appearances, on 13th October, she will say who she is and what she wants. The naturalness and simplicity with which they tell one this is extraordinary and impressive. . . . To hear these children, to see their candour and to observe them in general makes such a remarkable impression on one that one is led to conclude there is something in what they say. To be with them is an intensely moving experience. It is my conviction that we are confronted with something outside mere reason.[6]

The apparitions were now beginning to attract the attention of a large number of respectable people, many of whom carried a great deal of influence with the Church hierarchy. Consequently, it became increasingly difficult for the Church to remain aloof from the events at Fatima. It therefore fell upon one Reverend Doctor Manuel Nunes Formigao, canon of the Patriarchal See of Lisbon and professor at the Seminary and Lyceum at Santarem, to investigate the case. Although he had been present for the September apparition, he had not witnessed the globe of light or the sparkling "rain." Nevertheless, he had noted the dimming of the sun, which, at the time, he had attributed to the height of the mountains. However, the firmness of the witness of Mons. Quaresma and the other seminarians convinced him that there might be something to this affair. When he was asked by the Administrator of the Patriarchate in Lisbon to investigate these strange phenomena, he decided to interrogate the children at length. On Thursday, September 27, Rev. Dr. Formigao returned to Aljustrel and sent out messengers to procure the children for him. Here begins one of the many grueling interrogations that Dr. Formigao imposed upon the three young children.[7] He interviewed Francisco first:

"What did you see at the Cova da Iria these last months?"
"I saw Our Lady."
"Where does she appear?"
"On top of the holm oak."

6. Johnston, *Fatima: The Great Sign*, 47–48; de Marchi, 245–46; and Martins & Fox, *Documents on Fatima*, 137–42.
7. The following examples of interrogations are taken from de Marchi, 116–26; Johnston, *Fatima*, 48–50; Walsh, 128–36; and Martins & Fox, *Documents on Fatima*, 143 ff.

"Does she appear suddenly, or do you see her coming from somewhere?"

"I see her coming from the side where the sun rises and settling on the holm oak."

"Does she come slowly or quickly?"

"She always comes quickly."

"Do you hear what she says to Lucia?"

"No."

"Do you ever speak to the Lady? Does she ever speak to you?" (Dr. Formigao is trying to catch Francisco here.)

"No. I have never asked her anything: she speaks only to Lucia."

"At whom does she look? Also at you and at Jacinta, or only at Lucia?"

"She looks at all three of us, but longer at Lucia."

"Does she ever cry or smile?"

"Neither one or the other. She is always grave."

"How is she dressed?"

"She has a long dress and over it a veil which covers her head and falls to the edges of her dress."

"What is the color of the dress and the veil?"

"White, and the dress has gold lines."

"What is her attitude?"

"Like someone praying. She has her hands joined at the height of her breast."

"Does she hold anything in her hands?"

"She carries a Rosary round the palm and the back of her right hand. It hangs down over her dress."

"What color is the Rosary?"

"It is white."

"Is the Lady beautiful?"

"Yes, she is."

"More beautiful than that little girl over there?"

"Yes."

"But there are ladies who are much more beautiful than that girl."

"She was more beautiful than anyone I have ever seen."

After he had finished with Francisco, he called in Jacinta, who was passing the time playing with children outside. She came in and

150

was seated on a little stool by the side of the Professor. Her answers confirm those of her brother:

"Have you seen Our Lady on the 13th of each month?"

"Yes."

"Where does she come from?"

"She comes from the sky from the side of the sun."

"How is she dressed?"

"She has a white dress, decorated with gold, and on her head a mantle, also white."

"What color is her hair?" (Another trick question.)

"You cannot see her hair because it is covered by the mantle."

"Does she wear earrings?"

"I don't know because you cannot see her ears."

"How does she hold her hands?"

"Her hands are joined at the height of her breast, with the fingers pointing upwards."

"Are the beads in the right or the left hand?"

Jacinta first answered without hesitation that they were in the Lady's right hand. However, after a captious persistence on the part of Dr. Formigao, Jacinta became confused, trying to imagine which of her own hands corresponded with the hands in which the Vision held the Rosary.

"What was the chief thing that Our Lady told Lucia?"

"She said we were to say the Rosary every day." (One *tercet* or five decades of the Rosary, i.e., one set of mysteries.)

"And do you say it?"

"I say it every day with Francisco and Lucia."

Dr. Formigao dismissed Jacinta and awaited the arrival of Lucia. After half an hour, Lucia appeared. She came from one of the properties belonging to her family, where she had been helping with the vintage. The Doctor leaves us with this description:

Taller and better nourished than the other two with a clearer skin and a more robust, healthier appearance, she presented herself before me with an unselfconsciousness which contrasted in a marked manner with the shyness and timidity of Jacinta. Simply dressed like the latter, neither her attitude nor her expression denoted a sign of vanity, still less of confusion. Seating herself on a chair at my side, in response to my gesture, she willingly consented to be questioned on the events in which she was the principal protagonist in spite of the fact that she was visibly fatigued and depressed by the incessant visits and the repeated and lengthy questionings to which she was subjected.

This was to be one of the more lengthy interrogations.

"Is it true that Our Lady appeared in a place called the Cova da Iria?"

"Yes, it is true."

"How many times has she appeared to you?"

"Five times, once each month."

"On what day of the month?"

"Always on the thirteenth, except in the month of August, when I was taken to Ourem by the Mayor. In that month I only saw her a few days afterwards, on the nineteenth, at Valinhos."

"People say that Our Lady also appeared to you last year? Is there any truth in this?" The children had never mentioned the visitation by the angel in the previous year. Therefore, this could be yet another trick question.

"She never appeared to me last year, never before May of this year; nor did I ever say so to anybody because it is not true."

"Where does she come from? From the east?"

"I don't know because I don't see her come from anywhere. She appears over the oak tree and when she goes away she goes into the sky in the direction where the sun rises."

"How long does she stay? A long or a short time?"

"A short time."

"Enough to be able to recite an Our Father and Hail Mary, or more?"

"A good deal more, but it is not always the same time; perhaps it would not be long enough to say a Rosary." Here Lucia means only a *tercet* or five decades of the Rosary (about fifteen minutes).

"The first time you saw her, were you frightened?"

"I was, so much so that I wanted to run away with Jacinta and Francisco, but she told us not to be afraid because she would not hurt us."

"How is she dressed?"

"She has a white dress, which reaches to her feet, and her head is covered with a mantle, the same color and the same length."

"Has the dress anything on it?"

"You can see, in the front, two gold cords which fall from the neck and are joined at the waist by a tassel, also gold."

"Is there any belt or ribbon?"

"No."

"Her earrings?"

"They are little rings."

"In which hand does she hold the Rosary?"

"In the right hand."

"Is it a Rosary of five or fifteen decades?"

"I didn't notice."

"Had it a cross?"

"Yes, a white cross and the beads, too, were white, so was the chain."

"Did you ever ask who she was?"

"I did, but she said she would only tell us on the 13th of October."

"Did you ask her where she came from?"

"I did, and she told me that she came from heaven."

"When did you ask her this?"

"The second time, on the 13th of June."

"Did she smile sometimes, or was she sad?"

"She neither smiled, nor was she sad; she was always serious."

"Did she tell you and your cousins to say certain prayers?"

"She told us to say the Rosary [tercet] in honor of Our Lady of the Rosary, to obtain the peace of the world."

"Did she say that many people were to be present in the Cova da Iria during the Apparitions of the 13th?" This question alludes to the fact that Our Lady of Lourdes asked Bernadette to tell Fr. Peyramale to permit "processions to come forth." Was Lucia copying previous apparitions?

"She said nothing about that."

"Is it true that she told you a secret that you were not to tell to anybody at all?"

"Yes."

"Does it only concern you or your cousins also?"

"It concerns all three of us."

"Could you not tell it even to your confessor?"

At this question Lucia was silent and appeared confused. I judged it better not to insist by repeating the question.

"In order to free yourself from the Mayor on the day he imprisoned you, did you tell him something as if it were the secret, thus deceiving him and boasting of it afterwards?"

"That is not true. Senhor Santos really did want me to reveal the secret, but I could not and did not do so, although he tried in every way to make me do what he wanted. I told the Mayor everything the Lady said to me except the secret. Perhaps it was because of this that he thought I had told him the secret too. I never wanted to deceive him."

"Did the Lady tell you to learn to read?"

"Yes, the second time she appeared."

"But if she told you that she would take you to heaven in October next, what would be the good of learning to read?"

"That is not true. The Lady never said she would take me to heaven in October and I never told anyone that she had said such a thing."

"What did the Lady say was to be done with the money which the people left under the oak tree in the Cova da Iria?"

"She said that we were to get two 'andors' and that I and Jacinta and two more girls were to carry one and Francisco with three more boys the other, to the parish church. Part of this money was to be for the Festa of Our Lady of the Rosary and the rest to help to build a new chapel."

"Where does the Lady want the chapel built? In the Cova da Iria?"

"I don't know; she didn't say."

"Are you glad the Lady appeared to you?"

"Yes."

"On the 13th of October, will Our Lady come alone?"

"St. Joseph and the Holy Child will come, and a little time afterwards the world will have peace."

"Did Our Lady reveal anything more?"

"She said that on the 13th of October she would perform a miracle so that the people can believe that she appeared."

"Why do you often lower your eyes instead of keeping them on the Lady?"

"Because sometimes she blinds me."

"Did she teach you any prayer?"

"Yes, and she wants us to recite it after each mystery of the Rosary."

"Do you know this prayer by heart?"

"Yes."

"Say it."

"O my Jesus, forgive us and deliver us from the fire of hell. Take all souls to heaven, especially those who are most in need."

After these interrogations, there was no doubt in Formigao's mind of the sincerity and truthfulness of the children. Like Father Ferreira, he concluded that if it was false, it could only be accounted for by an hallucination induced by dark or evil forces. Some of the discrepancies in details (such as the earrings, the gold edging, the gold cords) resulted from differences in perspective and observation and were to be expected in most human testimonies. However, in order to be sure, Dr. Formigao decided to return to Fatima for a further interrogation, before the great day of the expected miracle.

By the time he made the journey from Santarem to Fatima, it was too late to interview the children. He spent the night in the home of the Goncalves family in Montelo, some two kilometers from Fatima. The eldest son of the family, Manuel Goncalves, was an intelligent man with acute powers of observation. He was able to furnish the Doctor with a number of facts about the children, their families, and village life, as well as details of the events that had transpired during the preceding months. After inquiring about the opinions of the local populace towards the apparitions, Dr. Formigao asked:

"On the days of the Apparitions, are there extraordinary signs? Many people claim to have seen them?"

"The signs are very numerous," replied Manuel Goncalves. "In August, almost everyone who was present saw them. A cloud came down on the oak tree. In July the same thing was seen and there was no dust. The cloud seemed to sweep the air clean."

"Were there any other signs?"

"In the sky, near the sun, there were some white clouds which turned successively bright red (the colour of blood), pink, and yellow. The people themselves turned this last colour. The light of the sun sensibly diminished in intensity, and in July and August, a noise was heard."

"Is it possible that anyone could have induced the children to play a hoax?"

"That would be impossible."

After asking other questions about the welfare of the families concerned, Dr. Formigao continued his journey to Aljustrel the next day (October 11). He found Lucia busily helping a mason who was repairing their roof. While he was waiting for her, he questioned Maria Rosa about Lucia's knowledge of the appearance at La Salette, which Maria Rosa had once read to her. It was firmly established that that story had made no real or lasting impression upon Lucia. In fact, Maria Rosa said, "I do not recall her ever having mentioned it."

Lucia entered, greeted the Doctor respectfully, and consented to yet another penitential interrogation, which was conducted in front of four witnesses. This time, the questions centered upon the signs that accompanied the apparitions, which Lucia said she did not see. He then rephrased some of his earlier inquiries: descriptions of the Lady, what she said, whether she requested prayers or sacrifices for sinners, etc. Lucia's answers were perfectly consistent with what had been said previously. Then he asked her the same question he had addressed to Maria Rosa:

"Do you remember your mother reading a book called the *Short Mission*, where there is a story of an Apparition of Our Lady to a girl?"

"Yes."

"Did you think much about this story or speak about it to other children?"

"I never thought about this story and I never talked about it to anyone."

Satisfied with this answer, Dr. Formigao, accompanied by his four witnesses, proceeded to the Marto house. He questioned

Jacinta further to see if she would confirm some of the details that Lucia had provided.

"Did you hear the secret or was it only Lucia who heard?"

"I heard too."

"When?"

"At the second apparition on St. Anthony's day."

"Is the secret that you will be rich?"

"No."

"That you will be good and happy?"

"Yes, it is for the good of all three of us."

"Is it that you will go to heaven?"

"No."

"Can you tell the secret?"

"I mustn't."

"Why?"

"Because the Lady said we were not to tell it to anyone."

"If the people knew it, would they be sad?"

"Yes."

"How did the Lady have her hands?"

"She had them stretched out. Sometimes she turned the palms up to heaven."

"Has she light round her head?"

"Yes."

"Can you look at her face?"

"No, because it hurts my eyes."

"Do you always hear well what the Lady says?"

"Last time I couldn't hear everything because of the noise the people were making."

Turning to Francisco, he asked whether he could hear the Lady, to which he replied that he could only see her. Francisco also confirmed the light around the Lady's head.

"Has the Lady's dress some decoration?"

"It has some cords of gold."

"What color is the crucifix?"

"White."

"And the chain of the Rosary?"

"White, also."

"Would the people be sad if they knew the secret?"
"Yes, they would."

In the face of the candor and innocence of these replies and their internal and external consistency, Dr. Formigao believed that the only crucial confirmation that remained was the predicted miracle on the day after the morrow. As far as he was concerned, the children had told the truth. If the Lady were genuine, the expected miracle, whatever its nature might be, would assuredly take place.

Although such interrogations were long and taxing for the children, Dr. Formigao was pleasant enough. A greater trial came when a parish priest by the name of Fr. Pocas, Prior of Porto de Mos, arrived the next day to inflict yet another penance on the children. He was purposely belligerent and domineering.

"Look here, child, you are just going to tell me that all this is stuff and nonsense and if you do not I will say so myself and tell everyone else, too. People will believe me and, besides, they are going to the Cova to destroy everything and you won't escape either."

Lucia said nothing. The Prior became furious and tried everything he could to overpower her reticence. He even turned on Jacinta, but she ran out the door. Then Manuel Marto intervened.

"Please leave the children alone. There is nothing to prevent your doing what you like about it!"

"Congratulations," the Prior said snidely, "you played your part well."

"Well or ill, that is my way," Ti Marto answered. "You have not succeeded in making the children deny their story, but even if you had, I should still believe in them!"

This prior was not the only one to make threats. As Lucia's sister, Maria dos Anjos, recalls, serious threats were made against the family if the miracle did not occur as promised.

> My family was much preoccupied. As the 13th drew nearer we kept telling Lucia that it would be better if she did not keep up the affair any longer because ill would come of it to her and to us and we should all suffer because of the things that were invented. My father scolded her very, very much. When he had been drinking he was very bad but he did not actually beat her. It was my mother

who did that most. It was said that they were going to put bombs down to frighten us and the children. Some people told us that if it were their children they would shut them up in a room until they came to their senses. We were all very much afraid. We wondered what would become of us all and said so behind Lucia's back. The neighbours said the bombs would destroy our houses and our belongings. Someone came to my mother and advised her to take Lucia right away where nobody would know where she was. Everyone said something different and gave different advice until we didn't know what to do for the best.[8]

One day, as the thirteenth of October drew near, Maria dos Anjos said to her sister and cousins: "Now, aren't you three going to say that nothing happened after all in the Cova da Iria? People are saying that they will put bombs down to destroy our houses. Just tell me and I will tell Fr. Ferreira and he can give it out in church. Shall I do that?"

Lucia, narrowing her forehead, merely scowled and said nothing. But Jacinta between her tears and in her tiny voice whimpered:

"Say it if you like, but we *saw* her!"

Maria Rosa, on the other hand, wondered why the Lady had not produced a spring like that at Lourdes. Apprehensive of where it would all end, she counseled Lucia:

"Lucia, we had better go to confession. Everyone says that we shall probably be killed tomorrow in the Cova da Iria. If the Lady does not do the miracle, the people will attack us, so we had better go to confession and be properly prepared for death."

"If you want to go, mother, I will come with you," Lucia said calmly, "but not for that reason. I am not afraid of being killed. I am absolutely certain that the Lady will do all that she promised tomorrow."

8. de Marchi, 127–28.

A Woman
Adorned with the Sun

I N THE FROZEN WASTES of Siberia, icy, cyclonic winds whipped up a vast weather front that shrieked across the tundra plain of Russia. Gathering strength, it howled over the village of Pokrovskoe, where Rasputin's widow and her four children were huddling for warmth around a meager fire. At the peak of its velocity, it surged into the Ural Mountains after dumping its cache of snow on the rude cabin at Ekaterinburg, where the Romanov family were awaiting their execution. The icy blasts tore across the peaks of the Urals and plunged into Finland. Comrade Lenin had been in hiding there ever since he had fled the July riots in Petrograd. He spent that frozen night in Vyborg near the Russian border, writing his pamphlet "The Crisis is Ripe." Russia had been without an effective government since March, and the people were starving. Cloud and snow only darkened their despair. The biting wind would harden their resolve.

In the path of this enormous weather system lay the battlefields of Europe. Its searing, icy winds drank thirstily from the moisture carried by the warmer air from the Gulf Stream. The saturated clouds spilled a torrent of rain upon the fields of Flanders and the trenches of the Western Front. Day after day the deluge fell, turning trenches into sewers and fields into swamps. The armies of General Douglas Haig were bogged down by the thick, oozing mud. His men, who were being decimated under relentless machine gun fire, could not mobilize because of the viscous mixture of mud, mustard gas, oil, blood, and portions of human flesh. Rain also fell mercilessly upon those refugees fleeing the Battle of Caporetto, where the Italian Front had fallen before the remorseless advance of the Austro-German armies into Venetia.

The rain surmounted the high Pyrenees. The air, now refrozen, became a sea of fog. Straddling Spain, it flowed into Portugal, turning the dawn into chilling darkness. The fog thickened and its moisture condensed into a fine drizzle, which the gale-force winds of the Serra da Aire lashed into rain. The rain pelted the land, flooding the fields and saturating the dusty roadways leading to Fatima.

It poured pitilessly upon the tens of thousands of pilgrims who were trudging wearily through the mud that dismal morning of the 13th of October, 1917. Fishermen from Vieira had abandoned their nets, boats, and wooden houses by the sea to tramp the oozing roads. Artisans from Marinha, farmers from Monte Real, sailors from the harbors of Porto or the Algarve, factory laborers from Lisbon, and serra folk from distant Minde or Soublio began to form little human rivulets that streamed together into rivers of souls. Delicate high-placed ladies and clever intellectuals were mixed together with simple charwomen and sturdy peasants in this splashing, heaving flood of human bodies.

The rain pounded relentlessly. It soaked the cotton skirts of women until they hung like lead around their squelching feet. It filled the brims of men's hats, flowed down their necks, and chilled their bowing backs. Boots were almost useless in the sticky mud. The bare feet of peasants, used to this sort of thing, made much easier passage through the marshy roadways.

Against the hissing background of spattering raindrops a chorus of *"Ave Maria cheia de graça..."* would ring out in the darkness. Prayers ascended to heaven. Laughter and conversation hung in the sodden air. Some seventy thousand people were converging upon the Cova da Iria. Some had come merely to scoff, some to pray; others sought healing or salvation, and still others surcease from the sorrow and futility of existence. But all would witness a miracle.

Back in Aljustrel, the Abobora house was preparing for disaster. Maria Rosa was still apprehensive of what would befall her youngest child if the miracle failed to occur. With tears streaming down her cheeks, she implored Lucia one last time not to go to the Cova.

"Do not be afraid, dear Mother," Lucia reassured her, "nothing will happen to us, believe me. Our Lady will do what she promised!"

However, Maria's concern for her daughter was sufficient to compel her to accompany Lucia to the place of the apparitions.

"If my child is going to die, I want to die with her!" she exclaimed.

On the way, they stopped by the Marto house. The place was in an uproar. Scores of people were outside, clamoring to catch a glimpse of the children. Dozens more had forced themselves inside. Water and mud were trodden all over the floor. Even the furniture and the beds were trampled on. Olimpia, who was trying to organize her children, was also frantically trying to control the mob. She, like Maria Rosa, took this confusion as an indication of how dangerously hysterical a mob could be. She prayed continuously that no harm would come to her children. Yet the children were unperturbed. "If they harm us," explained Jacinta, "we shall go to heaven, but the poor people who do it will go to hell!" But Olimpia was not reassured by this appeal to God's judicial economy on the part of a seven-year-old.

One of the intruders, a Baroness from Pambalinho, had brought a fancy blue dress for Lucia and a white one for Jacinta, which she insisted they wear. But the girls preferred to wear their own white communion gowns. However, they accepted her offer of two white wreaths, which she placed upon their heads. Francisco wore a dark jacket and matching trousers. When they were all ready to go, they stepped out into the rain.

We left the house in such rain as you never saw! (Ti Marto recalls.) The road was thick with mud but this did not prevent the women and even ladies from kneeling in front of the children. "Leave them alone, good people!" I cried. For they seemed to think that they had the power of saints. After a lot of trouble and interruptions we at last arrived at the Cova da Iria. The crowd was so thick that you couldn't pass through. It was then that a chauffeur picked up my Jacinta and pushed and shoved his way to the lantern arch, shouting: "Make way for the children who saw Our Lady!" I followed behind him, and Jacinta, who was frightened to see me among so many people, began to cry out: "Don't push my father, don't hurt him." The chauffeur at last put her down by the tree but there, too, the crush was so great that she began to cry. Then Lucia and Francisco made their way into the middle of it. My Olimpia was somewhere else, I don't know where, but Maria Rosa was quite close. At that moment I saw a man bearing down on me with a stick and I thought there was going to be trouble, but the people closed ranks in front and behind and when the moment came everything was quiet and orderly.[1]

Eventually Olimpia turned up at the *azinheira*, which Maria da Capelinha had lovingly bestrewn with ribbons and garlands of flowers. By this time, the Cova was a sea of black umbrellas that surrounded the holm oak on all sides, stretching for more than a thousand feet in one direction and five hundred in another. The Cova could adequately contain some 300,000 persons, and it was packed with people. An estimate made on the spot by Dr. Almeida Garrett, Professor of Coimbra University, places the size of the crowd at close to 100,000.

Suddenly, Lucia inexplicably shouted, "Put down your umbrellas, everyone!" In spite of the teeming rain, the crowd obeyed. Lucia began to say the Rosary. Seeing the flash of light that indicated the arrival of the apparition, she told Jacinta and Francisco to kneel, as the Lady was coming. Maria Rosa bent toward her and said: "Look closely, my child. Take care you make no mistake." Lucia never heard her. The people next to her observed that her face had begun to glow with a transparent radiance. Lucia and her cousins were transfixed upon the vision of the enchantingly beautiful Lady who had settled on the *azinheira*. They were bathed in a translucent halo of light that rose to a height of fifteen feet. The signs that had previously accompanied the apparition again occurred. Those nearby heard Lucia ask: "What do you want of me?"

"I want to tell you to have them build a chapel here in my honor. I am the Lady of the Rosary. Continue always to pray the Rosary every day. The war is going to end, and the soldiers will soon return to their homes."

"I have many things to ask of you: the cure of some sick persons, the conversion of sinners, and other things…"

"Some yes, others no. They must amend their lives and ask for forgiveness for their sins." Her tender demeanor became more sorrowful as she continued: "Do not offend the Lord our God any more, because He is already so greatly offended."

Having said this, she opened her luminous hands, which reflected

1. de Marchi, 134.

beams of light toward the sun. She ascended in its direction, continuing to project these rays of light. Instinctively, Lucia gasped, "Look at the sun!" Immediately, the darkened clouds dispersed to display the sun, which shone pre-eminent in the clearing sky. There, before the sun, the children saw in succession three tableaux which symbolized the three sets of mysteries of the Rosary. Firstly, there appeared a vision of the Holy Family, which represented the joyful mysteries: the Virgin Mary dressed in her traditional costume of white with a blue mantle, along with St. Joseph, dressed in white, standing beside her. In his arms he held the Christ child, who was dressed in red. "St. Joseph is going to bless us!" Lucia was also heard to say. He blessed the crowd three times with the sign of the cross. The image of the holy child did the same. Only the three children saw this.

The second tableau, seen only by Lucia, represented the sorrowful mysteries. Our Lady of Sorrows was seen wearing the customary somber attire of the stricken Mary on Good Friday, but lacking the traditional sword in her breast. Beside her stood her beloved Son, carrying the cross. Only the upper part of this figure was presented. The Christ of the passion was gazing with pity upon the crowd and blessing them with the sign of His cross.

Finally, Lucia was given to see a representation of the Lady of Mount Carmel, symbolizing the glorious mysteries. The vision dandled her infant son upon her knee and wore a crown of triumph upon her head. She also held the brown scapular, which, according to tradition, had been presented by her to Simon Stock, Prior General of the Carmelite Order at Aylesford, in 1251. Mary is believed to have promised him that "whoever dies wearing this shall not suffer eternal fire." The use of this well-known tradition[2] was a clear communication to Lucia, who would have to remain on earth to spread devotion to Mary's Immaculate Heart, that she would be assured of Our Lady's

---

2. The tradition of donning the brown scapular goes back to Elijah's conferring of his mantle—and, thereby, a double portion of his spirit—onto his successor, Elisha, upon Mount Carmel (2 Kgs 2:9–13). Since then, it has symbolized, within the Carmelite Order, the consecration of the individual to the Blessed Virgin who in return bestows her habit, promising her feudal protection—as vassal to liege—guaranteeing the wearer the grace of final perseverance to eternal life (Ez. 16:8; Ecclus. 6:25–32). In more modern times, it has also betokened the ordinary life of

eternal succor and consolation. Through this vision, Mary also indicated to Lucia the religious vocation she was to embrace.

While all this was happening, the crowd was experiencing something remarkably different. They had not seen the three heavenly tableaux, in spite of Lucia's suggestion to them that Saint Joseph was about to bless them. Rather, they were gazing admiringly at the sun, which was now alone in the cloudless sky. It had developed an opalescent luster like that of a huge pearl, and was singularly delightful to behold. After a moment the disc, in the language of the people, began to "dance." It started to rotate rapidly, like an enormous fire wheel. Then it stopped. Without warning, it began to whirl again, casting off flares of multicolored rays in all directions. It stopped. It spun a third time, bathing the dampened landscape in a dramatically beautiful spectrum of color, which radiated from prismic sectors within the madly gyrating disc. Earth, foliage, clothing, and upturned faces were painted, now red, now blue, now green as the flamboyant hues flashed in feverish succession. It stopped. It started to tremble. With a violent shudder, the fiery orb seemed to disengage itself from the sky. Then the frenzied fireball began to catapult headlong in a wild zigzag toward the terrified crowd. Throwing out a scorching heat, the orb plummeted to the earth until it reached such an awesome proximity that many thought they were about to be consumed in an apocalyptic conflagration.

"Save us, Jesus! Our Lady save us!"

"Oh, Lord, forgive me!"

"Oh my God, how great is thy power!"

Abruptly, the orb reversed direction and soared calmly back into the sky. For a moment it recovered its previously translucent appearance. Then it became the dazzling sun of the everyday.

"*Milagre! Milagre!* Miracle! Miracle!" shouted the crowd. The

---

one who consecrates to Mary the "sanctity of the everyday." According to Fr. Killian Lynch, Prior General of Carmel until 1985, Sister Lucia declared in an interview that "the Rosary and Scapular are inseparable" (*Our Lady of Fatima and the Brown Scapular*, 16). This is principally because both symbolize the simple, contemplative life lived by the *anawim*, of which Mary is the supreme exemplar.

A Woman Adorned with the Sun

Lady had fulfilled her promise! She had worked her miracle. Relieved and exhilarated, the people turned to one another to celebrate the event. As they congratulated each other, they suddenly realized that each of them was completely dry. Their clothing, scarves, and hats; their hair, shoes, and feet; even the ground, that a moment before was squelching mud and deep puddles, was now perfectly dry. To their astonishment, the sun had dried up all the rain in the course of some fifteen minutes. People scooped up handfuls of dusty soil to take home as souvenirs. "*Milagre! Milagre,*" they cried, with tears in their eyes.

As we have noted above, between seventy and one hundred thousand people witnessed the "Miracle of the Sun" on that autumn day in 1917. Atheists, newspaper reporters, scientists, priests, peasants, officials, gentry, and shopkeepers have left their testimonies to the authenticity of these incredible events. We shall now hear in their own words what some of them saw.[3]

The first account comes from the Lisbon paper *O Dia*, dated 17 October, 1917:

At one o'clock in the afternoon, midday by the sun, the rain stopped. The sky, pearl grey in color, illuminated the vast, arid landscape with a strange light. The sun had a transparent gauzy veil so that the eyes could easily be fixed upon it. The grey mother-of-pearl tone turned into a sheet of silver which broke up as the clouds were torn apart and the silver sun, enveloped in the same, gauzy grey light, was seen to whirl and turn in the circle of broken clouds. A cry went up from every mouth and people fell on their knees on the muddy ground. . . .

3. Unless otherwise stated, these testimonies come from: John M. Haffert, *Meet the Witnesses*; Fernando Leite, *Francisco de Fatima*; Fr. Antonio Maria Martins and Fr. Robert J. Fox, *Documents on Fatima*; Mabel Norton, *Eye Witness at Fatima*; Manuel Vilas-Boas (et al.), *Fatima: Os Lugares da Profecia* (see Bibliography).

The expressions of the crowd during the miracle of the sun.

Witnesses to the miracle of the sun.

168

A Woman Adorned with the Sun

The light turned a beautiful blue as if it had come through the stained-glass windows of a cathedral and spread itself over the people who knelt with outstretched hands. The blue faded slowly and then the light seemed to pass through yellow glass. Yellow stains fell against white handkerchiefs, against the dark skirts of the women. They were repeated on the trees, on the stones, and on the serra. People wept and prayed with uncovered heads in the presence of a miracle they had awaited. The seconds seemed like hours, so vivid were they.

The crowd falls to its knees before the dancing sun.
Note the dryness of the ground and the sharp shadows.

From this rather restrained report, we turn to the widely circulated newspaper, *O Seculo*. An article on the 15th October read: "Terrifying Event! How the Sun Danced at Midday in Fatima." The author was Avelino de Almeida, who was a witness to the event.

From the road, where the vehicles were parked and where hundreds of people who had not dared to brave the mud were congregated, one could see the immense multitude turn towards the sun, which appeared free from clouds and in its zenith. It looked like a plaque of dull silver and it was possible to look at it without the least discomfort. It might have been an eclipse which was taking place. But at that moment a great shout arose and one could hear the spectators nearest at hand shouting: "A miracle! A miracle!"

Before the astonished eyes of the crowd, whose aspect was Biblical as they stood bareheaded, eagerly searching the sky, the sun trembled, made sudden incredible movements outside all cosmic laws—the sun "danced" according to the typical expression of the people. Standing at the step of the Torres Novas omnibus was an old man, whose appearance in face and figure reminded one of Paul Deroulede. With his face turned toward the sun he recited the Credo in a loud voice. . . . I saw him afterwards going up to those around him who still had their hats on and vehemently imploring them to uncover before such an extraordinary demonstration of the existence of God. . . . People then began to ask each other what they had seen. The great majority admitted to having seen the trembling and the dancing of the sun; others affirmed that they saw the face of the Blessed Virgin; others, again, swore that the sun whirled on itself like a giant Catherine wheel and that it lowered itself to the earth as if to burn it in its rays. Some said they saw it change colors successively.

This particular report understandably provoked a considerable reaction among the liberals in Lisbon, who vehemently attacked Senhor Almeida for having gone back on the substance of a previous article. On the morning of the miracle he had published an article in which he confessed his own skepticism towards such apparitions. Now he was affirming a supernatural occurrence. Later, a friend persuaded him to write another article which was published in *Illustraçao Portuguesa* of 29 October, 1917. In that article, he states: "At the hour foretold, the rain ceased to fall, the dense mass of clouds parted, and the sun—like a shining disc of silver—appeared at its full zenith, and began to whirl around in a wild and violent dance, that a large number of people likened to a carnival display, with such lovely glowing colors passing successively over the sun's surface. A miracle, as the crowd cried out; or a natural phenomenon, as the learned say? It is not important for me to know the answer now, but only to tell you and confirm what I saw. . . . The rest we leave to science and the Church."

The professor of natural sciences at Coimbra, Dr. Almeida Garrett (who had estimated the crowd at 100,000), later wrote to Dr. Formigao at his behest. He was parked in his car on the roadway, looking down through the open door upon "the multitude which straggled out at my feet." Suddenly, he heard a shout, as the people in one mass turned away from the little oak tree towards the eastern sky.

A Woman Adorned with the Sun

It must have been two o'clock by the legal time and about midday by the sun. The sun, a few moments before, had broken through the thick layer of clouds which hid it and shone clearly and intensely. I veered to this magnet which seemed to be drawing all eyes and saw it as a disc with a clean-cut rim, luminous and shining, but which did not hurt the eyes. I do not agree with the comparison which I have heard made in Fatima—that of a dull, silver disc. It was a clearer, richer, brighter color, having something of the lustre of a pearl. It did not in the least resemble the moon on a clear night because one saw it and felt it to be a living body. It was not spheric like the moon nor did it have the same color, tone, or shading. It looked like a glazed wheel made of mother-of-pearl. It could not be confused, either, with the sun seen through fog (for there was no fog at the time), because it was not opaque, diffused or veiled. In Fatima it gave light and heat and appeared clear-cut with a well-defined rim.

The sky was mottled with light cirrus clouds with the blue coming through here and there but sometimes the sun stood out in patches of clear sky. The clouds passed from west to east and did not obscure the light of the sun, giving the impression of passing behind it, though sometimes these flecks of white took on tones of pink or diaphanous blue as they passed before the sun.

It was a remarkable fact that one could fix one's eyes on this brazier of heat and light without any pain in the eyes or blinding of the retina. The phenomenon, except for two interruptions when the sun seemed to send out rays of refulgent heat which obliged us to look away, must have lasted about ten minutes.

The sun's disc did not remain immobile. This was not the sparkling of a heavenly body for it spun round on itself in a mad whirl. Then suddenly, one heard a clamour, a cry of anguish breaking from the people. The sun, whirling wildly, seemed to loosen itself from the firmament and advance threateningly upon the earth as if to crush us with its huge and fiery weight. The sensation during those moments was terrible.

During the solar phenomenon, which I have just described in detail, there were changes of color in the atmosphere. Looking at the sun, I noticed that everything around was becoming darkened. I looked first at the nearest objects and then extended my glance further afield as far as the horizon. I saw everything an amethyst color. Objects around me, the sky and the atmosphere, were of the same color. An oak tree nearby threw a shadow of this color on the ground.

Fearing that I was suffering from an affection of the retina, an improbable explanation because in that case one could not see things purple colored, I turned away and shut my eyes, keeping my hands before them to intercept the light. With my back still turned, I opened my eyes and saw that the landscape was the same purple as before.

The impression was not that of an eclipse, and while looking at the sun I noticed that the atmosphere had cleared. Soon after I heard a peasant who was near me shout out in astonishment: "Look, that lady is all yellow." And in fact, everything, both near and far, had changed, taking on the color of old yellow damask. People looked as if they were suffering from jaundice and I recall a sensation of amusement at seeing them so ugly and unattractive. My own hand was the same color. All the phenomena which I have described were observed by me in a calm and serene state of mind and without any emotional disturbance. It is for others to interpret and explain them.

Many intellectuals tried to explain away the event by appealing to various natural phenomena. However, as Professor Oom of the faculty of sciences and director of the Lisbon Observatory pointed out in *O Seculo*, "If it were a cosmic phenomenon, astronomical and meteorological observatories would not have failed to record it. And this is precisely what is missing: that inevitable recording of all the disturbances in the world system, no matter how small they may be. . . ." What this astronomer declares is that, had the phenomena been caused by actual alterations in the solar orbit, their effects would have been catastrophic. For if the earth had jiggled in its orbit, and most certainly if the earth had moved that closely to the sun, the results would have been so extreme that no observatory would have missed it. Climatic and electromagnetic phenomena would have occurred all over the planet. Earthquakes and volcanic eruptions would have been triggered. Hurricanes, tornadoes, and tsunamis would have been unleashed. Animals would have been particularly disoriented, etc., etc. Clearly, the phenomena did not involve the sun in any direct way. However, there are no known indirect or atmospheric phenomena that could produce all these extraordinary manifestations. Had there been, as Professor Oom pointed out, they would have been recorded by meteorological observatories.

Another witness to the event was Lucia's tall stranger, the lawyer, Carlos Mendes, who was standing close to the spot of the apparition. He states:

"I saw the sun, as if it were a ball of fire, begin to move in the clouds. It had been raining all morning and the sky was full of clouds, but the rain had stopped. It lasted for several seconds, crushingly pressing down on us all. Wan faces, standing here, from every side great exclamations, acts of contrition, or the love of God. An indescribable moment!"

Maria da Capelinha, who had believed from the very beginning, leaves us this comment:

It turned everything different colors, yellow, blue, white, and it shook and trembled; it seemed like a wheel of fire, which was going to fall on the people. They cried out: "We shall all be killed, we shall all be killed." Others called to Our Lady to save them and recited acts of contrition. One woman began to confess her sins aloud, saying that she had done this and that.... At last the sun stopped moving and we all breathed a sigh of relief. We were still alive and the miracle which the children had foretold had taken place.

Another witness, who later moved to Oakland, California was a Mr. Higino Faria. In 1917 he lived only seven miles from Fatima. Two days before the miracle he noticed the crowds of pilgrims, and, although suffering from a severe cold, he decided he would go to see the miracle. He braved the rain and cold despite his wife's protestations to the contrary.

"When I arrived at eleven o'clock, I was surprised at the great number of people on the slope of the hill. Completely wet, dirty, and frozen, we waited. At one o'clock the clouds gathered into a very thick and dark form, giving the appearance of an eclipse. At that moment I looked at the multitude and had the impression that it was the day of final judgment. The faces of the people looked thin, long and yellow. Then the dark cloud broke into parts, and through the break we saw the sun shining, spinning in the shape of a wheel of fire. It seemed to approach the earth... Everyone was dried, cleansed. I who was sick, returned completely cured. In thanksgiving for such a great grace and my cure, I promised to recite the Rosary every day of my life."

Antonio Antunes de Oliveira, a farmer, was thirty-two years old when he witnessed the miracle.

"I looked at the sun and saw it spinning like a disc, rolling on itself. I saw the people changing color. They were stained with the colors of the rainbow. Then the sun seemed to fall down from the sky."

Another farmer, Manuel Francisco, twenty-two years old, was standing in the crowd with his wife. He recalls how he felt:

"The sun began to come down until it seemed we were almost near it, and it threw beams of light. It was getting dark and all the people screamed... I was so afflicted that I came home weeping... I went to say some prayers close to the spot where the vision appeared, then came home... My heart was afflicted. I could not help crying."

Maria do Carmo Marques da Cruz Menezes, a forty-six year old housewife at the time, leaves this account:

"Suddenly the sun appeared so that we could look at it as though it were the moon. It began spinning like a firework wheel, making us all turn into the colors of the rainbow, even the ground itself." It was asked of Maria da Cruz if she was wet and then dry afterwards. "Yes... I also saw four cures at the place of the apparitions: Two were of tuberculosis, one of a girl from Lisbon and the other from Alfarelos; two were crippled girls."

Maria Candida da Silva, a resident of Leiria: "I saw the sun coming down, feeling that it was falling to the ground. At that moment I collapsed, and when I awoke it was all over. . . . My clothes had been wet because it rained much, but quickly it was dry."

Doctor Jose Maria Pereira Gens also confirms this:

I still hold present in my spirit that singular and unforgettable scenario: the midday sun, suspended before us, unguarded, neutral, with those aggressive rays which characterized it. Suddenly, it began to gyrate and turn on itself, with a dizzying velocity and, at a certain height, like something advancing and menacing, fell headlong upon us. . . . The highly impressionable multitude knelt on the mud of the mesa praying, crying, shouting in agitation. Through the vale resounded an immense clamor, a high tide of enthusiasm and euphoria. For at the same time the sun stopped in order, after a brief pause, to recommence its strange dance. . . . Persons and things appeared to us illuminated by alternately different colors; and if it were true that the sun's luminosity was weakened, the heat remained, [so that] my suit though somewhat soaked, I felt it now almost dry. . . . Apart from everything, however, panic never manifested itself. No one fled. Everyone expected a sign from heaven; and given the circumstances of the moment which transpired, one hoped for a sign of peace; yet these signs sustained one with confidence and with serene surprise.

Father Joao Gomes Manitra leaves us with this reaction: "I looked and saw that the people were in various colors—yellow, white, blue. At the same time I beheld the sun spinning at great speed and very near me. I at once thought: 'I am going to die.' I knelt down on some stones and raised my hand, begging the pardon of God for every fault I might have committed. A few moments later the sun ceased to spin and went back into it place. I looked at the place and saw a truck beside me in which a man in an overcoat stood crying aloud the words of the creed. And I told myself that I was not the only one to be afflicted. . . ."

On the first of September, 1917, the Baron of Alvaiazere heard of the heroism of the three shepherd children while they were in the Ourem prison. Although he had not believed, he became an influential witness to the Miracle of the Sun. He was later instrumental in having Jacinta's body placed in his family's tomb for protection until the Church approved of the miracle. His sister, Maria Celeste da Camara e Vasconcelos, has left a deposition stating what they saw: "The sun began to spin with circles of every color. It was like a wheel of fireworks, and coming down to the ground."

Of the many testimonials from those who were there, we lastly quote Mario Godinho, an engineer from Vial do Paco: "I got out of the car. I could look straight at the sun without difficulty. It was like a disc of dimmed glass illuminated from behind, moving around and around, and then gave the impression of falling down. . . . At the end of the miracle it [his suit] got dry.... I was greatly impressed." On another occasion, he wrote: "I saw in a clear area of sky (where one should not be able to stare at the sun) the very sun. It was like a disc of smoked glass illuminated from behind and turning over itself, giving the impression that it was coming down over our heads. I could then see the sun more easily than I can see the moon on a full moon night. From those hundreds of mouths I heard words of belief and of love to the Blessed Virgin. And then I believed. I was sure I had not been the victim of suggestion. I saw the sun as I never saw it again."

The objection has been raised that the whole thing could have been mass hysteria or a collective hallucination. After all, Lucia did say "Look at the sun" just before the event transpired, and everyone was expecting a miracle to occur. Yet Lucia also said "St. Joseph is coming to bless us," and no one is known to have admitted to seeing him. If the crowd could respond to one suggestion, why not the other? It must also be remembered that no one, not even the children, knew what sort of miracle was going to take place on that day. The notion of suggestion is further discredited by the discovery that the miracle of the sun was observable over an area of 600 square miles by people who were completely indifferent to the events of Fatima. They hardly could have been susceptible to suggestions they never had heard.

One such witness to the Miracle of the Sun was Father Joaquim Lourenco, canon lawyer of the diocese of Leiria. At the time, he was only a schoolboy, observing the phenomenon with his brother and other children in the village of Alburitel, some nine miles from Fatima.

"I feel incapable of describing what I saw. I looked fixedly at the sun, which seemed pale and did not hurt my eyes. Looking like a ball of snow, revolving on itself, it suddenly seemed to come down in a zigzag, menacing the earth. Terrified, I ran and hid myself among the people, who were weeping and expecting the end of the world at any moment. It was a crowd which had gathered outside our local village school and we had all left classes and run into the streets because of the cries and surprised shouts of men and women who were in the street in front of the school when the miracle began. There was an unbeliever there who had spent the morning mocking the 'simpletons' who had gone off to Fatima just to see an ordinary girl. He now seemed paralyzed, his eyes fixed on the sun. He began to tremble from head to foot, and lifting up his arms, fell on his knees in the mud, crying out to God. But meanwhile the people continued to cry out and to weep, asking God to pardon their sins. We all ran to the two chapels in the village, which were soon filled to overflowing. During those long moments of the solar prodigy, objects around us turned all colors of the rainbow.... When the people realized that the danger was over, there was an explosion of joy."

San Pedro de Muel is a fishing town some thirty miles from Fatima. The Portuguese poet Afonso Lopes Vieira was relaxing on his veranda at noon. Overcome with astonishment, he called his wife and mother-in-law to witness the extraordinary spectacle occurring over the distant serra. His lengthy deposition confirms the familiar details of the solar phenomenon: the viewable sun, its spectrum of colors, its rotation, and its fateful plummet to earth.

Albano Barros lived in the village of Minde, about eight miles from Fatima. He was twelve years old at the time. "I was watching sheep, as was my daily task, and suddenly there in the direction of Fatima I saw the sun fall from the sky. I thought it was the end of the world."

Mrs. Guilhermina Lopes da Silva was living in Leiria, some sixteen miles from Fatima. She could not go there because her husband was an unbeliever. Although her vision was obscured by her proximity to the high mountains surrounding Fatima, she did observe "a great red flash in the sky" which was also witnessed by two workmen in her employ.

As a result of such confirmations made by distant witnesses, it is no longer possible to countenance any speculations of collective hallucination arising from suggestions verbally or non-verbally communicated to these people. They had no way of knowing what to expect, yet their reports coincide closely to those of the people who were actually present at the event.

We have already seen that no natural explanation can be proffered to account for the phenomena, which would not have registered their effects at some observatory. These points were made by another scientist, Pio Scatizzi, S.J., Professor of mathematics and astronomy at the Gregorian University, Rome, who has left an extremely detailed analysis of the event, from which we give the following excerpt:

> This opaqueness of the sun in a clear sky was but the beginning of events, for immediately there began to radiate from its centre thousands upon thousands of monochromatic lights in sectors, which in the form of spirals, began to whirl around the centre of the solar disc in such a manner that the sun itself seemed to turn on itself rather like a Catherine wheel, while the colored rays spread out in a centrifugal movement, covering the sky as far as the curtain of clouds and turning everything various colors as if by magic. Such a spectacle of red, yellow, green and violet rays from the sun, spreading and sweeping over the sky, cannot be explained by any known laws nor has such a thing been seen before.

It now remains to examine the third phase of the phenomenon, that is to say the movement of the sun, which appeared to detach itself from the sky and to fall on the earth in a zigzag path. It can be affirmed that such a phenomenon is outside and against all natural astronomical laws. It appears that with this final occurrence, all doubts as to the natural origins of the events, all scepticism on our part, must be laid aside.

At this point it would be well to refresh our motives for belief in such an unheard of incident. The number and nature of the witnesses exceed all requirements for verification. With twelve such, the law justifies the execution of a man. In this case eyewitnesses numbered some 70,000.

To resume our study: First, we have the rotation of the sun and the various colors; secondly, a movement outside the normal daily path of the sun in the heavens. In the first case there would be a normal admiration such as would be excited by a first view of an aurora borealis. There would be no cause for terror. Yet, suddenly, without the intervention of any new factor, the multitude is seized with terror as if menaced by a cataclysm. Everyone feels threatened by imminent catastrophe. There is a sensation that the sun is about to fall on the earth; that it is being torn from the cosmic laws of its eternal path. Hence the invocations, the prayers, the cries of affliction as in a universal cataclysm.

Observe well this second stage. It is not religious hysteria nor a species of Pentecostal fervor. It is sheer panic in the presence of Him Who alone can dominate the forces of the universe. Contemporary accounts will show that it was not a case of suggestion but that an objective vision was the cause of the panic which, when it had passed, left everyone perfectly calm, contented even, at having witnessed a prodigy which had been exactly foretold and anxiously awaited. How also could everyone have seen the danger pass at one and the same moment?

Of the historical reality of the event there can be no doubt whatever. That it was outside and against known laws can be proved by certain simple scientific considerations. . . . [Such as the enormous change in orbit that would have to be traversed to make such a noticeable change in the proximity of the distant sun.]

Conclusion: The above-mentioned solar phenomena were not noted in any observatory. Impossible that they should escape the notice of so many astronomers and indeed the other inhabitants of the hemisphere. It must then be admitted that there is no question of an astronomical or meteorological phenomenon as we have already said. We are thus confronted with an inescapable dilemma. Either all the observers in Fatima were collectively deceived and erred in their testimony or we must suppose an extra-natural intervention. Given the indubitable reference to God, and the general context of the story, it seems that we must attribute to Him alone the most obvious and colossal miracle of history.

Here, then, is the Miracle of the Sun of October 13, 1917, witnessed by some 70,000 people both proximate and distant and reported in various newspapers and periodicals of the time. This was an event that involved no known natural phenomenon that could be observed by scientific instruments. Yet it had an objective effect, not only upon the behavior of the witnesses, but upon the dampened condition of their clothing and the soaked earth itself. This event, whose historicity is beyond question, did not involve the sun in any direct sense—i.e., it did not result from some cataclysmic perturbation in either the earth's orbit or the fixity of the sun's position at the center of the solar system. We note from some of the more careful eyewitnesses that the sun appeared to look like it was covered with an opalescent membrane or "gauze" giving a "silvery" appearance like "mother-of-pearl." The engineer, Sr. Godinho, described it as "a disc of smoked glass illuminated from behind and turning upon itself." Professor Garrett said he noticed some clouds passing *behind* the disc, which is impossible if it were the sun itself. Clearly, something had interposed itself between the spectators and the sun at about the height of the clouds (passing before as well as behind), which acted like a filter or prism, casting a multicolored spectrum of light as it alternately rotated and stopped three times in succession. Moreover, this object could expand or move in such a way as to give the stereoscopic impression of a falling sun. The object would have to be large enough to cover the phenomenal sun at a height that would also permit it to be seen at a local distance away, but not any further than the angle permissible by the curvature of the earth. Finally, it would have to magnify the heat of the sun just enough to dry up all the moisture without burning the people. We have no known natural phenomenon that manifests these characteristics. There is no natural disc-like object that could simultaneously produce all these marvels and at the same time account for the lack of observable meteorological and astronomical phenomena.[1] Lucia implied that the luminous orb which conveyed the Lady moved toward the sun and projected itself there. If it were such an orb, it would clearly be a miracle.

Whatever it was that appeared in the sky, its occurrence at exactly the time foretold was miraculous enough. But given the entire context of Fatima—the messages with their profound theology; the faith and devotion of the children; their constancy in the face of disbelief, persecutions, and threats of death; their prophecies, which, as we shall see, have all been fulfilled—it becomes impossible not to acknowledge the hand of God. There is a unity in the events and messages of Fatima that forms a seamless fabric of truth. There is

---

1. Even ball lightning, which comes closest to being a candidate, would not be able to rotate and stop alternatively, produce the variety of colors, or descend and ascend in succession. Nor would it dry up the ground. It would certainly not be seen over an area of 600 square miles.

nothing in Fatima that cannot be affirmed by the Scriptures. There is nothing that does not uphold the sublime traditions of the Church. But more than this, there is a sense, when viewed as a whole, that we are in the presence of something holy.

We now know the identity of the Lady who appeared before the children six times in succession: she is the Lady of the Rosary, the Blessed Virgin Mary. Of course, the faithful had already made up their minds who she was. On this last and monumental visit, we have the confirmation in her own pure voice. However, in saying that she is the Lady of the Rosary, she is affirming much more than that she is a vision of the Blessed Virgin, the Mother of Jesus. She is declaring her solidarity with the spirit and truth expressed in the Rosary devotion. She is identifying with the analogue of her Immaculate Heart. Again she affirms its efficacy in ending the war, converting the lost, and making reparation for the offences committed against God. Once again, she calls the faithful to amend their lives and to fulfill their responsibilities towards God and the Church. Even if she had not told us that she was the Lady of the Rosary, her solicitude for the Church and her devotion to Our Lord would have convinced us that we were being confronted with an Immaculate Heart, a heart which in its deepest reflection consents to do God's will as Mother of the Church.

The urgency of her message was underscored by the awesome magnitude of the miracle she had performed by the power of God. For nearly one month later, on Tuesday morning, the 7th of November, the Bolsheviks under Trotsky seized the railway, the telegraph, the Tauride Palace, the State Bank, and the central telephone exchanges in Petrograd. By two o'clock the next morning, the Winter Palace was in Bolshevik hands. At 5:15 a.m. on Wednesday Lenin was established as President of the Communist government with Trotsky as Commissar of Foreign Affairs and Stalin as Commissar for Nationalities. And on 16 November, 1917, just one month after the Miracle of the Sun, the Kremlin fell to the Communists. The Russia was born that would spread its errors throughout the world, whose atheist, materialist, politically correct utopianism would pervade and persecute the Church, and whose unbelief was to become the crucible for the triumph of the Immaculate Heart.

After the miracle of October 13, the three children
pose under the makeshift arch that surrounded the
holm oak upon which Our Lady appeared.

The Call of Heaven

AFTER THE EVENTS OF October 13, the children were taken directly to Manuel Marto's house, where they were subjected to another long and grueling interrogation from Dr. Formigao. He wanted to be absolutely sure that the children would not be left alone together to compare notes before being examined. Also, he wanted to ensure that no other persons would have an opportunity to contaminate their testimonies. The children were so exhausted by the tumult of the day that their enthusiasm was considerably dampened and their concentration span curtailed. The lengthy interview which followed was surprisingly successful under the circumstances.

The children agreed perfectly on a number of details: all three had seen Our Lady on the oak tree, although Francisco did not hear her speak; all three had witnessed the rotation of the sun; and all had seen the vision of St. Joseph and the Christ child. They agreed perfectly with one another in their descriptions of the details of their dress, the location of the boy Jesus on the right side of Joseph, his approximate age (one to two years old), their actions of blessing the crowd, and their position near the sun. Lucia and Jacinta agreed substantially on the content of the message: that people must amend their lives, stop sinning, say the Rosary every day, and that a chapel must be built in honor of the Lady of the Rosary. Lucia mentioned nothing about the end of the war (nor was she asked), but Jacinta said in response to questioning that Our Lady promised the war would end that day. (Lucia had previously mentioned to an interviewer on the spot that the Lady of the Rosary said the war would end shortly. This fact was later quoted in *O Seculo*.)

The only real discrepancy in their collective testimonies concerned whether or not the Christ child was carried or was standing. Lucia said the little Jesus was carried in St. Joseph's right arm, while Jacinta and Francisco agreed that He was standing on Joseph's right side and that He did not quite reach to his waist. Given that Lucia had seen further visions of Our Lady of Sorrows and Our Lady of Mount Carmel, which her cousins had not seen, this discrepancy in detail is not an insurmountable difficulty. It had been prophesied that Francisco and Jacinta were soon to die. The vision of the boy Jesus standing to welcome these two children into heaven (as with St. Stephen, cf. Acts 7:55) fits in with this context. Lucia, who was to remain behind, simply saw the traditional tableau of the Holy Family followed by the two tableaux which indicated that she must continue to carry the cross and take up the devotion of a Carmelite. Moreover, Lucia was asked if these visions occurred simultaneously, which, as Dr. Formigao expressed it, "would have created a serious difficulty." He suggested to Lucia:[1]

"They all came at the same time, did they not?"

"No. First I saw Our Lady of the Rosary, then St. Joseph and the Holy Child. After that I saw Our Lord, then Our Lady of Dolors, and at the end what I think was Our Lady of Mount Carmel."

After this Dr. Formigao attempted to learn the secret from Francisco.

"Did you hear what the Lady said?"

"I heard nothing that she said."

"Who told you the secret; was it the Lady?"

"No, it was Lucia."

"Will you tell it?"

"No."

"You are afraid of being beaten by Lucia if you tell it, aren't you?"

"Oh, no!"

"Then, why can you not tell it to me? Would it be a sin?"

"Perhaps it is a sin to tell the secret."

"Is the secret for the good of your soul, and Jacinta's and Lucia's soul?"

"Yes."

"Is it for the good of Fr. Ferreira's soul also?"

"I do not know."

"Would the people be sad if they knew?"

1. Quoted in de Marchi, 142 ff.

184

The Call of Heaven

"Yes."

Because of the late hour, the interview was terminated until a subsequent date. A week later, on 19th of October, Dr. Formigao returned with another list of questions for the children. Again they were questioned about details of the visions, and again there was agreement between their various testimonies. However, a wider divergence emerged between Lucia and Jacinta over the exact wording of the prediction concerning the end of the war. Dr. Formigao asked Lucia this leading question:

"On the 13th of this month, Our Lady said that the war would finish on that same day? What were the words she used?"

"She said: 'The war will end today. You can expect the soldiers very shortly.'"

"But listen, Lucia, the war is still going on. The papers give news of battles after the 13th. How can you explain that if Our Lady said the war would end that day?"

"I don't know; I only know that I heard her say that the war would end on that day."

"Some people declare that they heard you say that Our Lady had said that the war would end shortly. Is that true?"

"I said exactly what Our Lady had said."

"On the 27th of last month I came to your house to speak with you. . . . On that day, you told me that Our Lady had said that on the 13th of October she would come with St. Joseph and the Holy Child and that *afterwards* the war would end, not necessarily on the 13th."

"I cannot remember now exactly how she put it. She might have said that or perhaps I did not understand her properly."

Later he questioned Jacinta while they were walking to Fatima.

"What did the Lady say this last time?"

"She said: 'I have come here to tell you that people must not offend Our Lord anymore because he is very much offended and that if the people amend their lives the war will end and if not the world will end.' Lucia heard better than I did what the Lady said."

"Did she say that the war would end on that day or shortly?"

"Our Lady said that the war would end when she arrived in Heaven."

"But the war has not ended."

185

"But it will end, it will."

"When will it end?"

"I think it will end on Sunday."

This interview with Jacinta sheds some light upon the nature of the confusion. For it is quite possible that the Lady could have used a conditional phrase such as "...if the people amend their lives the war will end; if not..." What we can affirm is that, had any definite date for the end of the war been given out at the time, and particularly if it had been that very day, newspapers all over the country would have seized the opportunity to draw attention to its obvious lack of fulfillment. Even so, the inconsistency in Lucia's testimonies is a difficulty which remains to this day. There is clearly some uncertainty in her testimony, which can be accounted for by the bewildering events of the day, the excitement and uproar of the crowd, the many petitions that were constantly requested that Lucia make, and the exhaustion of the three children. Jacinta evidenced a similar confusion. Yet it should be borne in mind that, even after a week, neither child made any attempt to harmonize her story with the other's. In all their recorded testimonies, this discrepancy remains the only real difficulty.

By the time this interrogation was completed, the children were so physically and emotionally debilitated that Dr. Formigao feared they would become gravely ill. He broke off the investigation to allow time for the children to recover.

As far as Lucia's family was concerned, the Miracle of the Sun did not have the expected transforming effect upon either Maria Rosa or upon Antonio Abobora. The events at the Cova da Iria, which had only exacerbated the economic circumstances of the family, weighed heavily upon Antonio. He had no fields left suitable either for cultivation or pasturage. By this time, the family had sold all their sheep. His livelihood was destroyed. He could never forgive God for that. Maria Rosa was somewhat tempered in her hostility towards the events, but she would still not permit herself to believe in the heavenly nature of the apparitions. She had heard from the priest that they might be demonic in origin, and, until the Church officially approved, neither would she. For Maria Rosa, obedience to the teaching authority of the Bishops was central to the faith. But

The Call of Heaven

she had softened enough to allow Lucia to learn to read. Enrolling her daughter in a school for girls which had recently been started in Fatima, she persuaded Olimpia to allow Jacinta to go also.

Francisco saw no reason to attend school. He would say to Jacinta and Lucia, "Listen! You go to school, and I'll stay here in the church, close to the Hidden Jesus. It's not worth my while learning to read, as I'll be going to heaven very soon. On your way home, come here and call me." His indifference towards school is apparent in an anecdote concerning two ladies who accosted him one day. They asked Francisco the inevitable question which adults expect all children to answer: "What do you want to be when you grow up?"

"Do you want to be a carpenter?"

"No, madam."

"A soldier?"

"No, madam."

"Surely you would like to be a doctor?"

"No, not that either."

"Then I know what you would like to be . . . a priest! Then you could say Mass and preach."

"No, madam, I do not want to be a priest either. I do not want to be anything. I want to die and go to heaven."

Later, when Lucia and Jacinta returned from school, they would find Francisco in the church as he said he would be, between the font and the altar, consoling the Hidden Jesus in the Eucharist. He prayed many hours in the church, often for specific petitions conveyed to him by pilgrims. One day, on her way to school, Lucia met her sister Teresa, who now lived with her husband in Lomba. She had come to bring the children various requests for prayers, one of which concerned a young man falsely accused of a serious crime, for which he might be imprisoned or exiled for many years. His anxious mother had asked Teresa to take her petition to the children. The girls had to go to school, but Francisco, deeply moved by the misfortune, said:

"Listen, while you two are at school, I will stay with the Hidden Jesus and ask for this grace."

After school, the children found Francisco still kneeling before the Eucharist. "Did you tell Our Lady about that?" Lucia asked.

"Yes and you can tell your sister, Teresa, that the boy will be home again in a few days."

On the thirteenth of the next month, the children saw the woman from Lomba, giving thanks to Our Lady for the release of her son.

While they were on their way to the Cova one morning, the three seers were ambushed by a group of questioning pilgrims as they came around a bend. In order better to hear what the children said, they decided to sit them on the wall. They placed Jacinta on the wall, but when they turned to Francisco, he edged his way out of their grasp and went to lean against a wall on the opposite side of the road. A poor, distressed woman and her son came out of the crowd and fell on their knees before Francisco. They were weeping for the boy's father, who was seriously ill. The woman implored Francisco to petition the Blessed Virgin to intercede for them, that her husband might be cured and would be kept out of the war. Francisco removed his cap, knelt down beside the anguished woman, and invited them to say a Rosary. The crowd of pilgrims came and joined them, and the entire troop went to the Cova, praying the Rosary as they walked. A few days later, the woman returned to the Cova, accompanied by her son and her husband, who had recovered from his illness. The three were afterwards seen regularly at the Cova, the husband always with them; he never went to the war.

Francisco's burning desire was to receive the Hidden Jesus in Holy Communion. During the period of the apparitions, he and Jacinta had begun to prepare for their first Communion. By May 1918, they were ready to be examined. Ti Marto relates the story:

About that time, it must have been after the second apparition, I took the two of them to the church to make their confessions. I went with them to the sacristy and said to Fr. Ferreira:

"Father, here are my two children; they want to go to confession. Your Reverence can ask them any question you like." (I confess that I put a little malice into those words!) Then the priest replied:

"These things (the apparitions) do not belong to confession, my friend!"

"That is true," I said, "and if they do not belong, I need not bring them here again."

But the children made their confession, though Fr. Ferreira thought they should wait another year for Holy Communion. The next year, in May, they went back to be examined in the Catechism. Jacinta answered well, but Francisco got muddled somewhere in the Creed—I cannot remember where—and so in the end Jacinta was allowed to make her Communion while Francisco could not. He went home in tears, but there was nothing to be done![2]

Francisco, who had experienced so many heavenly things with his sister and who was so drawn to his sorrowful Lord, was heartbroken to witness her going up to the altar and receiving their Lord without him. Francisco feared that time was short and that he would not receive his Lord before his death. All he could do was to offer up to God in reparation his sense of desolation: "It is for love of you, O my Jesus."

It was one year after the last apparition and the war was about to end. Yet at the beginning of October 1918, an influenza epidemic had broken out in Europe. It was to spread all over the world and would claim some 20 million lives. By the end of October, the epidemic had been brought to Aljustrel by the soldiers returning from the war, and before long the entire Marto family, with the exception of Ti Marto, were in bed with the disease. He was the nurse for the whole family.

When my wife went down, it was all I could do to look after them all and go about my work and the errands as well! One of the girls had to have a caustic plaster, another something else, and so forth. But the hand of God was here and He helped me. I never had to beg from anyone. We always had money enough.[3]

On All Saints Day, Ti Marto recalls having to turn away the children who came seeking sweets: "It's no use coming here, we are all ill." One by one the members of his family began to recover, except for Francisco and Jacinta. The little visionaries knew what this illness meant. They recovered for a short time, but in December they had a relapse. Francisco had contracted bronchial pneumonia and

2. de Marchi, 173.
3. Ibid., 178.

Jacinta pleurisy. Francisco was so ill that he could not move his hands or feet. During that time, they both had another visit from the Blessed Virgin, who told them that she would soon come to take Francisco to heaven, but that Jacinta must bide a little longer.

"Lucia," Jacinta murmured happily, "Our Lady came to see us. She told us she would come to take Francisco to heaven very soon, and she asked me if I still wanted to convert more sinners. I told her yes. She told me I would be going to a hospital where I would suffer a great deal; and that I am to suffer for the conversion of sinners, in reparation for the sins committed against the Immaculate Heart of Mary, and for love of Jesus. I asked if you would go with me. She said you would not, and that is what I find hardest. She said my mother would take me, and then I would have to stay there all alone."

Under Olimpia's conscientious care, Francisco's health gradually began to improve.

> The little boy took any medicine we gave him and was not difficult about anything (says Olimpia). I never knew what he liked and what he did not. If I gave him a little milk he took it, and if it was an egg he took that too. Bitter medicines he swallowed without making a face. Poor little boy! He was so good that we thought he would get better, but he always said that all the medicines were useless, because Our Lady was coming to take him to Heaven.
>
> In January he got better again for the second time and he even got up for a bit, which made us very hopeful. But he never believed he was better and always repeated the same thing, that Our Lady would soon come to fetch him.[4]

As his health improved, so Francisco began to return to the Cova to make reparation. Here he could contemplate that resplendent light in which He saw God. He said one day to Lucia: "I loved seeing Our Lord, but I loved still more seeing Him in that light where we were with Him as well. It is not long now, and Our Lord will take me up close to Him, and then I can look at Him forever." Occasionally he would go to the cave at the Cabeço to pray the angel's prayer: "My God, I believe, I adore, I hope, and I love You! I ask pardon of You for those who neither believe, nor adore, nor hope, nor love

4. Ibid., 179.

You." Then, though suffering from piercing headaches, he would even go to St. Anthony's Church in Fatima to console the Hidden Jesus for the indifferences of humanity. Lucia noticed one day that Francisco was walking very slowly.

"What's the matter?" Lucia asked. "You seem unable to walk."

"I have such a bad headache and I feel as though I am going to fall."

"Then stay at home."

"I don't want to. I would rather stay in the church with the Hidden Jesus, while you go to school."

Soon, however, he suffered a final relapse and returned to his wrought iron bed, never to leave it again. During this time, he received many visitors, who came to pay their respects. He generally remained silent, only speaking when spoken to. Some visitors remained for hours, preferring to sit quietly in his company. A neighbor woman once commented, "It seems to me that when we go to Francisco's room, we feel just as we do when we go into a church." Even children would come in to quietly stand by his bed, or else would peep in through the window to ask him if he were any better yet.

The holy ambiance which surrounded Francisco and pervaded his room left its mark upon his father also, as Sr. Marto attests:

> One night about one a.m. I awoke and I seemed to hear sighing within Francisco's room. I remained listening until I was certain that I was not mistaken; I jumped out of bed, lit a lamp, and entered anxiously into the room of my son. I found him lying face downwards, with his face buried in a pillow so as to stifle his sobbing. Convinced that he was feeling worse, I asked:
> "Why are you crying?"
> Surprised, he lifted his head, yet did not answer anything. To my insistent questioning, he responded in a tone both timid and devout:
> "I was thinking on Jesus, who is so sad because of the sins that are committed against Him."
> I remained possessed of an immense respect for my son. Unable to know what else to do except to convey my hand to his head, I ended with a caress.

"It is all right, Francisco, but sleep now."

Once again I lay down with all due care in order not to wake my wife; but sleep was difficult.

"Do you suffer much, Francisco?" Lucia asked him one day.

"Quite a lot, but it does not matter. I suffer to console Our Lord, and in a little while I shall be with him."

"When you go, don't forget to ask Our Lady to take me there soon as well."

"I won't ask that. You know very well that she does not want you to go there yet."

"Then listen to this. When you are there, don't forget to pray a great deal for sinners, for the Holy Father, for me, and for Jacinta."

"Yes, I will pray. But look, you had better ask Jacinta to pray for these things instead, because I am afraid I will forget when I see Our Lord. And then, more than anything else I want to console Him."

Then he handed over to Lucia the penitential rope that he wore during the day. "Take it before mother sees. No longer can I endure the cord. I am very ill. I shall go to heaven soon." Early one morning he sent his sister, Teresa, to bring Lucia to him, because he had something urgent to ask of her. Lucia dressed quickly and rushed to his bedside. He then asked everyone to leave the room as he had a secret to confide to Lucia. When they left he whispered to her:

"I am going to confession so that I can receive Holy Communion before I die. I want you to tell me if you have seen me commit any sin, and then go and ask Jacinta if she has seen me commit any."

"You disobeyed your mother a few times when she told you to stay at home, and you ran off to be with me or to go and hide."

"That's true. I remember that. Now go and ask Jacinta if she remembers anything else."

Lucia went to ask Jacinta, who thought for a while and said:

"Well, tell him that, before Our Lady appeared to us, he stole a coin from our father to buy a music box from José Marto of Casa Velha; and when the boys from Aljustrel threw stones at those from Boleiros, he threw some too!"

Lucia returned to convey the reminiscence to Francisco.

"I have already confessed those," he said, "but I will do so again.

Maybe it is because of these sins that I committed that Our Lord is so sad! But even if I should not die, I will never commit them again. I am heartily sorry for them now." He joined his hands and recited the new Rosary prayer: "O my Jesus, forgive us, save us from the fire of hell, and lead all souls into heaven, especially those most in need." Then he turned to Lucia and asked her to pray to the Lord to forgive him.

"I'll ask that, don't worry. If Our Lord had not forgiven them already, Our Lady would not have told Jacinta that she was coming soon to take you to heaven. Now I am going to Mass, and there I will pray to the Hidden Jesus for you."

"Then, please ask Him to let the parish priest give me Holy Communion."

Later that day, Fr. Morreira came to hear Francisco's confession. In spite of his weak condition, Francisco made a good confession to the priest. Satisfied, the priest assured Francisco he would return the next day. "Tomorrow I will bring Our Lord," he promised. And Francisco was radiant with joy. He was so pleased that he asked his mother not to give him any food after midnight, so that he could fast "like everyone else."

At last, the morning of April 3 arrived, when Francisco heard the tinkling of the bell rung by the acolyte which announced the arrival of the Sacred Host. In anticipation, Francisco struggled to sit up, but fell back weakly onto his pillow. "You can receive Our Lord lying down," his godmother, Teresa, advised. She had purposely come to assist at Francisco's first and last communion. As he looked around, he could see the lighted candles which his mother had arranged in the room. Then the priest entered and placed the pyx on the bedside table, which had been specially covered with a white, lace cloth. Conferring peace upon the house and all who lived in it, the priest placed the Body of Our Lord upon the tongue of the dying boy. His parents, sisters, and Lucia were weeping spasmodically, but Francisco was happy. "When will you bring me the Hidden Jesus again?" he asked.

Later, Jacinta was allowed in to see him. "I am happier than you are," Francisco said to her, "because I have the Hidden Jesus within my heart. I am going to heaven, but I am going to pray very much to Our Lord and Our Lady for them to bring you there soon." Jacinta and Lucia remained by his bedside the entire day. He was failing so rapidly that he could no longer pray the Rosary. The two girls prayed it for him. Then, with some difficulty, he said to Lucia: "I shall miss you very much in heaven. If only Our Lady would let you come soon, also."

"Miss me? Just imagine! And you right there with Our Lord and Our Lady! They are so good."

"That is true. Perhaps I won't remember."

"Perhaps you won't. But never mind."

When it came time for Lucia to go, she said, "Goodbye, Francisco. If you go to heaven tonight, don't forget me when you get there, do you hear?"

"No, I won't forget you." Then he seized her hand, which he clutched tightly for a long time as he gazed at her through his tears.

"Do you want anything more?" Lucia said uncomfortably, with tears streaming down her cheeks also.

"No," he murmured faintly.

"Goodbye then, Francisco. Till we meet in heaven... goodbye."

During the night his body was burning with fever and, even though he was thirsty, he was unable to swallow the small spoonfuls of water Olimpia offered him from time to time. "I am all right, I have no pain," he said to soothe her stricken heart. "Look, Mother, what a pretty light there, near the door... Now I don't see it anymore."

The next day, Friday, 4 April, 1919, at 10 p.m., after having begged everyone's pardon for any trouble he had caused, and after having once again confirmed that he had seen Our Lady in the Cova da Iria, the ten year old boy expired peacefully. He died sweetly and calmly, with a faint smile on his lips. The next day, his body was taken down the rough road to the cemetery at St. Anthony's, where he was buried in quicklime according to the custom. Later, in 1952, when Francisco's remains would be exhumed to be translated to the new Basilica of the Rosary in Fatima, they would find his Rosary still clutched in the fingers.

Afterwards, Lucia placed a simple cross upon the grave. Every day thereafter, Lucia went to his graveside to converse with her little friend. "I could never describe how much I missed him," she remembers. "This grief was a thorn that pierced my heart for years to come."

Jacinta was too ill to be present at Francisco's deathbed. But she was later moved into his room in order to be nearer the front door, so that she could see and hear what went on. Jacinta suffered acutely after the death of her brother. If anyone asked what she was thinking about, she would often reply, her eyes brimming with tears, "Oh, Francisco. I would give anything to see him again."

On another occasion, she replied to the same question, put by Lucia: "I am thinking of the war which will come. So many people will die and go to hell. So many houses will be destroyed and priests killed. Listen, I am going to heaven soon, but when you see that light that Our Lady told us would come before the war, you run up there too."

"Don't you see that nobody can just run off to heaven!"

"That's true, you cannot. But do not be afraid. In heaven I will be praying hard for you, for the Holy Father, for Portugal, so that the war will not come here, and for all priests."

Lucia often brought news about developments at the Cova da Iria to divert Jacinta's attention from her sufferings. Building had commenced on the little chapel and already disputes were arising. Some of these disputes concerned what should be done for the little oak tree, which was so stripped of foliage and branches that there was hardly anything left. Others involved how the money should be spent on the chapel, or how big it should be, or whom they could get to agree to bless the project, etc. In the thick of it was Maria da Capelinha, who took it upon herself to give advice as to what was fitting and proper. Jacinta heard these stories with delight, but then she would say pensively: "I will never see Cova da Iria or Valinhos again."

Her condition continued to worsen, to the extent that the doctor advised she be admitted to hospital. She had developed a purulent pleurisy which was causing such severe pains in her chest that it was felt she would require an operation to drain the fluid. On the morning of July 1, her father placed her enfeebled body on his donkey and set off for St. Augustine's hospital in Ourem, the town of the kidnapping. It was a large, whitewashed building with spacious rooms, and even though Jacinta's ward was bright and cheerful, she knew that she would not be cured. The Blessed Lady had said that she would go to two hospitals, and that she would be granted the grace of suffering for others.

Lucia managed to make two visits to the hospital during the two months that Jacinta was there. On the first visit, Lucia asked if Jacinta was suffering very much, and Jacinta answered that she was, but that she was happy to be able to offer it up in reparation for others. The second visit occurred after the death of Lucia's father. Antonio Abobora had died on 31 July from an attack of double pneumonia. Lucia later wrote: "My sorrow was so great that I thought I would die as well. He was the only one who never failed to show himself to be my friend, and the only one who defended me when disputes arose at home on account of me. 'My God! My God' I exclaimed in the privacy of my room. 'I never thought you had so much suffering in store for me. But I suffer for love of you....'"[5] Then, at one with the sufferings of Jacinta, she made a second visit to her at Ourem. She found Jacinta "as joyful as ever, glad to suffer for the love of Our Good God ... that was her ideal, and she could speak of nothing else."[6]

By the end of August, it was understood that the severe treatments administered to Jacinta were having no salutary effect upon her health. A large, festering wound remained in Jacinta's chest where a drain had been inserted. It had become infected and would not heal. Each day it had to be cleansed and dressed. On top of all this, she had contracted tuberculosis of the bone. Moreover, the expense of these ministrations was becoming burdensome for the Marto family. For these reasons, Jacinta was sent home on the 31 August. Dr. Formigao, visited Jacinta at her home and has left us a report of her condition.

> Jacinta is like a skeleton and her arms are shockingly thin. Since she left the hospital where she underwent two months' useless treatment, the fever has never left her. She looks pathetic. Tuber-

5. *Memoirs*, 91.
6. Ibid., 44.

culosis, after an attack of bronchial pneumonia and pleurisy, is undermining her enfeebled constitution. Only careful treatment in a good sanatorium can save her. But her parents cannot afford the expense which such a treatment involves. Bernadette, the peasant girl from Lourdes, heard from the mouth of the Immaculate Virgin in the cave of Massabielle, a promise of happiness not in this world, but in the next. Has Our Lady made an identical promise to the little shepherdess of Fatima, to whom she confided an inviolable secret?[7]

The fact of the matter was that Jacinta, like St. Bernadette, had been asked by her Heavenly Mother if she was willing to suffer in this world. The pain caused by the continual draining, cleansing, and dressing of wounds without anesthetic, and the soreness resulting from the infection for which there were no antibiotics, combined with the debilitating effects of the Koch bacillus that was eating away at her emaciated body, was excruciating. Like St. Bernadette, Jacinta was dying of tuberculosis. And she bore it with identical courage, even with joy, far beyond her eight tender years. She was empowered by a supreme grace.

"When I am alone," she confided to Lucia, "I get out of bed to say the prayer of the angel. But I cannot get my head on the ground any more because I fall, so I pray it on my knees."

Lucia spoke to the Vicar, Fr. Faustino, about this. He sent Lucia back to tell Jacinta that she was not to get out of bed to pray, but that it was perfectly acceptable to pray lying down, as King David did (Ps. 4:4), and then only so long as she could do so without tiring herself. When Jacinta heard this, she asked:

"And will Our Lord be pleased?"

"He is pleased," Lucia answered. "Our Lord wants us to do whatever the Reverend Vicar says."

"That's all right, then. I won't get up any more."

Towards the end of December, 1919, Jacinta had another visitation from the Blessed Virgin. "She told me that I am going to Lisbon to another hospital; that I will not see you again, nor my parents either, and after suffering a great deal, I shall die alone. But she said

7. Quoted in Fox, 87.

I must not be afraid, since she herself is coming to take me to heaven." Then she hugged Lucia and wept: "I will never see you again! You won't be coming to visit me there. Oh please, pray hard for me, I am going to die alone." A few days later, Lucia found Jacinta clasping a picture of Our Lady of Sorrows. She was frightened and was crying. "O my dearest heavenly Mother, do I have to die all alone?" This prayer reminds us of Christ's anguished cry in the garden, "Father, if it be possible…"

Lucia tried to comfort the trembling child: "What does it matter if you die alone, so long as Our Lady is coming to fetch you?"

"It's true, it doesn't really matter. I do not know why, but I sometimes forget Our Lady is coming to take me. I only remember that I will die without having you near me."

The family could not accept Jacinta's assurances that she would be taken to a hospital in Lisbon. After all, she had already been in one hospital, and it had done nothing except make her worse. It was obvious that she was not going to recover from her illnesses or her infected wound; she was virtually a skeleton. Besides, who would defray the expense of another sojourn in hospital? And why should it be a hospital in a city over ninety miles away? They simply thought Jacinta was becoming delirious.

Suddenly, in the middle of January 1920, an automobile pulled up outside the Marto home. Out of the car stepped Dr. Formigao, who by this time was an intimate friend of the family, and one Dr. Eurico Lisboa and his wife, who had just been for a run to the Cova da Iria to try out their brand new car. Dr. Lisboa has left a description of what transpired that day.

> On our way through Santarem we went to pay our respects to Dr. Formigao, who we knew could tell us all about Fatima and the events of which he had been a witness. Dr. Formigao, whom we had not known personally before, but who has been our intimate friend ever since, had the kindness to accompany us to Fatima on that occasion and it was through him that we came to know the seers, Jacinta and Lucia.
>
> After a visit to the Cova with Lucia, in whose company we prayed the Rosary with unforgettable faith and devotion, we returned to Fatima, where we spoke to Jacinta and the mothers of

the two seers. They told us about Francisco, who had been a victim of the wide-spread epidemic of pneumonia influenza which had swept with such tragic results through Europe. He has, we learned, realized his only wish since the apparitions, which was to go to Our Lady. He refused all help and advice from the people, who knew him in his life and only desired death, with the least possible delay.

Little Jacinta was very pale and thin and walked with great difficulty. The family told me she was very ill, which they hardly regretted, because Jacinta's only ambition also was to go to Our Lady, whose will it was that she should die in the same way as Francisco.

When I censured them for their lack of effort to save their daughter, they told me that it was not worthwhile, because Our Lady wished to take her, and that she had been interned for two months in the local hospital without any improvement in her condition.

I replied that Our Lady's will was certainly more powerful than any human efforts and that in order to be certain that she really wished to take Jacinta, they must not neglect any of the normal aids of science to save her life.

Impressed by my words, they went to ask the advice of Dr. Formigao, who supported my opinion in every respect. It was therefore arranged on the spot that Jacinta should be sent to Lisbon and treated by the best doctors in one of the hospitals of the capital.

And in fact, some days later, on 2nd February, 1920, Jacinta was interned in Ward 1, bed no. 38 of the Dona Estefania [St. Stephen] Hospital, under the care of Dr. Castro Freire, then, and now, one of the most famous children's specialists in Lisbon. The diagnosis was as follows: purulent pleurisy, osteitis of the 7th and 8th ribs.[8]

This decision by Dr. Lisboa was a shrewd one, since it quashed any rumors that Jacinta died because of a neglect purposely contrived to fulfill Our Lady's prophecy. The doctor had connections in Lisbon, which enabled him to expedite the arrangements very quickly. Expenses were no difficulty, either. Dr. Lisboa had several wealthy friends who were willing to cover the costs. Among these was the Baron Alvaiazere, whose sister, Maria Celeste, was one of the witnesses to the Miracle of the Sun. Little did she know, that day

8. Quoted in ibid., 90–91.

at Fatima, that she would be contributing to the fulfillment of another of Our Lady's prophecies.

Reluctantly, the Martos had consented to the doctor's proposal. When they informed Jacinta of the decision she remarked between sobs: "Yes, Father, I am in a fine way to go to Lisbon!"

"It has to be, dear. Otherwise everyone will say that we have neglected to have treatment. Perhaps, after all, you will be all right."

"Father dear, even if I recover from this illness, I should get another straight away. If I go to Lisbon, it means goodbye."

"Indeed," comments Ti Marto, "she was a sorry sight. Her heart was enlarged and her digestive organs ruined. It did seem as if she would not recover."

Before leaving, Jacinta requested that she be taken one last time to the Cova da Iria where she could gather some of the flowers she loved so much. After placing the flowers in the chapel, she paused to say a Rosary. Then she prayed in her own simple fashion. Turning to Olimpia, she said: "Mother, when Our Lady went away, she passed over those trees, and afterwards she entered heaven so quickly that I thought she would get her feet caught!"

In the meantime, Ti Marto had gone to Ourem to see the Baron Alvaiazere, who had agreed to assist with the train fare. It had been arranged that Olimpia and their son, Antonio, who could read, would take Jacinta from Chao da Macas to Lisbon, and that a white handkerchief would identify Jacinta to the personages who were to escort her to her destination. That night, Ti Marto gave his last-minute instructions to Olimpia:

When you get into the train you must ask the other people to excuse you because your little girl is very ill, and it is because of this that she has an unpleasant smell. Be very careful that she doesn't lean out of the window when another train is passing. When you are going through the Rossio tunnel [into Lisbon] do not forget to tie on the white handkerchief and do not worry.[9]

Early next morning the time approached for Jacinta and Lucia to

9. de Marchi, 195.

part for the last time. Lucia recalls the heartbreak of this final farewell.

> For a long time, she clung to me with her arms around my neck,
> and sobbed: "We shall never see each other again! Pray a lot for
> me, until I go to heaven. Then I will pray a lot for you. Never tell
> the secret to anyone, even if they kill you. Love Jesus and the
> Immaculate Heart of Mary very much, and make many sacrifices
> for sinners."[10]

On 21 January 1920, Jacinta was taken to Lisbon. After some difficulty in locating temporary accommodation, she was finally admitted to an orphanage attached to a convent run by a Franciscan nun
named Madre Godinho. Olimpia stayed with her for over a week
until she was called to the bedside of her other daughter, Florinda,
who had taken ill. She also had to discuss with her husband the
advisability of allowing Jacinta to undergo another operation. Sor-
rowfully, Olimpia returned to Aljustrel, wondering if she would
ever see her youngest child again.

During the few days that she spent in the convent, Jacinta was
extremely happy. She loved being surrounded by other children,
and Madre Godinho was very pleasant and kind. All the children
loved her whom they called *Madrinha* (Godmother), and Jacinta
was happy to do so also. Attached to the convent was a small chapel.
Jacinta felt very privileged to be able to live under the same roof as
Jesus in the Blessed Sacrament and to receive her Lord daily. She
was allowed to sit in a little chair in the choir loft, where she con-
templated the Real Presence in the Eucharistic Host. She remained
for hours with her eyes fixed upon the Tabernacle, praying and
meditating. Whenever people in the church below were not composing themselves with the proper respect and dignity, she would
complain to Madre Godinho, pointing out that such behavior
offended Our Lord and Lady. Madre Godinho wrote of her:

> I soon began to realise that a little angel had come into my house.
> Although I had long wanted to see the privileged children of

10. *Memoirs*, 46.

Fatima, I never imagined that I would have the good fortune to shelter one under my roof.

We had some twenty to twenty-five children in the asylum. Jacinta was friendly with them all, but she preferred the company of a little girl about her own age to whom she would give little sermons. It was delightful to hear them, and hidden behind the half-open door, I assisted at many of these conversations.

"You must not lie, or be lazy or disobedient, and you must bear everything with patience for love of Our Lord if you want to go to heaven." She spoke with such authority; hardly like a child.[11]

Madre Godinho wrote down many of Jacinta's sayings:

"The sins which cause most souls to go to hell are the sins of the flesh." (That little Jacinta had no understanding of what "the sins of the flesh were" is revealed in an episode later recalled by Olimpia. One evening at home Jacinta said to her mother: "Mother, you must never eat flesh (meat) on Fridays, nor give it to us, because Our Lady said that sins of the flesh brought many people to hell.")

"Fashions will much offend Our Lord. People who serve God should not follow the fashions. Woe to women wanting in modesty. Women are worse than men on account of the fashions. The Church has no fashions. Our Lord is always the same."

"Wars are punishments for sin. Our Lady cannot at present avert the justice of her Son from the world. Penance is necessary. If people amend their lives, Our Lord will even yet save the world, but if not, punishment will come. If men knew what eternity is, they would do everything to change their lives."

"Madrinha, you must pray much for sinners and for priests and for religious. Priests should concern themselves with the affairs of the Church. Priests should be very, very pure. The disobedience of priests and religious to their superiors and to the Holy Father offends Our Lord very greatly."

"Pray, Madrinha, for those who govern. Heaven forgive those who persecute the Church of Christ. If the government would leave

11. Fox, 94.

the Church in peace and give liberty to religion, it would have God's blessing."

"Madrinha, do not walk in the midst of luxury. Flee from riches. Love poverty and silence. Have charity even for the wicked. Speak evil of no one and avoid those who do. Mortification and sacrifice are very pleasing to Our Lord. Our Lady likes those who mortify their senses, and those who help one another to have faith, hope, and charity."

"Confession is a sacrament of mercy. For this reason it is necessary to approach the confessional with confidence and joy. Without confession, there is no salvation. God does not wish the death of the sinner; He wants them to be converted to give glory to God on earth and in heaven."

"The Mother of God wants more virgin souls, who bind themselves to her by the vow of chastity. To be a religious, it is necessary to be very pure in soul and body."

Madre Godinho asked Jacinta if she understood what it means to be pure. "To be pure in body means to be chaste, and to be pure in mind means not to commit sins; not to look at what one should not see, not to steal, never to lie, and always to speak the truth even when it is hard."

"Who taught you these things?" asked Mother Godinho.

"Our Lady, but some of them I thought myself. I love to think."

Such was the simple wisdom which nine-year-old Jacinta loved to share with her Madrinha and the children. However, this happy interlude was soon curtailed, as Our Lady had further sufferings with which to grace her. On February 2, the Feast of the Purification of Our Lady, Dr. Lisboa had arranged to have Jacinta transferred to Dona Estefania Hospital. On the way, she had to endure a preliminary examination at St. Joseph's teaching hospital. So great was her love for modesty that she wept with embarrassment when she was exposed to the scrutiny of doctors and students.

Madre Godinho accompanied her to Dona Estefania, where she was placed in bed 38 of the children's ward. She visited Jacinta every day. On one occasion, she related to Jacinta a fine sermon given by a visiting priest, who was much praised by fashionable ladies for his theatrical style of delivery. Jacinta replied: "When you least expect it, you will see that that padre is wicked." A few months later, he abandoned the priesthood under scandalous circumstances. Jacinta also prophesied that her two sisters, Florinda and Teresa, would die—a prophecy that was fulfilled shortly after her own death. Jacinta told a doctor, who had asked her to pray for him in heaven, that both he and his daughter would die shortly after her death— and they did. She also foretold that Madre Godinho would visit the Cova da Iria after her death, "and so will I," Jacinta said of herself.

On another occasion Jacinta asked to have a medal coined with Our Lady of Fatima on one side and an angel on the other. A tiny medal was coined with an image of Our Lady of Fatima on one side, but, instead of the requested angel, it had "Souvenir of Fatima" written on the other side. Jacinta was given this medal to hold. It was not until many years later that Lucia disclosed the apparition of the angel in her memoirs. Madre Godinho also remembers having heard Jacinta praying one of the prayers taught by the angel.

On February 10, Jacinta was taken to the operating room. Because of her weakened condition, she could only receive a local anesthetic. Dr. Castro Freire proceeded to extract the two infected ribs, leaving a gaping wound in her side the size of his fist. Jacinta cried out in agony, "*Ai, Nossa Senhora,*" "Oh, Our Lady." Then she would tell herself, "Patience! . . . It is for love of you, my Jesus." After it was over, she was taken back to the ward, and placed in bed number 60. Her daily dressings also brought her extreme agony, causing her to cry, "*Ai, Nossa Senhora,* now you can convert many sinners, for I suffer much." Yet she accepted all this pain and discomfort without any complaint.

One week later, on the 17th, Our Lady visited Jacinta on this earth for the last time. Jacinta confided to Madre Godinho, "Now I am much better. Our Lady said that she would soon come to fetch me and that she would take away the pain." A report by Dr. Lisboa confirms this:

> And in fact, with the apparition there in the middle of the ward, her pain completely disappeared and she began to be able to play and enjoy certain distractions. She liked to look at holy pictures,

one among them in particular—given me later as a souvenir—of Our Lady of Sameiro which she said most closely resembled the Lady of the apparitions. I was told several times that Jacinta wished to see me, but as my professional duties were heavy and Jacinta was apparently better, I, unfortunately, put off my visit until too late.[12]

At six o'clock on the evening of Friday, February 20, Jacinta asked for her nurse, Aurora Gomez, and told her that she was about to die and that she wanted the sacraments. Two hours later, Rev. Dr. Pereira dos Reis, priest of the Church of the Holy Angels, heard her confession. Although Jacinta had urged that the Blessed Sacrament be brought to her as Viaticum, Dr. Reis disagreed, as she appeared quite well. He promised to bring her Holy Communion the next morning, even though she again requested Viaticum, insisting that she would shortly die.

At 10:30 that night, Sister Aurora left Jacinta for a few moments, and returned just in time to witness Jacinta's last gasp. Her cheeks were a rosy pink, and she was smiling peacefully. Our Lady had come to escort Jacinta into heaven just three weeks before her tenth birthday.

The next day, Jacinta was laid out according to her wishes, in a white communion dress and a blue, silk sash—the colors of Our Lady. Madre Godinho, who washed the body, noticed tears of dried blood on her flushed cheeks. She was laid in a little white coffin which was taken to the Church of the Holy Angels, where it was placed on two stools in a corner of the sacristy. News of the death of the little visionary spread rapidly, and many of the faithful of Lisbon sent money for the funeral expenses. The funeral was to be held that very Sunday. However, the fervency and devotion of these people, who were constantly praying before the coffin and touching Rosaries, crucifixes, and images to her body, was such that Dr. Reis decided to order them out of the sacristy. This otherwise charitable and courteous priest did not want to offend against official procedure, which does not permit honors to the dead until such time as their sanctity has been approved. Moreover, there was a real danger

12. Ibid., 99.

of the spread of disease from the open coffin. So he had the body transferred to a leaden coffin, which was sealed and deposited in the confraternity room above the sacristy. A firm of undertakers, Antonio Almeida and Co., dressed the body. Sr. Almeida, who assisted at the undertaking process himself, later remarked:

> I seem to see Jacinta still, looking like a little angel. In her coffin she seemed to be alive; her lips and cheeks were a beautiful pink. I have seen many corpses, large and small, but I have never seen anything like that. The beautiful perfume which the body exhaled could not be explained naturally and the hardest skeptic could not doubt it. One remembers the smell, which so often makes it repugnant to remain near a corpse, and yet this child had been dead three days and a half and the smell of her body was like a bouquet of flowers.[13]

It was arranged that the coffin would be taken to Ourem, where Jacinta's family could attend the funeral. When Ti Marto met the train, he broke down and cried like a child. He felt that all the ministrations had been useless. "She had been in the hospital here two months and then gone to Lisbon and in the end she died all alone . . . !" he said. On Tuesday, February 24, the body of the little mystic was laid to rest in the family vault of the Baron of Alvaiazere. Lucia, back in Aljustrel, heard the ringing of the funeral bells. Realizing that they were tolling for Jacinta, she ran to the Loca do Cabeço and flung herself upon the ground, sobbing her heart out until nightfall. Only then did she return home, her eyes red from weeping.

Later in 1935, after a canonical inquiry had been made into the extraordinary facts of Jacinta's life, the Bishop of Leiria felt it desirable to have Jacinta's body brought to Fatima to be laid next to the mortal remains of Francisco. Upon opening the coffin, to everyone's astonishment the body of Jacinta was found to be incorrupt, despite the quicklime used in the burial. The body also exuded a noticeable fragrance like flowers. Photographs were taken and the body was touched with religious objects. The coffin was sealed and

---

13. Ibid., 104.

transported to the Cova da Iria, fulfilling Jacinta's prophecy. Later, on 5 May, 1951, the body was once again exhumed and taken to its final destination in the Basilica at Fatima, when it was again found to be in a remarkable state of preservation. Thus, Jacinta, like St. Bernadette of Lourdes, St. Catherine Labouré of Paris, and many other saints and venerables before her, joined the worthy lineage of incorruptibles within the Church.[14] Above her tomb in the floor of a room in the Basilica were the words: "Here lie the mortal remains of Jacinta Marto, to whom Our Lady appeared." On 13 March of the following year, Francisco was brought to the same room to lie opposite his sister's tomb under a similar epitaph.

A photograph taken in 1951 of Olimpia and Manual (Ti) Marto outside their home in Aljustrel.

14. See Joan Carroll Cruz, *The Incorruptibles*, for descriptions, photographs, and the locations where one can see today the remarkably preserved bodies of those worthies who have remained incorrupt since death.

The incorrupt remains of Jacinta unearthed in 1935
when she was moved to St. Anthony's, Fatima.

Lucia's family, taken shortly after the death of her father.
Maria Rosa is seated with Lucia standing by her side.

Triumph of the Immaculate Heart

LUCIA WAS ALONE with her memories. She could not attend to her daily tasks without something to remind her of her little companions. She would touch a wall, and there would be Francisco reclining on the top, blowing his flute; or smell a flower and recall how Jacinta would pick them and weave them into garlands for her hair. The bleating of lambs at springtime would evoke an image of Jacinta skipping home from the Cabeço with a lamb round her shoulders. An oak tree would conjure up a boy climbing to pick bitter acorns for mortification. At Mass, the Eucharistic host would remind her of Francisco praying to console the sorrowing Jesus. The moon at night, was that not Our Lady's lamp? Or the brilliant sun of day, was that not Our Lord's lamp? She had but to tread on a coil of rope for her saintly friends to appear before her. Such intimacies as these always belong to those who experience things in common. But who has seen Our Lady? Who has been bathed in the light of God? They alone had beheld the angel who taught them how to pray and to make sacrifices for others. An enchanting and beautiful Lady had entrusted them with many special and secret things. Together, they had endured persecutions and threats of death, had seen miracles and had suffered death in their own ways. Now that her cousins were gone, she no longer had anyone with whom she could share the wondrous and ominous things they alone had in common. Never again on this earth would Lucia have anyone who could possibly understand what she alone understood.

Lucia had to remain behind, for she had a task to fulfill. Our Lady had said to her on her second visitation:

"I will take Jacinta and Francisco soon. But you are to stay here some time longer. Jesus wishes to make use of you to make me known and loved. He wants to establish devotion to my Immaculate Heart."

"Am I to stay here alone?"

"No, my daughter. Are you suffering a great deal? Do not lose heart. I will never forsake you. My Immaculate Heart will be your refuge and the way that will lead you to God."

Now that Lucia remained the only visionary of Fatima, she became the focus of the attention of the world and the Church. She was even called upon to supervise the sculpting of the first statue of Our Lady of Fatima by Jose Ferreira Thedim. Commissioned by Gilberto dos Santos, of Torres Novas, the image, made of cedar wood from Brazil, was enthroned in the Little Chapel on 13 June, 1920.

Bishop of Leiria-Fatima, Dom José Alvares Correia da Silva

In 1918 Leiria had been restored as a diocese independent from Lisbon so that the Church could oversee the developments at the Cova more closely. On May 15, 1920, three months after Jacinta's death, Dr. José Alves Correia da Silva was consecrated Bishop. Born near Braga in 1877, Dom José was of medium height, dark and stocky. He suffered from a limp received from having been forced by republican inquisitors to stand in ice water day and night. He had a singular devotion to Our Lady of Lourdes and had made six pilgrimages to her shrine. His scholarship and popularity as Professor at the Seminary at Porto earned him recognition as far away as Rome, which secured for him his appointment as Bishop.

Upon taking up his duties on August 5, Dom José immediately found himself in the midst of a furor. Firstly, he had to decide what to do with the 357,000 reis collected by Maria da Capelinha. Then, a delegate from the Patriarchate of Lisbon delivered to him a complete dossier on Fatima for him to scrutinize and adjudicate. For there were also detractors of Fatima who called for the new Bishop to take action to suppress the devotions there. It was obvious that a thorough examination must be made before any decisions could be executed. Therefore, discretion demanded that Dom José remove Lucia to a place where she could be observed free from the pressure of those innumerable questions and visits inflicted upon her by pilgrims. With the last of the seers absent from Fatima, the constancy of their devotion could be tested.

After much deliberation, the following year Bishop da Silva sent word to Maria Rosa to bring Lucia to be interviewed on the Feast of St. Anthony (June 13). After a long chat, the Bishop asked Lucia how she would feel about leaving Aljustrel to attend a good school. He pointed out that she would be free from the endless questions and controversies, that she would be in new surroundings that would take her out of her grief, that she would learn to read and to write, and that her family would at last be able to return to a normal life. Maria Rosa was relieved at the suggestion, since the events of Fatima had caused her nothing but trouble. Lucia's attitude was one of obedience and submission to her Bishop. Thus, it was decided that Lucia should enter a boarding school run by the Sisters of Saint Dorothy in Vilar, a suburb of Oporto, and that she must start preparing to leave within a few days.

The day of departure was to be the 16th of June, 1921. Lucia had been instructed to say nothing of her parting to anyone. "When you go away you must come and say goodbye to me," Maria Capelinha had requested of her a fortnight earlier. But Lucia was bound to obey her Bishop and could not bid farewell even to this dear lady, who had given her so much solid support. The evening before her embarkation, Lucia visited the familiar haunts which had come to hold so many precious and intimate memories. She went first to the Cabeço, where the angel had first appeared. There she prostrated herself on the ground and prayed the angel's prayer to the Holy Trinity. Next, at Valinhos, she recalled the consoling apparition after their beautiful Lady had delivered them from the kidnappers. Then she visited the cemetery where the remains of her father and Francisco were buried. She prayed for her father and asked Francisco to pray for her. Returning home, she stopped at the well at the bottom of the garden, where she recalled the many trysts the children held there and the special prayers they uttered.

At two o'clock in the morning Lucia departed Aljustrel without saying a word to anyone. She was accompanied by her mother and by a poor laborer who was also travelling to Leiria. On the way, she made her last visit to the Cova da Iria. There she knelt down and offered up a Rosary to the Blessed Lady who had so loved this prayer. As Lucia departed the Cova, she kept looking back in order to imprint the miraculous spot on her memory exactly as it was. Almost a quarter of a century would pass before she would see it again.

At eleven a.m., Lucia and her mother arrived in Leiria, where they were met by Dona Filomena Miranda, an envoy of the Bishop. At two o'clock, Lucia gave her mother her last embrace. With copious tears drenching her cheeks and a heart filled with sorrow, Lucia boarded the train for distant Oporto.

Lucia and her guide arrived at the Asilo of the Sisters of Saint Dorothy. Because they had arrived during Mass, Lucia was taken directly to the chapel, where she was able to receive Holy Communion before being presented to the Mother Superior. The Reverend Mother was unimpressed by the simple girl of fourteen. She had refused to accept her at first, remonstrating with the Bishop that she wanted no simpletons exerting a backward influence upon the other pupils in her school. "Yes, she is simple," Dom José had agreed, "but I do not think you will find her a simpleton, and I desire that you take her for a while." As she looked upon the tired and disheveled shepherdess standing before her, sullenly staring back under her dark brows, and with a stubborn pout fixed upon her thick, extended lips, the Reverend Mother had even greater reservations about admitting her. However, she had already promised the Bishop.

"When they ask you your name you will reply, 'Call me Maria of the Sorrows.'"

"Yes, Reverend Mother."

"When they ask you where you are from, you will say, 'I am from Lisbon.'"

"Yes, Reverend Mother."

"As for what happened at Fatima, never again mention it to anyone, either by question or by answer."

"Yes, Reverend Mother."

Lucia as a Sister of Dorothy in Tuy, Spain.

Lucia, now Maria das Dores, was taken to her room and given her new uniform of black-and-white checkered gingham. For the next four years, she was to lead the unobtrusive and obedient life of a convent student. After daily Mass, she would attend her lessons, where she learned grammar, reading, writing, needlework, and typewriting. She also received religious instruction and Church history. Then there followed endless chores, such as scrubbing floors, cooking, and polishing the brass and silver. All of these were interspersed with periods of prayer and recreation. None of this was taxing or oppressive to Lucia, who was used to manual work and loved the peaceful, reflective atmosphere.

Soon, Maria das Dores found herself an accepted part of convent life. The sisters at the convent came to respect her simple obedience and her unselfish willingness to sacrifice for others. Then there was her extraordinary devotion to prayer and to the sacrament. Much of her leisure time was spent in the chapel, kneeling before the Blessed Sacrament, praying quietly the adoring prayers taught her by the angel. She began to read the lives of the saints, becoming especially fond of the autobiography of St. Therese (the "Little Flower") of Lisieux, beatified in 1923.

After four years of convent life, Maria das Dores decided that, like the "Little Flower of Lisieux," she wanted to enter the Carmelite order. However, the Mother Superior objected, remarking that she was not strong enough for such austerities. It was eventually agreed that she should become a Sister of Saint Dorothy instead. In 1925 she entered the Dorothean order in Tuy, just across the Spanish border. One year later, on November 2, 1926, at the age of nineteen, she became a novice. Two years later she took her vows and six years after that, on October 3, 1934, she made them perpetual. She was then transferred to the convent at Pontevedra and only returned to Tuy in May 1937, where she was to remain until she returned to Portugal in May 1946.

While she was at Tuy, Sister Dores had further visions. At the Cova, the Lady of the Rosary had promised to return another time to ask for the reparation of the five first Saturdays and at a still later time to ask for the consecration of Russia. On the night of 10 December, 1925, the most holy Virgin appeared, elevated and standing on a cloud with the Christ child by her side. The Blessed Virgin rested her right hand on Lucia's shoulder, while in her left hand she held a heart encircled with thorns. The apparition of the Christ child said:

"Have compassion on the Heart of your most holy Mother, covered with thorns, with which ungrateful men pierce it at every moment, and there is no one to make an act of reparation to remove them."

Then the Blessed Virgin responded:

"Look, my daughter, at my Heart, surrounded by thorns with which ungrateful men pierce me at every moment by their blasphemies and ingratitude. You, at least, try to console me and say that I promise to assist at the hour of death, with the graces necessary for salvation, all those who, on the first Saturday of five consecutive months, shall confess, receive Holy Communion, recite five decades of the Rosary, and keep me company for fifteen minutes while meditating on the fifteen mysteries of the Rosary, with the intention of making reparation to me."

Here we have the first secret of Fatima: devotion to the Immaculate Heart of Mary. Until this moment, none of the children had revealed this secret to anyone. Now Sister Lucia was being asked to make this devotion known to the world. Of course, we are aware that this devotion is linked to the second secret—the conversion of Russia—but here, Our Lady promises to assist those who make this devotion with the graces necessary to ensure their final perseverance in the faith.

The following February, on the 15th, the child Jesus, symbolizing the childlike acceptance and trust inherent in this devotion, appeared again to Sister Lucia, asking: "What is being done to establish devotion to the Heart of my Mother?" She was assured that, in spite of the difficulties she would experience, through His grace she would succeed. At that time, the Mother Superior strongly desired the propagation of this devotion. However, Sister Lucia's confessor and spiritual director, Fr. P. Apparicio, admonished her that she should understand that her Mother Superior could not achieve this by herself. Hence Jesus's reply to Lucia's objection: "It is true that your superior alone can do nothing, but with my grace she can do all." Fr. Apparicio then asked her to write an account of this apparition. Since it involved betraying the first secret, Sr. Lucia was unsure what to do.

On December 17, 1927, Sr. Lucia was kneeling before the tabernacle, beseeching her Lord how she could comply with her confessor's request to establish this devotion. Through an inner locution, she obtained these words, which she understood were from Jesus: "My daughter, write what they ask of you. Write also all that the most holy Virgin revealed to you in the Apparition in which she spoke of this devotion. As for the remainder of the secret, continue to keep silence."

Thus, Sr. Lucia was directed to reveal the first secret, while suppressing for the time being the portion concerning Russia. A few days later, Sr. Lucia wrote a full account of this apparition, which she forwarded to Msgr. Manuel Pereira Lopes, who had been her confessor during her stay at Vilar do Oporto. Although this account was left unpublished for some time,[1] Dr. Formigao, who had learned of it, became one of the chief propagators of the devotion, which began to spread throughout Portugal and then throughout the world.

Meanwhile, Sister Lucia had been given permission to observe a Holy Hour, in the chapel at Tuy, between the hours of eleven p.m. and midnight each week. During one of these vigils, on 13 June 1929, she received the most wondrous of all her visions. It was a fulfillment of the Blessed Virgin's promise to her in the July apparition: "I shall come to ask for the consecration of Russia to my Immaculate Heart." Sister Lucia describes in her own words this enigmatic vision:

> I had sought and obtained permission from my superiors and confessor to make a Holy Hour from eleven o'clock until midnight, every Thursday to Friday night. Being alone one night, I knelt near the altar rails in the middle of the chapel and, prostrate, I prayed the prayers of the Angel. Feeling tired, I then stood up and continued to say the prayers with my arms in the form of a cross. The only light was that of the sanctuary lamp. Suddenly the whole chapel was illumined by a supernatural light, and above the altar appeared a cross of light, reaching to the ceiling. In a brighter light on the upper part of the cross could be seen the face of a man and his body as far as the waist; upon his breast was a dove of light; nailed to the cross was the body of another man. A little below the waist, I could see a chalice and a large host suspended in the air, on to which drops of blood were falling from the face of Jesus Crucified and from the wound in His side. These drops ran down on to the host and fell into the chalice. Beneath the right arm of the cross was Our Lady and in her hand was her Immaculate.

---

1. It was inserted by Rev. Dr. Sebastiao Martins dos Reis in his book *A Life in the Service of Fatima*, 336–57 and in Lucia's *Memoirs*, 189–97.

Triumph of the Immaculate Heart

(It was Our Lady of Fatima, with her Immaculate Heart in her left hand, without sword or roses, but with a crown of thorns and flames.) Under the left arm of the cross, large letters, as if of crystal clear water which ran down upon the altar, formed these words: "Grace and Mercy."

I understood that it was the Mystery of the Most Holy Trinity which was shown to me, and I received lights about this mystery which I am not permitted to reveal.

Our Lady then said to me: The moment has come in which God asks the Holy Father, in union with all the Bishops of the world, to make the consecration of Russia to my Immaculate Heart, promising to save it by this means. There are so many souls whom the Justice of God condemns for sins committed against me, that I have come to ask reparation: sacrifice yourself for this intention and pray.

This sublime vision contains all the elements that we have discussed previously: the Holy Trinity, the Real Presence in the Eucharist, the Immaculate Heart of Mary, and the need for personal sacrifice for others in spite of hardship and suffering. We have also mentioned before why the consecration of Russia had to be done through the union of all the Bishops: Our Lady's intention was to bring about a singleness of mind and unity of spirit among contemporary Bishops. Clearly, this has not yet been accomplished, since many modern Bishops have deliberately chosen to swallow just those errors spewed forth (Rev. 12:15) by those promoting the ideology which Russia had embraced. These errors essentially deny the traditional teaching of the Church that salvation and the kingdom come through the blood of Christ alone, i.e., it is Eucharistic in substance.

On the contrary, the contemporary view holds that salvation is to be sought and achieved through the construction of a social order that will rectify the ills which come only from society. According to this view, the problems of humanity are social in origin, such that if we can only correct the present-day evil of social and economic structures, the Kingdom of God will arrive on earth. It is the *sine qua non* of Marxist teaching that change in the infrastructure of society (namely ownership of the means of production) determines everything else in the superstructure of society (namely crime, oppression, injustice, poverty, violence, and war). The whole of contemporary theology is permeated with this materialistic, indeed, consequentialist view that social and personal problems derive solely from faulty social and personal relationships.

However, the traditional teaching of the Church and the canonical teaching of Sacred Scripture has been that social, personal, and economic problems are rooted in our fundamental alienation from God (Gen. 3:17–19, 22–24; Rom. 5:12–14; 1 Cor. 15:21–22), and that a solution will not be achieved in any of these areas until we are reconciled to Him (Jn. 15:5; 2 Cor. 3:5; Phil. 2:13, 4:13; Col. 3:1–3; Rev. 21:5–7). This reconciliation is effected through the sacrifice of Christ on the cross, whence we are directed to seek union with God. The reason for this is essential to the Divine Nature: whatsoever the Father does is for the honor and dignity of His Son, whose image He is. Therefore, He would not call us to walk a path different from that chosen by His beloved Son, the way of the cross, the way of loving self-sacrifice for others. The Eucharistic emphasis in this vision is obvious: the source of our life and strength, our wisdom and compassion, comes only from the Divine Bread of Life given up for us, upon which we must feed in order to regain that fullness of life from which the fiery angel has barred us (Gen. 3:22–24).

This truth is emphasized in the sublime vision of Sr. Lucia: Christ alone can give us eternal life (Jn. 14:6). We must not allow this supreme Source to be eclipsed by some other arbitrary and all-too-human path. For in the July apparition, Our Lady of the Rosary had already denounced the materialist-historicist aspirations of the Marxists as error. It is in order to demonstrate this error and to save the Church from its tribulation that she came to provide the only possible alternative: devotion and imitation of that Immaculate Heart which constantly and reverently reflects upon and consents to obey the sublime mysteries of the life, death, and resurrection of Our Lord and Savior, Jesus Christ. As we have seen, the Rosary prayer is the very analogue of this Heart. In other words, to reflect deeply upon the Person of Christ and to consent to follow His Truth is to have the Immaculate Heart of Mary, and, vice versa, to possess the Heart of Mary is to reflect upon and consent to the Truth manifested in the very Person of Our Lord. For the Rosary prayer contains all the teachings and mysteries traditionally held by the Church, guided by the Holy Spirit (Mt. 16:19; Jn. 16:13–15)—traditions which are given heavenly sanction by the apparitions of Fatima and the visions vouchsafed to Sister Lucia.

The repercussions of Fatima upon modern error are clear. That is why the Mother of the Church asked for a collegial consecration of Russia to Her Immaculate Heart. In a flash of heavenly brilliance, she points out the source of modern error, its nature, and the means to its end. The prayers and sacrifices of the faithful, centered upon the Eucharistic devotion of the five first Saturdays, will lead to a spiritual awakening that will compel the Church to act in collegial unison. That very unison will heal the divisions in the Church by identifying and acting upon the source of all error: lack of universal, personal consecration to and imitation of the Immaculate Heart which God first gave to that Woman of Zion, upon whom the entire Old Testament expectation devolved.

Everything God does is in honor of the dignity of His Son, who is the reflected image of the Father. This is the reason why the image of the Trinity overshadows the image of Our Lady in the vision given to Sr. Lucia. Even the Immaculate Heart that Jesus gave to His Mother would have to reflect that loving Holy Spirit, that Blessed Life of the Trinity, shared by the Father for the Son, and the Son for the Father. It is impossible that God should give the Mother of Our Lord any other Heart. And it is impossible that we should be called to imitate any other Heart than the Heart of Jesus, given to the Blessed Mother of Our Lord and, through Him, of the Church.

No wonder that Jesus wants to establish devotion to the Immaculate Heart of His Mother, and no wonder that Russia has been made the crucible for this devotion: they exclude each other. The materialistic and anthropocentric aspirations of Marxist ideology oppose the Spiritual and Christocentric nature of the Immaculate Heart given to Mary. Where one's treasure is, there is one's heart (Mt. 6:21). A heart centered upon the world is ruled by the world. A heart centered upon Christ, as Mary's is, is ruled by Christ. The message of Fatima is that the latter will triumph.

The Blessed Virgin Mary, through her solicitude for the Church, has selected a pre-eminently practical devotion to this end: the prayers of the Rosary. The truths they express, the spirit of grace and mercy they evoke, the discipline and obedience they require, their ambiance and sublimity, their faith and devotion, express and imitate that Heart which has been made the exemplar of perfect discipleship. The Rosary devotion is the analogue, the disciplinary process that can render us immaculate, too. To recite the Rosary and to meditate upon the mysteries of the gospel is to have the Heart of Mary which kept all these things. And to have the Heart of Mary is to quietly reflect upon Our Blessed Lord and Savior and to willingly follow Him.

But why has Our Lady, in this current vision, asked for the *five* first Saturdays? Why not seven, for the seven sorrows of Our Lady? The answer was given in a letter dated the 12 June, 1930, addressed simply "Reverend Father."[2] In that letter, Sr. Lucia tells us that during her Holy Hour of 29–30 May, she received the following locution:

> My daughter, the motive is simple. There are five kinds of offences or blasphemies uttered against the Immaculate Heart of Mary: (1) blasphemies against the Immaculate Conception; (2) blasphemies against her virginity; (3) blasphemies against her divine maternity and, at the same time, refusal to recognize her as Mother of men; (4) blasphemies by those who openly seek to foster in the hearts of children indifference, contempt, or even hatred for the Immaculate Mother; (5) offences by those who insult her directly in her sacred images.

Of course, any insult directed towards anyone (let alone the Mother of Our Lord) who comes in the name of Christ is an insult directed to Jesus (Mt. 25:40); any encouragement to such a sin is a dishonor to Our Lord (18:5–7); and to dishonor the Mother whom He honors, dishonors the Son also (Lk. 10:16; Jn. 12:48; Lk. 2:34–35; Jn. 19:27). Yet Jesus replied to Sr. Lucia that the effect of this reparation (of five first Saturdays) would be that He "will show compassion by forgiving those souls who have had the misfortune to offend her [Mary]." "As for you," Our Lord said to Sr. Lucia, "strive without

---

2. Quoted in Pelletier, *Exciting Fatima News*, 46; Cf. Martins & Fox, *Documents on Fatima*, 245–46.

ceasing by your prayers and sacrifices to move Me to compassion toward these poor souls."

Meanwhile, after exhaustive investigations into the events of Fatima, after critical analyses of personal testimonies, depositions, and official reports, and after comparison of reams of material from lengthy interrogations, the Church was ready to pronounce on the authenticity of the apparitions at Fatima. Such a pronouncement must have been cautiously made, for if it should ever be shown that Fatima resulted from a hoax, hysteria, or natural causes, the Church would find itself discredited. This holds especially true regarding the numerous cures which pilgrims claimed to have received while praying at Fatima or as a direct result of prayers offered there. In order to establish that such cures were indeed miraculous, rigorous criteria established by Pope Benedict XIV needed to be satisfied. These criteria were executed by the Lourdes Medical Bureau, which examines all such cases.

The investigations into the phenomena at Fatima, which began in 1922, were completed by April 14, 1929. On October 1, 1930 Bishop da Silva issued a pastoral epistle entitled "The Divine Providence" in which he declared the visions of Lucia, Francisco, and Jacinta worthy of belief. After having described in some detail the virtues, visions, and sufferings of the shepherd children, the Bishop declared:

> In virtue of the consideration made known, and others which for reason of brevity we omit; humbly invoking the Divine Spirit and placing ourselves under the protection of the most Holy Virgin, and after hearing the opinions of the Rev. Advisers of this diocese, we thereby:
>
> First, declare worthy of belief, the visions of the shepherd children in the Cova da Iria, parish of Fatima, in this diocese, from the 13th of May to October, 1917.
>
> Secondly, permit officially the cult of Our Lady of Fatima.

After the vision of the Trinity, Sr. Lucia began to work even more diligently to obtain the consecration of Russia to the Immaculate Heart of Mary. On 29 May 1930, Sr. Lucia wrote to Fr. Jose Goncalves, her confessor, that "the good Lord promises to end the persecution in Russia, if the Holy Father deigns to make and command the bishops of the Catholic world to also make a solemn and public act of reparation and consecration of Russia to the Very Holy Hearts of Jesus and Mary, and (if he also) promises that at the conclusion of this persecution, he will approve and recommend the practice of the devotion of reparation mentioned above." (This last referred to the devotion of the five first Saturdays.)

Another letter, written May 18, 1936, further elucidates the issue of why Russia must be consecrated in this particular way—by the college of Bishops in unison with the Pope—and why the Saturday devotion must be carried on in the precise manner indicated. We quote the relevant part of the letter.

> Intimately, I have spoken to Our Lord about this matter, and not too long ago I asked Him why He did not convert Russia without the Holy Father making the consecration? "Because I want my entire Church to acknowledge that consecration as a triumph of the Immaculate Heart of Mary, in order to later extend its cult and to place the devotion to this Immaculate Heart alongside the devotion to my Sacred Heart."
>
> But, dear Lord, the Holy Father will never believe me, if you yourself do not influence him with a special inspiration.
>
> Oh Holy Father! Pray very much for the Holy Father! He will make the consecration, but it will be late—*mas sera tarde!* However, the Immaculate Heart of Mary will save Russia. It has been entrusted to her.[3]

Here we have clear confirmation of the reason for the particular nature of this consecration: in order to make the world realize that the Lord Jesus Christ has entrusted the conversion of Russia to Mary's Immaculate Heart. The eventual conversion of Russia would be a sign to the world of what the Lord had done.

Two months later, civil war began in Spain, as prophesied by Jacinta, and two years later (25 January, 1938) there appeared in the skies above Europe that strange light foretold during the July apparition. Starting in March 1938, Germany invaded first Austria, then the Sudetenland, Albania, and finally Poland (March, 1939), precipitating the Second World War. In the following year (December 2, 1940), Sister Lucia wrote to Pope Pius XII asking for the Collegial

3. Quoted in Pelletier, 9.

Consecration. On the Silver Jubilee of Fatima (31 October, 1942), the Pope complied, but, instead of Russia alone, consecrated the entire world to Mary's Immaculate Heart. The request was not made in concert with the entire college of Bishops.

In May 1946, Sr. Lucia was invited to return to Aljustrel for the first time in over twenty years. There she identified the various places of the apparitions and submitted to further interrogations. Two years later, Sr. Lucia's original desire to enter the Carmelite order was granted by Pope Pius XII. On March 25, 1948, she entered the Discalced Carmelites in Coimbra, Portugal, a contemplative order based upon the sixteenth century reforms of St. Theresa of Avila. Thus was fulfilled Our Lady's intention, revealed to Lucia at the apparition of the sun. Lucia remained in this order, living a life of constant prayer, penance, and contemplation.

On the Golden Anniversary of Fatima, 13 May, 1967, Sr. Lucia was invited to share the dais with Paul VI when he made his own personal consecration of the world to the Immaculate Heart. This time, mention was made of "those nations, in which religious liberty is almost totally suppressed and where the negation of God is proclaimed as representing the truth of these times and the liberty of the people." But there was still no unity among the Bishops. For this reason, Sister Lucia did not feel that Our Lady's request had yet been properly fulfilled. She said, "the Pope will make the consecration, but it will be late. . . . The consecration of Russia and also the final triumph of the Immaculate Heart of Mary which will follow it, are absolute and will be realized despite all the obstacles."[4]

By this time, the faithful all over the world were keeping the Saturday devotion, maintaining overnight vigils, undergoing pilgrimages to Fatima (oftentimes walking the last hundred meters on their knees), and performing penance and mortification while reciting the Rosary, all to the end that Russia might be consecrated to Mary's Immaculate Heart. Increasingly, petitions were made for the collegial consecration. One of the strongest of these petitions came from a communist-dominated country: a group of Polish Bishops who approached Paul VI in the late seventies, among whom was one

4. Johnston, *Fatima*, 91

Sister Lucia, now a Carmelite, with Pope Paul VI
at the Golden Jubilee in Fatima.

Cardinal Karol Wojtyla (later Pope John Paul II). They requested
that the consecration be made, not solely by the Pope, as Pius XII,
John XXIII, and Paul VI had done, but rather "in union with all the
Bishops of the world."[5]

On October 16, 1978, late in the afternoon, the chimney of the
Sistine Chapel emitted the white smoke announcing the decision
that a new Pope had been elected to succeed the late John Paul I,
following the latter's tragically short reign of only thirty-four days.

5. Fox, 226.

This successor, who took the name of John Paul II, has since been widely regarded as one of the greatest Popes that the Catholic Church has had. Nobel Prize-winning writer Alexander Solzhenitsyn said of him, "This Pope is truly a gift from God." The fact that the first non-Italian Pope in four hundred years should come from a country oppressed by communism is not without significance as far as Fatima is concerned. He would be the pope who, as Our Lady had prophesied in July, 1917, would "have much to suffer." He would also be the one to consecrate Russia to her Immaculate Heart.

On 13 May 1981, while Pope John Paul II was greeting the faithful in St. Peter's Square, he was gunned down at point-blank range. The hired assassin was Mehmet Ali Agca, a supposed "Gray Wolf" member of a Turkish right-wing extremist organization, who also had apparent connections with the communists in Bulgaria. In addition to the wound, which severed his intestines, causing internal hemorrhage, the Pope had contracted a cytomegalovirus, which some say came from contaminated serum and which others attribute to the contaminated bullet. This virus brought him within inches of death. The assassination attempt occurred on the anniversary of Our Lady's first apparition at Fatima. The Pope took this as a sign.

The following May 13, Pope John Paul made a special visit to Fatima to thank Our Lady for her intercession in his remarkable recovery. He also used the anniversary of his assassination to consecrate Russia.

Before leaving for Fatima, the Pope dispatched a letter to the Bishops of the world, calling them to unite in collegial consecration. Writing on the Pope's behalf, the Cardinal Secretary of State said: "I now fulfill the honored task of informing you that in the course of his visit to Fatima on 13 May next, when he intends to thank the Blessed Virgin for having saved his life on the occasion of the attack of 13 May last year, the Holy Father also intends, in spiritual union with all the bishops of the world, to renew the two acts whereby Pope Pius XII entrusted the world to the Immaculate Heart of Mary."

Speaking at the Cova da Iria on May 13, 1982, Pope St. John Paul II averred: "I am here united with all the pastors of the Church in that particular bond whereby we constitute a body and a college, just as Christ desired the Apostles to be in union with Peter. In the bond of this union, I utter the words of the present act, in which I wish to include, once more, the hopes and anxieties of the Church in the modern world." He went on to confirm and renew the previous consecration made in 1942 by Pius XII, mentioning Russia by name: "The appeal of the Lady of the message of Fatima is so deeply rooted in the Gospel and the whole of Tradition that the Church feels that the message imposes a commitment on her. She has responded through the servant of God, Pius XII (whose Episcopal ordination took place precisely on 13 May, 1917): he consecrated the human race and *especially the peoples of Russia* to the Immaculate Heart of Mary." At the mention of Russia, a shout of praise and thanksgiving rang out from the congregation.

We now record further relevant extracts from the Pope's moving and memorable speech:[6]

> And so I come here today because on this very day last year, in Saint Peter's Square in Rome, the attempt on the Pope's life was made, in mysterious coincidence with the anniversary of the first apparition at Fatima, which occurred on 13 May, 1917.

> My heart is oppressed when I see the sin of the world and the whole range of menaces gathering like a dark cloud over mankind, but it also rejoices with hope as I once more do what has been done by my Predecessors: namely, I entrust the world to the Heart of the Mother, *I entrust especially to that Heart those peoples which need particularly to be entrusted.* By doing this, I am entrusting the world to Him who is infinite Holiness. This Holiness means redemption. It means a love more powerful than evil. No "sin of the world" can ever overcome this Love.
>
> Once more this act is being done. Mary's appeal is not for just once. Her appeal must be taken up by generation after generation, in accordance with the ever new "signs of the times." It must be unceasingly returned to. It must be ever taken up anew.

---

6. See Timothy Tindall-Robertson, *Fatima, Russia and John Paul II,* Appendix iii. Also see de Marchi, 243 ff; Fox, 249 ff.

Triumph of the Immaculate Heart

✠ ✠ ✠

In entrusting to you, O Mother, the world, the individuals and peoples, we also entrust to you the consecration itself, for the world's sake, placing it in your motherly Heart.

Oh, Immaculate Heart! Help us to conquer the menace of evil, which so easily takes root in the hearts of the people of today, and whose immeasurable effects already weigh down upon our modern world and seem to block the paths toward the future!

From famine and war deliver us.

From nuclear war, from incalculable self-destruction, from every kind of war, deliver us.

From sins against the life of man from its very beginning, deliver us.

From hatred and from the demeaning of the dignity of the children of God, deliver us.

From every kind of injustice in the life of society, both national and international, deliver us.

From readiness to trample on the Commandments of God, deliver us.

From attempts to stifle in human hearts the very truth of God, deliver us.

From sins against the Holy Spirit, deliver us, deliver us.

Accept, O Mother, of Christ, this cry laden with the sufferings of all individual human beings, laden with the sufferings of whole societies. Let there be revealed, once more, in the history of the world the infinite power of merciful love. May it put a stop to evil. May it transform consciences. May your Immaculate Heart reveal for all the light of hope.

During this speech, yet another attempt was made upon Pope John Paul II's life, this time from an attacker who came within five feet of the Pope. Once again, Our Lady protected him; the man was stopped before he could raise his weapon against him.

After this first consecration, events began to move swiftly in the Soviet Union and in Eastern Europe. On November 10, 1982, Leonid Brezhnev, Soviet leader for eighteen years, after toppling Khrushchev, died of a heart attack at the age of seventy-five. He was succeeded by Andropov who, in turn, died of a kidney disease fifteen months later. He was succeeded by Chernenko who was only to live for one more year.

On March 24–25 1984, in Rome, St. John Paul II renewed his consecration of Russia to the Immaculate Heart of Mary. The Holy Father had invited the Rector of the Shrine of Fatima to visit Rome with a statue of Our Lady of Fatima sculpted under Sr. Lucia's direction by Father Thomas M. McGlynn, the Dominican priest, playwright, author and sculptor. Sr. Lucia had commented that the statue was a reasonably good likeness of Our Lady of Fatima. The statue was followed by the Pope as it was paraded through St. Peter's Square. At the end of the Mass which followed, the Pope repeated the words of consecration in unity with the college of Bishops. In that speech, the Holy Father included the consecrations made by his predecessors:[7]

> Forty years ago and then years later, your servant Pope Pius XII . . . entrusted and consecrated to your Immaculate Heart the whole world, *especially the peoples for which by reason of their situation you have particular love and solicitude.* . . . And therefore, O Mother of individuals and peoples, you who know all their sufferings and their hopes, you have a mother's awareness of all the struggles between good and evil . . . accept the cry that we, moved by the Holy Spirit, address directly to your Heart. Embrace, with love of the Mother and Handmaid of the Lord, this human world of ours, which we entrust and consecrate to you, for we are full of concern for the earthly and eternal destiny of individuals and peoples.
>
> In a special way we entrust and consecrate to you those individuals *and nations* that particularly need to be thus entrusted and consecrated.

✠✠✠

The power of this consecration lasts for all time and embraces all individuals, peoples, and nations. It overcomes every evil that the spirit of darkness is able to awaken, and has in fact awakened *in our own times,* in the heart of man and in his history.

---

7. Tarcisio Cardinal Bertone, *The Last Secret of Fatima*, 153–56.

Triumph of the Immaculate Heart

✠✠✠

Mother of the Church! Enlighten the People of God along the paths of faith, hope, and love! *Enlighten especially the peoples whose consecration and entrustment by us you are awaiting.*

Pope St. John Paul II then repeated the prayer offered in the 1982 consecration quoted above.

Sr. Lucia repeatedly testified that the consecration of Russia had been fulfilled, in the prominent international Catholic journal 30 *Days,* in letters to the *Fatima Family Apostolate,* and in letters and conversations with Vatican Secretary of State Cardinal Tarcisio Bertone. Indeed, His Eminence states clearly that "Lucia confirms the validity of this act of consecration: 'Yes, it has been done, as Our Lady asked, on March 25, 1984.'"[8] There can be no doubt that the witness of Sr. Lucia, whose life and testimony is above reproach, is unimpeachable. Her life has been examined and cross-examined, studied and scrutinized. She has never ceased from this affirmation that, in her own words: "Yes, it was accomplished, and since then I have said that it was made. And I say that no other person responds for me, it is I who receive and open all letters and respond to them."[9]

Indeed, no sooner was the 1984 consecration made than the world became witness to the collapse of Russia. The following year, on 11 March, 1985, Mikhail Gorbachev became General Secretary of the Communist Party of the Soviet Union. Almost immediately, he began making numerous reforms to the communist system in Russia. In November 1985, he attended the first Summit with President Reagan. The following February, he stood before the first Party Congress and attacked the Brezhnev years as wasteful and repressive. The following year, he began introducing his policies of *glasnost* (openness) and *perestroika* (reconstruction). These involved devolution of central authority, an end to the State's economic monopoly, the encouragement of private enterprise, the introduction of electoral procedures, and increased freedom of speech and

---

8. Ibid., 161. See also Fr. Antonio Maria Martins and Robert J. Fox, op. cit. and Timothy Tindall-Robertson, op. cit.

9. Fr. Antonio Maria Martins and Robert J. Fox, 86.

of the press. Agreements to remove all short-range missiles from Eastern Europe were followed on December 8, 1987 by the signing of the Arms Treaty at the Washington summit. The following December, he also unilaterally cut troops in Eastern Europe by 500,000 men over the next two years. Six tank divisions (5000 tanks) were to be removed from East Germany and another six from the Soviet Union.

That same year (1988) saw the celebration of the millennium of the Baptism of Vladimir, Prince of Kiev, which date (988) represented the birth of the Orthodox Church in Russia. From June 3 to June 14, religious leaders from all over the world representing many faiths participated in the celebrations. The Vatican's representative was Cardinal Cassaroli. Nine new saints were canonized during the festivities, in which greater religious freedom was also promised to the Russian people. The following year (1989), 1000 Orthodox dioceses were established, two new seminaries were opened, and several monasteries restored. That July, the first Catholic Bishop to a Soviet Republic (Byelorussia) was appointed by the Vatican. In November, 1989, Gorbachev visited Vatican City, where he had an audience with the Pope. Official relations were established between the Soviet Union and the Holy See. Pope John Paul promised to visit Moscow (in 1992 or 1993), and Mrs. Gorbachev was presented with a Rosary. By this time, the Jewish exodus to Israel was in full force, with 20,000 emigrating in 1988 and 60,000 in 1989. That year (1989) also witnessed the withdrawal of Russian troops from Afghanistan.

Then the unthinkable began to happen. In November 1989, East German Party Boss Gunter Shabowski had declared that traffic could move freely between East and West Germany. The resulting flood of humanity led to the collapse of the Berlin Wall and Gorbachev's agreement to the unification of Germany. The spirit of dissent began to spread all over the Eastern Block. Since 1988, rioting had broken out in various Republics of the Soviet Union in Azerbaidzhan, Georgia, Uzbekistan, and Moldavia. Then, in March 1990, the Ukraine declared its intention to become a republic, followed by Estonia and Latvia. The Soviet Union was breaking up under the immense economic problems it was suffering.

Triumph of the Immaculate Heart

May 13, 1991 represented the tenth anniversary of the attempted assassination upon Pope St. John Paul II. To commemorate Our Lady's intervention in his recovery, the Pope made a return visit to Fatima. During his visit, the Holy Father made a sacred Act of Entrustment "in which he thanked Mary for protecting his life, and particularly consecrated Europe once again to her."[10]

> How many times we have invoked you! And today we are here to thank you because you always listened to us. You showed yourself a mother: Mother of the Church, a missionary on this earth's roads towards the awaited third Christian millennium; Mother of all the people by your constant protection which sheltered us from disaster and irreparable destruction, and promoted progress and modern social conquests. Mother of the Nations by the unexpected changes which restored confidence to the peoples who were oppressed and humiliated for so long. Mother of life, by the many signs with which you have accompanied us, defending us from evil and the power of death; My Mother forever, and especially on 13 May, 1981, when I felt your helpful presence at my side; Mother of every person who fights for life which does not die. Mother of the humanity redeemed by the blood of Christ. Mother of perfect love, of hope and peace, Holy Mother of the Redeemer.

> In collegial unity with the pastors, in communion with the entire People of God spread to the four corners of the earth, today I renew the filial entrustment of the human race to you. With confidence we entrust everyone to you. With you we want to follow Christ, Redeemer of mankind.

Then, on August 19, 1991, just three months after this renewed collegial consecration, Communist intransigents attempted to stage a coup. Their purpose was to recover the power that had been eroded during the Gorbachev years, to repair the crumbling Soviet economy, and to preempt Gorbachev's proposed Union Treaty, which would have given even greater autonomy to the republics, thereby reducing the Soviet Union to a loose confederacy. Taking advantage

10. *L'Osservatore Romano*, 20 May 1991, 7.

of Gorbachev's absence from power while he was on holiday in the Crimea, Gennady Yanayev announced that Gorbachev was suffering from ill health, and that he was assuming power as acting president. A state of emergency was declared, and an eight-man committee was formed to rule the country. Hundreds of tanks and armored, personnel carriers moved into Moscow throughout the morning. Meanwhile, the KGB had blockaded the runway of the airfield near Gorbachev's summer house. That afternoon, Boris Yeltsin, the Russian Federation President, called for a general strike and national protests on the part of the people. A stalemate emerged between the communist intransigents and the people of Russia under Yeltsin.

The next day, the military commandant of Moscow imposed a curfew on the capital. A war of nerves developed when tanks were brought to bear upon the Russian Parliament building where Yeltsin and his supporters were sequestered. However, popular resistance conveyed directly to the hard-liners that they had misread the hearts of the Russian people. The people pulled down statues of Lenin and daubed a huge bust of Marx with graffiti, one of which read, "Workers of the world, forgive me."

On the Wednesday, Latvia and Estonia declared their independence from the Soviet Union. Lithuania and Albania were to follow. Tanks and armored personnel began first to withdraw from the Russian Parliament and then to leave Moscow entirely. That evening, leaders of the national legislature demanded Gorbachev's reinstatement and proceeded to nullify all the emergency decrees made by the intransigents. Gorbachev appeared on television to state that he had resumed power. The rumor of his illness was thus shown for what it was. The next day, Thursday, August 22, he returned to Moscow. Thousands of Russian people streamed into Red Square to celebrate their victory over communism.

The coup—which, incidentally, had started on the same date (August 19, 1917) as the visitation of Our Lady of Fatima to the three shepherd children on the Sunday after their release from Ourem prison, and had ended on the traditional feast of the Queen of Heaven (August 22), when Gorbachev was restored to power and the intransigents had surrendered—had failed. It was doomed from before its inception. All that it had accomplished was to propel Gorbachev into further reforms. Gorbachev began by resigning from the Communist Party, which he then abolished as a political entity. No longer could Party officials hold any position within the KGB. All military links with the Communist Party were to be broken. All property previously owned by the Party—and it was substantial—had to be returned to the people. *Pravda*, the official media organ for the Communist Party, was temporarily silenced, and all Party archives were seized. The Central Committee was disbanded and more powers were ceded to the Republics. The Soviet Union itself was to be broken up.

Our Lady's Immaculate Heart had triumphed. The triumph had occurred, as she had said it would, quite late, after Russia had spread error throughout the world, and when Sr. Lucia was nearing the end of her life. When she first knelt with her two cousins before Our Lady, when she appeared to them above the little oak tree, the Soviet Union was nonexistent. Its conversion to communism and its ideological imperialism was yet to be. Yet, in a period of seventy-four years, the seer of Fatima lived to see Russia come full circle. One month after the Miracle of the Sun, the Communist Revolution launched modern Russia. Three months after Pope John Paul's third collegial consecration of Russia to the Immaculate Heart of Mary, it recovered its heart. It has become a Christian nation once more. We now anticipate the accomplishment of the remainder of Our Lady of Fatima's message.

The fulfillment of Our Lady's promise that Francisco and Jacinta would be taken into heaven was confirmed by St. John Paul II on 13 May, 2000, when at Fatima he beatified the two seers in the presence of the Bishop of Leiria Fatima, Serafim de Sousa Ferreira e Silva, and the Vatican Secretary of State, Cardinal Angelo Sodano, accompanied by the Postulator General, numerous Cardinals and Bishops from all over the world, many other dignitaries and, of course, Sr. Lucia of the Immaculate Heart.

> Gathered here at the expressed wish of our Brother Serafim, the Bishop of Leiria-Fatima, and of many of our Brothers in the episcopate, and of all the faithful in Christ, and having heard the findings of the Congregation of the Causes of Saints, with our

Apostolic Authority we agree that, from this day on, the venerable Servants of God, Francisco and Jacinta Marto may be called Blessed and may have their feast celebrated each year, locally according to the norms of the privilege, on the 20th February. In the name of the Father and of the Son and of the Holy Spirit.

Pope John Paul II with Sister Lucia.

In so doing, he proclaimed to the world that the children were truly in heaven and could intercede for the Church and the faithful. What a privilege to be among the 600,000 people, mostly Portuguese, who, along with Sr. Lucia, heard the Holy Father's valediction celebrating the virtues of their own beloved Francisco and Jacinta:

What most impressed and entirely absorbed Bl. Francisco was God in that immense light which penetrated in the inmost depths of the three children. But God told only Francisco "how sad" he was, as he said. One night his father heard him sobbing and asked him why he was crying; his son answered: "I was thinking of Jesus who is so sad because of the sins that are committed against him." He was motivated by one desire—so expressive of how children think—"to console Jesus and make him happy."

A transformation takes place in his life, one we could call radical: a transformation certainly uncommon for children of his age. He devotes himself to an intense spiritual life, expressed in assiduous and fervent prayer, and attains a true form of mystical union with the Lord. This spurs him to a progressive purification of the spirit through the renunciation of his own pleasures and even of innocent childhood games.

Francisco bore without complaining the great sufferings caused by the illness from which he died. It all seemed to him so little to console Jesus: he died with a smile on his lips. Little Francisco had a great desire to atone for the offences of sinners by striving to be good and by offering his sacrifices and prayers. The life of Jacinta, his younger sister by almost two years, was motivated by these same sentiments.

Little Jacinta felt and personally experienced Our Lady's anguish, offering herself heroically as a victim for sinners. One day, when she and Francisco had already contracted the illness that forced them to bed, the Virgin Mary came to visit them at home, as the little one recounts: "Our Lady came to see us and said that soon she would come and take Francisco to heaven. And she asked me if I still wanted to convert more sinners. I told her yes." And when the time came for Francisco to leave, the little girl tells him: "Give my greetings to Our Lord and to Our Lady and tell them that I am enduring everything they want for the conversion of sinners." Jacinta had been so deeply moved by the vision of hell during the apparition of 13 July that no mortification or penance seemed too great to save sinners. She could well exclaim with St. Paul: "I rejoice in my sufferings for your sake, and in my flesh I complete what is lacking in Christ's afflictions for the sake of his body, that is, the Church" (Col. 1:24).

Then, for the first time, we all sang, *Cantemos alegres a uma so voz: Francisco e Jacinta, rogai por nos!* (Happily we sing with only one voice: Francisco and Jacinta, pray for us.)

At the end of the ceremony, the third secret, given to the children on the 13 July, 1917, was finally revealed by Cardinal Sodano: (We transcribe this secret in the form officially transmitted to Bishop Correia da Silva, by Sister Lucia on 3 January, 1944.)

The third part of the secret revealed at the Cova da Iria, Fatima, on 13 July, 1917.

I write in obedience to you, my God, who commands me to do

so through his Excellency the Bishop of Leiria and through your Most Holy Mother and mine.

After the two parts which I have already explained, at the left of Our Lady and a little above, we saw an Angel with a flaming sword in his left hand; flashing, it gave out flames that looked as though they would set the world on fire; but they died out in contact with the splendour that Our Lady radiated toward him from her right hand: pointing to the earth with his right hand, the Angel cried out in a loud voice: *"Penance, Penance, Penance!"* And we saw in an immense light that is God: "something similar to how people appear in a mirror when they pass in front of it," a Bishop dressed in White; "we had the impression that it was the Holy Father." Other Bishops, Priests, men and women Religious going up a steep mountain, at the top of which there was a big Cross of rough-hewn trunks as of a cork tree with the bark; before reaching there the Holy Father passed through a big city half in ruins and half trembling with halting step, afflicted with pain and sorrow, he prayed for the souls of the corpses he met on his way; having reached the top of the mountain, on his knees at the foot of the big Cross he was killed by a group of soldiers who fired bullets and arrows at him, and in the same way there died one after another the other Bishops, Priests, men and women Religious, and various laypeople of different ranks and positions. Beneath the two arms of the Cross there were two Angels each with a crystal aspersorium in his hand, in which they gathered up the blood of the Martyrs and with it sprinkled the souls that were making their way to God. Tuy: 3.1.1944.[11]

Sister Lucia had already indicated the conditional interpretation of this final part of the secret in a letter to the Holy Father, dated 12 May, 1982:[12]

The third part of the secret refers to Our Lady's words: "If not [Russia] will spread her errors throughout the world, causing wars

11. Tarcisio Cardinal Bertone. *The Last Secret of Fatima*, 137–38. (Italics and punctuation as in the original.) For a prolonged discussion of the context and history of the third secret, this is a useful book. It also contains a foreword and an official interpretation of the secret by Pope Benedict XVI.

12. *The Seers of Fatima: Organ for the Causes of Canonization of Francisco and Jacinta*, ed. Fr. Luis Kondor. April/June, 2000. Fatima, 3.

and persecutions of the Church. The good will be martyred; the Holy Father will have much to suffer; various nations will be annihilated" (13 July, 1917). The third part is a symbolic revelation, referring to this part of the Message, conditioned by whether or not we accept what the Message itself asks of us; "If my requests are heeded Russia will be converted, and there will be peace; if not, she will spread her errors throughout the world, etc."

As this message has clearly not been heeded, the errors of secular materialism, along with the relativism and political correctness that follow, have pervaded the whole of Western culture, leading to the degrading of the human person, denial of the fundamental right to life, distortion of the nature of the family, and persecutions of the Church, involving the murder of thousands of priests, religious and lay people worldwide.

Yet, as the then Cardinal Ratzinger has asserted,[13] there is some hope provided within the imagery of this final part of the secret: namely, the consoling vision of the angels gathering the blood of the martyrs that dripped down the cross of Christ, and which was then given to the souls making their way to God. This is a poignant affirmation of the doctrine of vicarious atonement whereby the sacrifices of the just are to be united with the atoning sacrifice of Christ to obtain intercession for others—the heart of the message of Fatima . . . and of the Holy Sacrifice of the Mass, which is in turn the pulse of the Church offering Life to the world.

Sister Lucia of Fatima died in the Carmel at Coimbra on February 13, 2005 at 5:25 in the afternoon, aged 97. Doctor Branca Paul, who had been her personal doctor for years, was at her bedside. Like her little cousins so many years earlier, Lucia died from an influenza that was spreading through Portugal at the time. Lucia's advanced years, combined with the flu, were more than her feeble body could bear. Her last words were:

13. Ibid.

"For the Holy Father!... Our Lady, Our Lady,
Holy Angels, Heart of Jesus, Heart of Jesus!
We are going, we are going."
"Where?" asked Mother Celina.
"To Heaven..."
"With whom?" asked Mother Celina.
"With Our Lord... Our Lady... and the little Shepherds."

A national day of mourning was declared in Portugal. Her body was laid in state at Coimbra for public viewing. In 2006 Lucia's remains were transferred to the Basilica of Fatima, as she requested, to lie next to her beloved Jacinta.

Two months after Lucia's death, Pope John Paul II died on 2 April, 2005, at 9:37 local time. The Holy Father—whose pontificate had been closely linked to Fatima and the events associated with the fall of the U.S.S.R.—had a deep devotion to Our Lady of Fatima and to her message. It seemed as though a chapter had been closed.

Nevertheless, Fatima was not finished. On October 13, 2010, Pope Benedict XVI visited Fatima with this message for the world:

> We would be mistaken to think that Fatima's prophetic mission is complete. Here there takes on new life the plan of God which asks humanity from the beginning: "Where is your brother Abel [...] Your brother's blood is crying out to me from the ground!" (Gen. 4:9). Mankind has succeeded in unleashing a cycle of death and terror, but failed in bringing it to an end.... In sacred Scripture we often find that God seeks righteous men and women in order to save the city of man, and he does the same here, in Fatima, when Our Lady asks: "Do you want to offer yourselves to God, to endure all the sufferings which he will send you, in an act of reparation for the sins by which he is offended and of supplication for the conversion of sinners?" (Memoirs of Sister Lúcia, I, 162).
>
> At a time when the human family was ready to sacrifice all that was most sacred on the altar of the petty and selfish interests of nations, races, ideologies, groups and individuals, our Blessed Mother came from heaven, offering to implant in the hearts of all those who trust in her the Love of God burning in her own heart. At that time it was only to three children, yet the example of their lives spread and multiplied, especially as a result of the travels of the Pilgrim Virgin, in countless groups throughout the world ded-

icated to the cause of fraternal solidarity. May the seven years which separate us from the centenary of the apparitions hasten the fulfilment of the prophecy of the triumph of the Immaculate Heart of Mary, to the glory of the Most Holy Trinity.

Pope Benedict XVI had also decided to speed up the opening of the cause of beatification and canonization of Sr. Lucia. In a communiqué released on February 13, 2008, late in the afternoon, the Congregation for the Causes of Saints announced that the pope had chosen to dispense with the mandatory five-year delay usually required after the death of this servant of God before the opening of her cause.

During the first year of his pontificate, on 13 October, 2013, Pope Francis consecrated the world to the Immaculate Heart of Mary in the climactic ceremony of a Marian Day of celebration—a mass in St. Peter's Square in Rome—before a crowd of over 150,000.[14] Repeating the acts of consecration that had been made by Pope Pius XII and Pope John Paul II, the Holy Father prayed: "Protect our lives in your arms; bless and strengthen every desire for goodness; revive and nurture faith; sustain and illuminate hope; rouse and invigorate charity; guide us all on the path to holiness."

In 2015, Pope Francis had confirmed to Bishop Antonio Augusto dos Santos Marto of the diocese of Leiria-Fatima that "if God gives him life and health," he will be in the Cova da Iria to celebrate the centenary of the Apparitions of Fatima on 13 May 2017. Then on 20 April, 2017, the Vatican duly approved the canonization of Francisco and Jacinta. The Pope is to confirm the sainthood of the little shepherds during that centenary celebration. This is consequent upon a second miracle having already been attributed to them. Felipe Marques, the son of a Portuguese couple residing in Switzerland, was born with type-one diabetes. In May, 2000 his mother and grandmother took their infant son to the Shrine of Fatima and placed him near the tombs of the two Blesseds in the Basilica. While watching the beatification ceremony on television, the mother

---

14. http://www.parra.catholic.org.au/news---events/latest-news/latest-news... events/latest-news/-aspx.pope-francis-consecrates-world-to-immaculate-heart-of-Mary.

prayed to Francisco and Jacinta for his healing. Felipe has been completely cured of his diabetes and is no longer dependent on insulin.

Our Lord said to Lucia in the letter of May 18, 1936 quoted above, "I want my entire Church to acknowledge the consecration [of Russia] as a triumph of the Immaculate Heart of Mary, in order to later extend its cult and to place the devotion to this Immaculate Heart alongside the devotion to my Sacred Heart." And as Our Lady said to the three visionaries on 13 June, 1917, it is Our Lord's wish that devotion to the Immaculate Heart of Mary be established throughout the world. We now turn to consider what response that asks from each of us.

Epilogue

A S WE CAST OUR MINDS BACK over the remarkable events of Fatima, we discover in its tapestry an image of profound truth and sublime holiness. From the supplications of the angel to the messages of Our Lady, from the purity, devotion, and endurance of the shepherd children to the panic of the people before the apocalyptic Miracle of the Sun, and from Our Lady's warnings of tribulation and the ominous vision of hell to the majestic triumph of her Immaculate Heart and the promise of peace, we find ourselves in the presence of something majestic and ponderous that beckons us to decision.

What is our response to the message of Fatima? Do we, like the little shepherds, commit ourselves to a life of prayer and devotion to God, a life of penance and reparation? Or do we, like Arturo Santos, refuse to acknowledge His omnipotence?[1] For who can fail to recognize the finger of God in the pious and poignant lives of these blessed children—fledglings who exemplified a religious maturity and wisdom far beyond their tender years? Who can refuse to notice the harmony between the uniform message of Fatima and the Gospel, when, at every point, Fatima is supported by the entire canon of sacred Scripture? Who can deny that at Fatima, in its holiness, purity, majesty, and prophetic compass, heaven has once again

---

1. Artur Oliveira Santos was born on 22 January, 1884 in Vila Nova de Ourem. In 1907 he founded the Democratic Republican Centre which became a source of republican propaganda in the region. He became president, vice-president and town councillor between 1911 and 1915 when he was appointed Administrator Interior of the Council on the Revolution, a post which he held until 8 December, 1917. After occupying administrative positions on the council in 1919, 1922, and 1924, he was removed from office in 1926. He was exiled to Spain from 1931 to 1940, having worked in that country in various hospitals during the Spanish civil war. He died in Lisbon on 27 June, 1955 never abandoning his commitment to Marxist republican sentiments. His mortal remains were translated to Ourem on 29 June, 1974.

touched the earth? Given that in Fatima we do encounter the finger of God, what shall our response be if we are to be obedient to Our Lord, who wants to establish in the world devotion to the Immaculate Heart of Mary, His mother?

In order to answer this question, we must return to the Fatima message to consider it more closely. So far we have followed it piecemeal. Now we shall proceed more thoroughly. We start where all things begin: within the Heart of the Holy Trinity.[2]

It was the angel who first drew our attention to the Holy Trinity in that beautiful prayer he taught to the children in the Loca do Cabeço: "Most Holy Trinity, Father, Son and Holy Spirit, I adore you profoundly, and I offer you the most precious Body, Blood, Soul, and Divinity, of Jesus Christ, present in all the tabernacles of the world, in reparation for the outrages, sacrileges and indifference with which He Himself is offended. And, through the infinite merits of His most Sacred Heart, and the Immaculate Heart of Mary, I beg of you the conversion of poor sinners." Our attention was next drawn by the Trinitarian prayers of the Rosary: the Apostles' Creed and the Gloria. Lastly, we learned of Sister Lucia's wondrous Eucharistic vision of the Holy Trinity overshadowing the image of Our Lady. Thus, the Holy Trinity is at the very heart of the Fatima message.

We previously discovered, within the Holy Trinity, an attribute which we, being made in the image of God, can readily (if only analogically) recognize in ourselves: the attribute of consciousness. God, the Holy Trinity, is, among so many other wonderful things, supremely self-aware. God is both the agent and the recipient of His own act of self-reflection: He both directs His awareness and accords with its light. This direction is both immediate and perfect, for every divine act is eternal and comprehensive of itself.

---

2. For this section on the Trinity and its relationship to our hearts, I am indebted to Norbert Hoffman's fine technical discussion in his essay "Atonement and the Spirituality of the Sacred Heart: An Attempt at an Elucidation by Means of the Principle of 'Representation'" in Leo Scheffczyk (ed.), *Faith in Christ and the Worship of Christ*, 141–206. However, we short-circuit his discussion somewhat by utilising the notion of God as supremely self-aware, an attribute we, being made in the image of God, readily recognize in ourselves.

Epilogue

Thus, God is perfectly transparent to Himself. "Do you not believe that I am in the Father and the Father in me? The words that I say to you I do not speak on my own authority; but the Father who dwells in me does his works. Believe me that I am in the Father and the Father in me. . . ." (Jn. 14:10–11). The Son proceeds from the Father as His perfect self-expression (Mt. 26:39; Heb. 10:9); and the Father begets the Son as the sublime resplendence of His own will. The Word emanates immediately from the Divine Substance, and is like it in having the same nature as the Father, but also expresses it by being its perfect form (Phil. 2:6). Thus, the Son comprises the whole substance, nature, excellence, majesty, and perfection of the Divinity, possessing a complete and well-defined image of the Father. The Word is properly and truly proclaimed to be the natural and best-beloved Son of the Father, distinct in Person, but of identical and singular essence and divinity.

There is an eternal reciprocation whereby the Father begets (conceives) the Son for the sake of the Son, who, in turn, submits to the Father for the sake of the Father. "I glorified thee on earth, having accomplished the work which thou gavest me to do; and now, Father, glorify thou me in thy own presence with the glory which I had with thee before the world was made" (Jn. 17:4–5). The Father glorifies His name for the sake of the Son who loves Him; and the Son glorifies the Father for the sake of the Father whom He loves. The essence of this movement of surrender and begetting is love (*agape, caritas*).[3]

From this eternal communion between the Father and the Son, there emanates the creative Life (Spirit) of the Trinity. The Holy Spirit proceeds from the Father and the Son as from one spiration, for the love which the Father and the Son share is one breath, one Spirit. The essence of this fruitful Spirit is love. Out of this outpouring ecstasy of love within the Life of the Holy Trinity flows the impulsion to bring into being creatures upon whom God's grace can rest. This does not reflect a lack or a need within the Godhead,

---

3. I.e., self-giving love wholly for the good of the other; not *eros* (amor), *philos* (friendship), *storgé* (affection), concupiscence (desire), or any of the other human "loves."

for God is complete and perfect and wants for nothing. It simply expresses the loving nature of a Being who delights to have beings that He can love, precisely because He is love (1 Jn. 4:8).

Since God's delight is to create beings that can enjoy His love, it is necessary that God creates them free. He does not force His will upon them, but wants them freely to accept His gift, so that they, too, can delight in His love. His purpose is to create "sons" (Gal. 4:4–5) who can participate, like His own beloved Son, in the loving Life of the Holy Trinity: creatures who willingly delight in serving God, because they love Him, because He first loved them (1 Jn. 4:19), and because He knows what is best for them, since, being God, He cannot deny Himself. Hence the text: "Let us make man in our image, after our likeness" (Gen. 1:26): children who are self-aware and self-directing—autonomous, free beings, who are capable of returning love for love, and who will rejoice in it. Indeed, it is important that the children know Him and love Him as just the sort of God who loves them and would only do what is good for them. This is important for their own sakes, so that they can have confidence in Him and exult in Him. Because God loves them, He wants them to have this happiness.

Yet this freedom also necessitates the possibility that they may forsake Him. Coiled within the self-reflective autonomy of His children, like a serpent in a tree, is the moral freedom to decide to take that liberty upon themselves and to choose for themselves just what they will esteem and desire (Gen. 3:1–5). They then can will to turn their devotion from God towards created things (v. 6), taking these idols up into themselves and constituting their egos[4] thereby, lest their souls be naked and vulnerable (vv. 7, 10).

The essence of original sin is alienation from God. The root cause is pride born of desire (concupiscence). The tendency of human beings to direct their concern to the things of this world (symbolized by the tree of knowledge of good and evil) in order to prize these

---

4. Here "ego" is used to refer to false self-conceptions, not to the core of our selfhood, as in most secular psychologies. Rather, the essence of our selfhood is that spark *(scintilla)* of awareness of our being sustained *(synderesis)* in the image and likeness of God. In this, our ontological dignity is founded.

Epilogue

things as more worthy than God, leads by degrees to beguilement and enslavement (Mt. 6:19–24). Because humans treasure these things, they identify with them; their egos coalesce around these idols, so that they resent relinquishing their determination to do with them as they please. The result is the illusory world into which humanity has fallen. "It is my right... It is my body... I did it my way..." These are the clichés of original sin, which refuses to recognize that all things belong to God and are to be used for his glory (1 Cor. 6:19–20). Humanity no longer dwells in the garden of innocent communion with God; humans have become autonomous beings, weighed down by the perpetual arbitration between values, loyalties, desires, ideologies. This is the burden of being, that anguish, that sore that poets and philosophers are fond of scratching.

However, since only God has His Being in, from, and of Himself (*aseity*), His fallen children cannot recover the Reality which they have lost. Our being is derivative: we are created to derive our substance from the Father (2 Pet. 1:4), though the Son is of one substance with the Father (Jn. 17:20–26). Like the Son, we should "not count equality to God a thing to be grasped," but should empty ourselves, "taking the form of a servant" (Phil. 2:6). By so doing, we acknowledge that God is God, and not we ourselves. Therefore, the way to sanctity has been barred for those who leave the paradise of communion with God for attachment to created things (Gen. 3:24). To the extent to which their hearts become set upon the things of this world (Mt. 6:21), they become carnal beings (Ro. 8:3–8; Ja. 4:4–5) subject to the gods of this world (2 Cor. 4:4), fallen into structures (values, ideologies, possessions, status) which dominate and oppress them (Ro. 6:16ff.). In attempting to actualize themselves, egos have come into being, generating the conflict of each against each (Ro. 1:24–32). Mutual need then necessitates the emergence of political alignments, which spin out of their false selves an intricate web of tragedy and suffering stretched upon brambles (Gen. 3:18). This futile world of suffering and toil is such that any attempt to solve its problems leads only to the injection of more complexity into the system. Each attempt to overcome adversity only generates more difficulties, calling for more intervention and generating ever-greater complexity—all because they aspire to the aseity of God.

Because human beings are created free, there will always be those who will reject God and His commandments. Such is the error of secular utopian movements: they demand a deterministic or totalitarian system to ensure conformity. Unless the people are completely determined by the desired social system, or unless this system is thoroughly policed, human freedom will ensure that injustice and selfishness will inevitably resurrect itself (Mt.13:24–30; 24:6; 26:11). Some will choose to do what is right in their own eyes (Deut. 12:8; Jud. 17:6; 21:25), and, thereby, fall out of communion with the Triune life of God (the mutual love the Father shares with the Son in the Holy Spirit) into the structures of the world (structures of our own devising). To love this fallen world is to be at enmity with God (Ja. 4:4; 1 Jn. 2:15–17; Mt. 6:24). Therefore there must be a change in heart, a surrender of the will to God. That is why God has so designed things that we can only come to Him through faith, through loving acceptance and devotion to Him alone. For that is exactly how His Son loves Him, and all that the Father does is for the dignity, honor, and glory of His Beloved Son.

The entire world and all that it contains are of less value to God than the grace of a single human soul created in God's image and likeness. So God permits the fall, that He may love us even more. "Though we are faithless, he remains faithful, for he cannot deny himself" (2 Tim. 2:13). He will even suffer His Beloved Son to die for us so that the Son can demonstrate to the Father the depth of His love. The Father permits this because He loves the world and because He honors His Son, who loves to do His will: "For God so loved the world that He gave His only Son, that whosoever believes in Him will not perish, but have eternal life" (Jn. 3:16). By willingly suffering in our stead, Jesus says to the Father, "See how much I love them for your sake, even unto the death of the cross!" (Heb. 2:9–10, 13–15; 12:2; 1:3; Is. 53:10–12). Therefore, "Father, forgive them, for they know not what they do."

Jesus has accomplished the reparation of the broken communion between humanity and God by willingly suffering in His own Person that alienation from God which is the essence of the fallen human condition and converting it into love. In so doing, Christ bridges the gulf between humanity and God. Humanity is reconciled to God by the essential conversion of sin into love which Christ accomplished on the cross. Although this is a profound mystery, we are able to discern its outline. We have seen that humanity is alienated from God because of a misdirected love: love of self rather than love of God (2 Tim. 3:2–5). The life of the Holy Trinity is the opposite of this; it is characterized by mutual embrace, eternal love. God desires to bring humanity into this eternal life of surrender and begetting by adopting us as "sons" (Gal. 4:5). For our sakes and for the sake of the love He bears for His Son, God sends His Beloved Son, born of a woman, into this human condition. His Holy Spirit overshadows this young woman, Mary, and a human life is conceived in her that, from the moment of conception, is appropriated into the life of the Trinity, the life of begetting and surrender. The human nature is appropriated into the divine nature as the Second Person of the Trinity is received into the womb of the Virgin. "And the Word became flesh and dwelt among us, full of grace and truth; we have beheld his glory, glory as of the only Son from the Father" (Jn.1:14). In Jesus Christ, the Wisdom of God is perfectly realized, because he is the incarnate Word of God. Precisely because the Divine Wisdom lives in Him, Jesus can procure for us reconciliation with God.

> The Logos enters sinful flesh, sinful nature . . . and acts as "Son," is "Son," in the sinner's place, that is, where the sinner is. Far from holding himself aloof from sinners, he, sinless (2 Cor. 5:21; Heb. 4:15; 1 Pt. 2:22), enters the Godlessness of their sin, yet as Son. And this signifies the conversion of sin. For if "the Son" enters sin and absorbs it, sin has no choice but to become its own opposite: and as for the Son, in the Godless void of sin, all he can do is to become the nameless, yet somehow still personal, absence of the Father. Jesus's death-cry (Mk. 15:34) is the Son's cry of dereliction. As the Son experiences the nature of sin, however, sin is converted in its very nature: the proud self-assertion against God, the sinful desire to be free from God, is changed into pain, a pain that is as great as this Son's love.[5]

5. Ibid., 167–68.

Jesus, within the crucible of His Sacred Heart, has transformed estrangement into reconciliation. The transforming catalyst in this interaction is love itself. By willingly embracing forsakenness upon the Cross and offering it up in love for the Father—"Into thy hands I commit my Spirit"—and in love for us—"Forgive them, for they know not what they do"—Jesus has perfected love and reconciled humanity: "It is finished (i.e. perfected)." There, on the cross, we witness "the eternal Father-Son relationship transposed into the drama of sin and salvation history."[6] Only Jesus can fully do this. Only the Son who is perfectly reconciled to the Father through the divine love they share, can undergo utter forsakenness without losing His love for the Father, without falling—simply because His essence, which the Son shares with the Father, is love, the Holy Spirit. God cannot deny Himself.

Being without sin, Jesus suffered solely for the sins of the world. He had no personal sins to repair. Jesus willed to endure the rejection of God by humanity in order to demonstrate, in His passion and suffering, the extent and depth of His love for the Father. "For this reason the Father loves me, because I lay down my life, that I may take it up again. No one takes it from me, but I lay it down of my own accord. I have power to lay it down, and I have power to take it again; this charge I have received from my Father" (Jn. 10:17–18). This passage not only alludes to the cross, but serves as a profound affirmation of the life of the Holy Trinity that we have been describing.

The essence of atonement is that love which, by taking estrangement upon itself, transforms it into reconciliation. Thus, this extension of the life of the Trinity into our world is itself an act of redemption. The life of the Holy Trinity, realized to its fullest extent in the Person of Jesus of Nazareth, leads inevitably to suffering and reparation. To accept suffering in love is to transform suffering into something new. To suffer sin willingly and to offer it up to God *is* an act of reparation and of reconciliation. "Penance, penance, penance," cries the angel of the third secret. Anyone who absorbs sin in this way atones for it, because it is willingly transformed into that

6. Ibid., 170.

248

love which reconciles: the love which is the life of the Trinity, which the Son freely gives to the Father and the Father begets in the Son.

Even though only the Son can do this perfectly, nevertheless, whenever we suffer the effects of sin and offer it up in this way, we too, "complete what is lacking in Christ's afflictions for the sake of his body, that is, the church" (Col. 1:24). Suffering is an inevitable part of the Christian path, as we have seen: "All who desire to live a godly life in Christ Jesus will be persecuted" (2 Tim. 3:12). As Our Lord declared, "a servant is not greater than his master. If they persecuted me they will persecute you" (Jn. 15:20). Even so, God does not ignore our sighs and groans, but out of the honor He holds for His Son, accepts our offering, too, for His sake. "For God is not so unjust as to overlook your work and the love which you showed for his sake in serving the saints" (Heb. 6:10; 1 Pet. 2:19; 3:14; 4:14; 5:9–10). This is only fitting; otherwise suffering and Christian service lack all meaning. But it is the relation of the Son to the Father that gives meaning to our sacrifices. They are the mark of our union with Him (2 Cor. 4:7–12; Gal. 6:17; Phil. 3:10–11). "When we cry 'Abba! Father!' it is the Spirit himself bearing witness with our spirit that we are children of God and fellow heirs with Christ, provided we suffer with him in order that we may be glorified with him" (Ro. 8:17). Our Lady asked, at her third visit to the children, that we "make sacrifices for sinners." The willing acceptance and loving offering of suffering to God the Father reflects the sacramental nature of the relationship of the Son to the Father, and, in like manner, transforms sin (alienation) into reconciliation.

Our Lord requires that we not return evil for evil, but rather return good for evil (Mt. 5:44). In so doing, we participate in the sacramental body of Christ. We, too, offer ourselves to the Father in emulation and honor of the love the Son has shown Him. Our Father receives our offering for the sake of His Son, simply because our willing endurance, by the grace and Spirit of Christ which lives within us, has atoning value. The Church has the power to forgive sin (Jn. 20:23).

This is the deeper meaning of the Eucharist. When we come to the altar, having first reconciled ourselves with our neighbor (Mt. 5:24), we too repair the rent in the created order which sin has rendered. By forgiving and being forgiven, we also participate in the sacrificial offering of the body and blood of Christ, making reparation for the sins of the world. We, "like living stones built into a spiritual house," are "a holy priesthood," who must offer "spiritual sacrifices acceptable to God through Jesus Christ" (1 Pet. 2:5). "I appeal to you therefore, brethren, by the mercies of God, to present your bodies as a living sacrifice, holy and acceptable to God which is your spiritual worship" (Ro. 12:1).

"Therefore, [we] endure everything for the sake of the elect, that they also may obtain salvation in Christ Jesus with its eternal glory" (2 Tim. 2:10). This is the essential meaning of that beautiful prayer which Our Lady taught the little shepherd children to say whenever they suffered: "O my Jesus, it is for love of you, in reparation for the offences committed against the Immaculate Heart of Mary, and for the conversion of poor sinners." By offering up our sighs and groans to Our Lord in an attitude of forgiveness, we heal in ourselves the breach caused by sin and "complete what is lacking in Christ's afflictions" by voluntarily transforming our pain into that love the Son gives to the Father. That is the meaning of reparation.

When such repentance is undertaken by the entire Church acting in concert (i.e., when the entire Church exercises its power to forgive sins in this way) and when this power is directed to a people which has become unfaithful, then God will respect the penances and reparations of the entire Body of Christ for the sake of His Son and for the sake of the Church for which He so compassionately suffered. If the Church has the power to forgive sins and to make reparation, then it has the power to convert nations! That is why Jesus said to Sr. Lucia, "I want my entire *Church to acknowledge* the consecration [of Russia] as a triumph of the Immaculate Heart of Mary." Millions of ordinary people within the Church, for many years, have faithfully made reparation for Russia, so that it might be consecrated by a collegially united Church and thereby be converted. The successful conversion of Russia from communism is directly attributable to this devotion and evidences Our Lord's wish that devotion to the Immaculate Heart of Mary be established throughout the world. Why?

The answer lies within the nature of Mary's heart. Her heart, which has been created Immaculate for the sake of her dear Son and Lord, who has honored her as Mother from before the foundation of the world, is characterized by two essential features: reflection upon the life and words of Jesus and her consent to do His will. "Let it be to me according to your word." Indeed, this consent ("let it be") already entails her reflection ("according to your word"). Out of this reflective fiat emerge all her other virtues: obedience, meekness, gentleness, solicitude, kindness, faithfulness, hope, love, etc.

Yet all these virtues are manifested in her simply because Mary considered herself to be but the handmaid of the Lord. Recall what Brother Thomas Merton has said of her: "The sanctity of Our Lady was great indeed, but so great that it cannot adequately be expressed in anything other than the ordinary ways of human existence." It is precisely because Mary has made herself the servant of God, living a poor and hidden life, having nothing of her own, but receiving everything from God, that she could truly be called full of grace: full of the grace of God. The nature of Divine Love is to give the fullness of being to the other, and there is nothing in Mary to obstruct or hinder this Holy Spirit. Mary's sanctity is the sanctity of God, since there is nothing of Mary and all of God in her heart. This is the secret of Mary and the secret of her holiness.

By becoming nothing, Mary makes God the holy principle of her life: "He who is mighty has done great things in me, and holy is his name." Through Mary's self-abandonment and self-emptying, God is able to work through her in the most extraordinary way, bringing forth the gift of Christ to the world. In her *fiat*, her "let it be," we have the key to her sanctity, which insight we too can adopt in order that we may also, as it were, bring forth the life of Christ in us and into the world. But the essential feature of this reflective, consenting attitude, which so typifies Mary's heart, is that it is in perfect imitation of the Trinitarian life. The Father conceives His beloved Son, and the Son lovingly consents to conform to the Father's will. Similarly, Mary contemplates her beloved Son and, in joy and adoration, consents to accede to the will of her Lord.

Submission to the will of God is the essence of true discipleship. Mary in the Gospel tradition typifies the exemplary disciple. She, of all the characters in the Bible, exemplifies, among created beings, the essential nature of the life of the Holy Trinity. She alone willingly contemplates and accepts the will of God in perfect imitation of the Son's relationship to the Father.

Given the nature of the tribulations afflicting the Church today, we can see why such a heart is required of us as well. Any attempt to create a utopia through human effort alone is a delusion. We can never achieve paradise on earth, not only because of the human tendency towards selfishness and willfulness,[7] or because we cannot comprehend and control complexity, or because human behavior is indeterminate, or because society can never be perfectly policed nor individuals perfectly conditioned, but because of the limits of human reason. Over the past eighty years, methodological studies have demonstrated the failure of rational methods to model social systems or to correct human behavior. Within the philosophy of science, fundamental difficulties and restraints to rationalist claims to knowledge and control have emerged. Yet modernist (liberal) errors contend that humanity, solely by its own cleverness and effort, can determine the truth and secure social justice. We now know that such confidence is illusory.[8] The poor will always be with us (Mt. 26:11; Mk. 14:7; Jn. 12:8) and war and famine will persist until the end of time (Mt. 24:4–8; Mk. 13:5–8; Lk. 21:5–11).

Therefore, even though the political apparatus of Marxism and its communist ideology have been defeated, nevertheless those errors of Russia which Our Lady of Fatima has warned us about continue to be parasitic upon Western Christian culture. Materialism, relativism, irreligion, political correctness, and blind faith in social progress still condition many people's thinking both outside and inside the Church. Furthermore, those dark specters which accompanied Rasputin also linger: the spread of dissipation, occultism, and esoteric knowledge, a fascination with evil and superstition, and an obsession with fads, fashions, and celebrity still haunt society. Such errors will continue to plague us despite all our sociopolitical and technological innovations.

7. The denial of this is the heresy of Pelagianism.
8. See *The Catechism of the Catholic Church*, 675–77.

Epilogue

There is nothing new in these errors: "Your eyes will be opened, and you will be like God, knowing good and evil," the serpent said to Eve in the primordial garden. Eve, seeing "that the tree was good for food, and that it was a delight to the eyes, and that the tree was to be desired to make one wise, she took of its fruit and ate, and she also gave some to her husband and he ate" (Gen. 3:5–6).

How different and distinctive is Mary's response: "let it be to me according to your word." The contrast between the avarice of Eve's concupiscence, on the one hand, and the humility and selflessness of Mary's consent, on the other, is absolute. Unlike Eve, Mary did not seek personal gain, but embraced poverty. She did not turn her eyes to the world, but kept them on her Lord. She did not seek political sophistry, but reflected upon the word of God. In doing so, she evidenced in her heart the fundamental option that God requires of each of us.

Given the limitations of human reason, what matters essentially is the intention of one's heart. Rather than capitulating to this fallen world, Our Lady has asked that we make reparation for the errors and deceptions of this world, transforming them into works of loving devotion. Our hearts will then become the crucible whereby evil is atoned for and our own hearts purified. We also are called to enter the life of the Holy Trinity by this sincere and loving consent to the word of the Father; it is the pure in heart who shall see God (Mt. 5:8).

Such is the Immaculate Heart of Mary, which was in the Divine plan of salvation from before the beginning. Propriety demands that a pure-hearted yes had to be freely given to God by the one who was to become the "Mother of the Most High." It would be unfitting for God to have acted upon Mary if there had been the slightest reluctance, impediment, or doubt on her part. Her assent had to be perfect, given from an Immaculate Heart:

> When [Mary] says yes, she will throw her whole self into the wholeness of God without wanting to grasp or know any particular. Feeling the whole fullness of God within and around her, she knows that God's offer continues and will always continue and that she can peacefully entrust her entire soul, her entire being, to this offer to be newly formed. She allows it to happen. She places

her soul so much at the Son's disposal that he can use it as he wills. And he not only forms her nature with its natural qualities in order to exalt them but he also uses her as a vessel in order to pour his entire divine nature into her and form from her a mother for himself.[9]

So profound and inexhaustible is this mystery that the human mind cannot contain it, since such consent implicates, in an intimate manner, the person of the Virgin in the very life of the Holy Trinity. Because her Motherhood was foreordained, Mary is enfolded in the mutuality of the processions of the Divine Persons. Mary is at once the daughter, the spouse, and the Mother of God.

Mary, by a unique privilege and singular grace, has God for her Father in an inestimable way. She has been created immaculate by the Father out of love for the Son that she is to bear. She is the innocent, pure Eve, yet an Eve preserved from any stain of even venial sin. God the Father cannot but regard with singular complacency and favor the Mother of His Son. In return, she, espoused to the Holy Spirit, loves the Father with a love which is perfect and sublime, beyond that of any creature in heaven or on earth: for she loves the Father in and through God the Son.

Moreover, Mary loves her Son, not only with a love exceeding any natural love of a mother, but with the love which the Father has for the Son in the Holy Spirit. She loves Jesus with an infinite love, which is hers not from her natural capacity as a woman, but from the supernatural grace bestowed upon her as Spouse of the Holy Spirit. Her love surpasses that of any transforming union, or mystical marriage. Its superabundance overflows endlessly in the exquisite intermingling of the Divine relations into which she has been assumed. St. Bernard addresses the divine Mother in these words: "The Father is with thee who makes the Son His and thine; the Son is with thee who makes thee His Mother; the Holy Ghost is with thee, who with the Father and the Son sanctifies thy womb."

We cannot speak too highly of the privileges and dignity of the Mother of God, for it is from this office that all her sanctity derives. Mary is our Mother because she has been ordained to be the

9. Adrienne von Speyr, *Handmaid of the Lord*, 20.

Epilogue

Mother of salvation; it is through her that salvation has come into the world. The mind can only marvel at the complexity of what to God is a single vision: the image of a "woman adorned with the sun, with the moon under her feet, and on her head a crown of twelve stars . . . who brought forth a male child, one who is to rule all the nations with a rod of iron" (Rev. 12:1, 5). How can one comprehend the enormity of this design: that Mary was graced to be the Mother of the Son of God who, to honor her, made her His supreme creation; that, through her immaculate consent, He would be born of her, having espoused her to the Holy Spirit; thereby bringing salvation to the world, simultaneously showing to us his human nature which he took from her, and, by virtue of her virginity, the miracle that evidenced his divine origin from His heavenly Father? The hearts of the Son and the woman are so intricately entwined, both in the life of the Holy Trinity and in the physical natures which they share, that devotion to the one necessarily invites devotion to the other. This is the essential meaning of the vision in the *Apocalypse* which caused a third of the angels to rebel.

Mary's Immaculate Heart is inferior only to the Sacred Heart of Jesus. Her heart is the greatest happiness of our Savior here on earth, next to the bliss his soul enjoyed from the Beatific Vision. In his Mother's love, Jesus finds abundant consolation for the outrages and indifference of those who would not receive Him. Jesus gave Himself to Mary so intimately, and Mary corresponded so completely, that after the union of the Divine Persons in the Holy Trinity we cannot conceive a communion more perfect or sublime.[10]

For these reasons, our indebtedness to Mary is second only to that of her Son. She is literally our Mother according to grace, inasmuch as we are indebted to her, by and under her Son, for our spiritual life. By freely accepting her office as Mother of the Redeemer, by donating the physical elements of His body and blood—and His Sacred Heart—and by willingly consenting to His death, despite her own grievous suffering, Mary has merited her proper titles. Her titles of mediatrix and dispenser of grace, of advocate, refuge of sin-

---

10. Fr. Timothy Harris, *Mary: The Blessed the Beloved*, 118.

255

ners, comfort of the afflicted, and gate of heaven, etc., rightly belong to her, because she is the Mother of our God, the Savior who has associated her in our redemption. This is why Mary was present at Calvary. Her exemplary faith and hope in God the Savior empowered her to offer up her Son, that we might live.

We will never plumb the depths or circumscribe the boundaries of the role that the "woman adorned with the sun" has in the mystery of salvation. Nevertheless, with deep humility and gratitude, we thankfully receive the words Our Lady spoke to us in Fatima: "I will never forsake you. My Immaculate Heart will be your refuge and the way that will lead you to God." We hope thereby to find consolation in her Heart, as we do in the Sacred Heart of her Son, who has willed from all eternity to give to us this treasure.

Our Lord at Fatima has offered the world the pre-eminent gift of Mary's Heart. He desires that the entire Church embrace this Heart of contemplation and consent as an alternative to the dissension that has persecuted the Church. This Heart is like His own Sacred Heart, which suffers with such compassion on behalf of recalcitrant and indifferent human beings. Mary's Heart is a heart of tenderness and solicitude, of kindness and devotion, and of constancy and submission. It is a heart of mercy and succor. It is an adoring heart, loving the Lord in the truest way by imitating Him. Out of its desire to emulate the compassionate life of the Savior, such a heart consents to accept the will of God absolutely by entering into human suffering, embracing it, and transforming it into a holy love. It bleeds in sympathy with the Triune passion, willingly making reparation and penance for the conversion and reconciliation of poor, lost sinners. It is a merciful heart, reaching out to the lost, the afflicted, the oppressed, the sick, the frail, the misguided, the willful, the lonely, the despairing, the proud, the fallen, the desperate, the perverse— seeking to recover them, to recall them, to correct them, to guide them, to restore them, in the only way this can be done: by bringing them the word of the Lord in love. It is a yearning heart, reaching out to its Savior on behalf of those oppressed by wealth, power, sensuality, and intellectual pride. It is an understanding heart, realizing the necessity of suffering and the reason for its constancy. This Heart of Mary is an Immaculate Heart, a fiery furnace of love refining and purging all that it embraces, renewing and restoring, healing and completing. It is a Holy Heart that sanctifies and perfects, a prayerful heart that intercedes for others. It is the fount of blessing and grace, of Spirit and Truth, because within it beats the meek and lowly Heart of the Savior. It is a necessary heart, because no one can enter the kingdom without such a heart that so readily consents to do the will of the Father. It is the heart of salvation, because there the Father makes His home with the Son.

This is the Heart that the Lord wishes to give to the world. Only by making the fundamental decision to "let it be to me according to your word" can we come to know the Lord fully. Only by such self-emptying can we be filled with His Wisdom. This submission in itself honors and emulates the Immaculate Heart of Mary. In return for such devotion, Mary gives us sanctity, not only by dispensing her grace upon us, but by disposing the individual to discover his true self in her: she is a mirror in which we can see the person that we will eventually become. The eternal God sees us as we will be, not as we are. The kingdom that is to come has already been reified in Mary and has been made visible in her. Mary reveals to us a sanctity, "hid with Christ in God" (Col. 3:3), which will one day be apportioned to us.

> Which virtues and gifts become our treasure in Jesus Christ. For in that same time that God knit himself to our body in the maiden's womb, he took our sensual soul. In taking which, having enclosed us all in himself, he oned it to our substance. In this oneing he was perfect man; for Christ, having knit in himself every man that shall be saved, is perfect man. Thus Our Lady is our Mother in whom we are all enclosed; and, of her, born in Christ. For she that is Mother of our Savior is Mother of all that are saved in our Savior. And our Savior is our true Mother, in whom we are endlessly borne; and we shall never come out of him.[11]

This inheritance is kept "imperishable, undefiled, and unfading" (1 Pt. 1:3–5, 23) by Our Blessed Mother, who is the dispenser of all our graces.

---

11. Julian of Norwich, *Revelations of Divine Love*, 157.

Yet, not only then, but even now, this sanctity which we see in Mary is transforming us through that single stimulus which forms the double life of the Christian: to sanctify oneself, and to be a light to the world. Secure in the hope of a world beyond this one, we may advance with confidence, fortified against all odds, and dare to hope for the restoration of this present world. The certainty of this future kingdom inspires us not to abandon the present in the name of some all-too-human ideology. Victory is certain, even in the face of failure, because Our Heavenly Father does not regard the bundles of wheat we gather, but the number of grains we have sown in the soil.

And what Our Lady of Fatima has asked of us is neither burdensome nor difficult. Firstly, we must consent to accept the will of God in all things. This means fulfilling our daily duty in our vocation in life in which God has placed us, and in our daily walk with Jesus to which God has called us.[12] In doing so, we cooperate in God's eternal purpose (Phil. 2:12–13).[13] God's grace does not require us to act in a manner contrary to our natures, for grace respects nature. Rather, God calls us to fulfill our natures in harmony with his will (2 Pet. 1:10–11). This simply means "unswerving fidelity to our religious obligations, performing our daily tasks to the best of our ability, being honest, truthful, patient, and charitable in our dealings with others, and being constantly on guard against temptation, especially as regards the custody of our eyes."[14]

Since this is not easy in our current self-centered, dissipated, and hedonistic culture, it will invariably involve us in much personal sacrifice. But, as the Angel of Portugal said to the children at the well, "Make of everything you can a sacrifice, and offer it to God as an act of reparation for the sins by which He is offended, and in supplication for the conversion of sinners. You will thus draw down

---

12. Mt. 25:14–30; Luke 17:10; Ro. 13:1–10; 1 Cor. 7:26–27; Tit. 3:1–2; 1 Pet. 2:13–17.

13. The doctrine of predestination to eternal life (election) is a *de fide* teaching of the Roman Catholic Church. See Ludwig Ott. *Fundamentals of Catholic Dogma*, 239, 242–44 and *CCC* 600, 1037. However, the Jansenist-Calvinist teaching of positive reprobation (predestination to damnation) has never been taught by the Catholic Church.

14. Johnston, *Fatima*, 103.

peace upon your country. . . . Above all, accept and bear with submission the suffering which the Lord will send you." Here again we have the deep mystery of the Body of Christ, which can make reparation for the evils in our society and bring peace upon it. The kingdom of God grows like a mustard seed planted within our hearts (Mt. 13:31–32). Performance of our daily duty injects the message of God into the system, so that it grows from within outwards. As each of us looks after the little things in our lives, so the collected contribution of all these noble acts spreads outwards to sanctify the whole. The kingdom of God begins with His word planted in the heart (Mt. 13:18–23). It cannot be imposed on civilization (Mt. 13:37–43), but must, like yeast, be allowed to leaven the entire loaf (Mt. 13:33). Only God can give us the kingdom (Lk. 12:32)—a Kingdom that is not of this world (Jn. 18:36; Lk. 17:20–21; Jn. 3:3, 5). And it comes through much suffering (Acts 14:22; Mt. 7:14; Mk. 10:29–30; 2 Thess. 1:5–7; Rev. 1:9). Nevertheless, Our Lady has promised to be with us always: "Do not lose heart. I will never forsake you. My Immaculate Heart will be your refuge and the way that will lead you to God."

Secondly, consecration to the Immaculate Heart of Mary means Eucharistic reparation. By willingly accepting whatever the Lord brings us and gladly offering it up in reparation for the conversion of poor sinners, we truly participate in the Body of Christ and "complete what is lacking in Christ's afflictions" on behalf of the Church, both present and future. Such actions are essentially Eucharistic insofar as they recall and re-enact the passion and sacrifice of Our Lord. But more than this, Eucharistic reparation means regular celebration of the sacrament of Holy Communion with the intention of making this offering. For thus we console the sorrowing Hearts of Jesus and Mary as young Francisco did before the tabernacle which housed the Real Presence of Our Lord. It means preparing oneself for Communion by confessing our sins and repenting of them with a definite resolve not to repeat them. It means being heartily sorry for offending Our Lord and willingly taking that sorrow upon ourselves in a penitential manner. We must be prepared to forgive within our hearts all transgressions committed against us, so that our transgressions also will be forgiven (Mt. 6:14–15). We must heal, reconcile, and repair in our broken and contrite hearts (Ps. 51:17) the alienation and estrangement suffered by others. Then God will hear us for the sake of His Son and reconcile them to Him (Jn. 20:23). "For he has not despised or abhorred the affliction of the afflicted; and he has not hid his face from him, but has heard, when he cried to him" (Ps. 22:24). Eucharistic reparation is the heart of intercessory prayer.

Thirdly, consecration to the Immaculate Heart of Mary entails daily recitation of the Rosary. At every visitation to the three children of Fatima, Our Lady requested this devotion. We have witnessed its power to convert nations, and we have seen that it is the analogue of Mary's reflective and consenting heart. Regular repetition of these beautiful prayers, done while contemplating scenes from the life of Jesus, will nourish our faith and conform our spirits to His Sacred Person. "Whatever is true, whatever is honorable, whatever is just, whatever is pure, whatever is lovely, whatever is gracious, if there is any excellence, if there is anything worthy of praise, think about these things" (Phil. 4:8). Meditating upon the teachings of the Creed, repeating Our Lord's Prayer, contemplating the life of Christ while blessing His honored Mother for her Providential participation in salvation history on our behalf, glorifying the Holy Trinity in the Doxology, praying for the conversion of poor sinners, all these things will nourish in our hearts that devotion to Jesus which so typified the Heart of the Blessed Virgin Mary. "It is a deep mistake," writes Bishop Hedley, "to suppose that the best progress is made by efforts to acquire virtues and to root out vices. Such efforts must be made; but there is another and a better way. That other way is the contemplative union of our intelligence, will, and heart with the Sacred Humanity of Jesus Christ."[15]

The role of Mary, even in the highest degrees of contemplation, can never be incidental to the Christian life. It has been made evident just how intimately her sinless soul is embraced within the life of the Holy Trinity. Thus, when the Holy Mother inclines to form her children, she procures for them the Spirit of Jesus, with whom she is spiritually united, so that for those consecrated souls Mary's

---

15. Quoted in Fr. Timothy Harris, *Mary: The Blessed the Beloved*, 105.

spirit pervades their devotion as well. It is material to those prayers devoutly offered to Our Lady that they cannot but penetrate that *"cloud of unknowing* that is betwixt you and your God."[16] For, although God is imperceptible to our senses and incomprehensible to our intellects, so that "clouds and darkness surround Him" (Ps. 97:2), and even though our sins and our worldly attachments, or our willfulness and selfishness, constantly obtrude between us and God, nevertheless Our Lady's heart is eternally joined to His. Only love can pierce the cloud: "By love may He be gotten and holden; but by thought never."[17] Yet no creature in heaven or on earth loves the Son more perfectly than Our Holy Mother, who forever beholds the Divine beauty: "pure and clear and unalloyed, not clogged with the pollutions of mortality and all the colours and vanities of human life . . . holding converse with the true Beauty simple and divine."[18] Therefore, just as her appearance at Fatima dispersed the clouds to disclose the resplendent Sun, so through Mary's intercession we shall have a ready and intimate access beyond those clouds that separate our vision from His Divinity. Did she not promise that she would never forsake us, and that her Immaculate Heart would lead us to God? It is for this reason that she has commended this devotion. The final prayer of the Rosary entreats that such be granted unto us: "Our Father, whose only begotten Son, by His life, death, and resurrection, has purchased for us the rewards of eternal life, grant, we beseech thee, that in meditating upon these mysteries of the most Holy Rosary of the Blessed Virgin Mary, we may imitate what they contain and obtain what they promise, through the same Jesus Christ, Our Lord. Amen."

These are the devotions which Our Heavenly Mother came to Fatima to ask us to perform, the treasures she is calling us to contemplate within our hearts, and the sacramental life we are invited

16. Anon. *The Cloud of Unknowing*, cp. 4.
17. Ibid., cp. 6; cf. also cps. 24, 46, & 49.
18. Plato, *Symposium*, 211.

to embrace. Thus may we obtain the sort of heart necessary to enable us sincerely to utter the consent: "Let it be to me according to your word." It has been the will of Our Lord that we receive the heart of Mary in this way: "And He said to the disciple 'Behold, your Mother!' And from that hour the disciple took her to his own home."

Our Lady prays, surrounded by light, while the man works in the darkness. Original statue of Our Lady of Fatima in the workshop of Jose Thedim for repainting (1951).

Select Bibliography

Aumann, Jordan. *Spiritual Theology*. London: Sheed and Ward, 1980.

Bertone, Tarcisio Cardinal. *A Ultima Vidente de Fatima*. Lisbon: A Esfera dos Livros, 2007.

_____. *The Last Secret of Fatima*. New York: Doubleday, 2008.

Brown, R. E. et al. *Mary in the New Testament*. London: Geoffrey Chapman, 1978.

Calvat, Melanie (Maria of the Cross) (1878). *Apparition of the Blessed Virgin on the Mountain of La Salette the 19th of September, 1846*. Quebec: St. Raphael's Publications, 1984.

Carroll, W. H. 1917: *Red Banners, White Mantle*. Crossroads Books, 1981.

Cosgrove, J. J. and Kreiss, J. K. *Two Centuries*. Sydney: Whitcombe and Tombs, 1977.

Cristiani, Leon. *St. Bernadette*. New York: Alba House, 1965.

Cruz, Joan Carroll. *The Incorruptibles*. Rockford: Tan Books, 1977.

De Jonge, Alex. *The Life and Times of Grigorii Rasputin*. New York: Coward, McGann and Geoghegan, 1982.

De Marchi, John. *Fatima: The Full Story*. Washington: World Apostolate of Fatima, 1990.

Denzinger, H. (C. Rahner) *Enchiridion Symbolorum* (30th ed.). Fitzwilliam: Loreto, 1955.

Fox, R. J. *Fatima Today*. Virginia: Crossroads Books, 1983.

Haffert, J. M. *Meet the Witnesses*. Washington: World Apostolate of Fatima, 1961.

Harris, Fr. Timothy. *Mary: The Blessed the Beloved*. Dublin: Clonmore & Reynolds Ltd., 1949.

Jelly, Frederick M. *Madonna: Mary in the Catholic Tradition*. Huntington: Our Sunday Visitor, 1986.

John Paul II, St. *Reconciliatio et Paenitentia*. Sydney: St. Paul Publications, 1985.

_____. *Redemptoris Mater*. Sydney: St. Paul Publications, 1987.

_____. *Salvifici Doloris*. Sydney: St. Paul Publications, 1984.

Johnston, Francis. *Fatima: The Great Sign*. Rockford: Tan Books, 1980.

Julian of Norwich, *Revelations of Divine Love*. Tr. James Walsh, S.J. Wheathampstead: Anthony Clarke Books, 1973.

Kondor, Louis (ed.) *Fatima in Lucia's Own Words*. Fatima: Postulation Centre, 1989.

_____ (ed.) *Memorias da Irma Lucia,* vols. 1–2. Fatima: Postulation Centre, 1996.

Leite, Fernando. *Francisco de Fatima.* (4ᵗʰ ed.) Braga: Editorial A.O., 1986.

Lynch, Fr. Kilian, *Our Lady of Fatima and the Brown Scapular.* Faversham: Carmelite Press, 1956.

_____. *The Scapular of Carmel.* Faversham: Carmelite Press, 1955.

McGlynn, Thomas. *Vision of Fatima.* London: Skeffington and Son, 1951.

Manteau-Bonamy, H.M. (O.P.) *Immaculate Conception and the Holy Spirit.* Libertyville, IL: Franciscan Marytown Press, 1977.

Martindale, C.C. *The Message of Fatima.* London: Burns and Oates, 1950.

Martins, Fr. Antonio Maria and Fox, Fr. Robert J. *Documents on Fatima.* Alexandria, SD: Fatima Family Apostolate, 1992.

Moorehead, Alan. *The Russian Revolution.* London: Collins, 1960.

Norton, Mabel. *Eye Witness at Fatima.* Dublin: C.J. Fallon, 1950.

O'Carroll, Michael. *Theotokos.* Wilmington: Michael Glazier, Inc., 1988.

Ott, Ludwig. *Fundamentals of Catholic Dogma.* Rockford: Tan Books, 1974.

Paul VI. *Marialis Cultus.* Sydney: St. Paul Publications, 1974.

Pelletier, Joseph A. *Exciting Fatima News.* Maryland: Assumption Publications, 1973.

Scheffczyk, Leo (ed.). *Faith in Christ and the Worship of Christ.* San Francisco: Ignatius Press, 1986.

Sierra, A. Martinez. *Maria, Caminho do Homem.* Lisboa: Sao Paolo, 1993.

Tambasco, Anthony J. *What Are They Saying About Mary?.* New York: Paulist Press, 1984.

Tindal-Robertson, Timothy. *Fatima, Russia and Pope John Paul II.* Devon: Augustine Publishing Co., 1992.

Vatican Council II. *Lumen Gentium. Dogmatic Constitution on the Church.* Boston: St. Paul Editions, 1965.

Vilas-Boas, Manuel et al. *Fatima: Os Lugares da Profecia.* Lisbon: Circulo de Leitores, 1993.

Von Balthasar, Hans Urs. *Mary for Today.* San Francisco: Ignatius, 1987.

Von Speyer, Adrienne. *Handmaid of the Lord.* San Francisco: Ignatius, 1985.

Select Bibliography

Walsh, William Thomas. *Our Lady of Fatima*. New York: Doubleday, 1954.

Werfel, Franz. *The Song of Bernadette*. New York: Pocket Books, 1940.

Zicardi, M. James. *Blessed John Duns Scotus: The Case for the Existence of God and the Immaculate Conception*. (self-published work), 2013.

Made in the USA
Lexington, KY
26 May 2017